Russian Civilisation and Islam

Russian Civilisation and Islam

Arun Mohanty

KNOWLEDGE WORLD

KW Publishers Pvt Ltd
New Delhi

ISBN 978-93-83649-80-8

Published in India by Kalpana Shukla

KNOWLEDGE WORLD

KW Publishers Pvt Ltd
4676/21, First Floor, Ansari Road, Daryaganj, New Delhi 110002
Phone: +91 11 23263498/43528107
Email: knowledgeworld@vsnl.net • www.kwpub.com

2011 FPBA BEST PUBLISHERS AWARD (ENGLISH)

Printed and Bound in India

Contents

Acknowledgements

The current volume is the result of an ICSSR project on the "Role of Islam in Shaping Russia's domestic and foreign policy." It is my pleasure to acknowledge the support received from ICSSR in the execution of the project. I thank Bandita Bhol and Gyan Ranjan Panda who participated in the project for its successful completion. My thanks are due to my students, particularly Sukanya, Suravi, Nivedita, Tahira and others for their work in preparing the text. I am grateful to His Excellency, Ambassador of the Russian Federation to India, Alexander Mikhailovich Kadakin, for kindly writing the foreword for the current volume. I would be failing in my duty if I do not express my gratitude to my Russian friends, particularly Executive Director of World Public Forum on Dialogue of Civilizations—Vladimir Kulikov, Vice-President of the Russian National Glory Foundation—Mikhail Yakushev, Senior Counsellor of Russian embassy in Delhi, Sergey Karmalito and eminent Russian scholar on Islam, Prof Roman Silantiyev, for their assistance and encouragement in completion of the book.

Preface

Russia is a multi-confessional and multi-ethnic state where Islam, according to the constitution, has been declared as one of the four traditional religions. President Vladimir Putin in his address to the Russian Muslim leaders in 2007 emphasized that the multi-religious co-existence as an "absolutely new form of cultural cooperation between different peoples and religions constitutes Russia's inner strength as a great and important world power."

If we look at the evolution of the Russian state, we will find the foundations of its multi-ethnic and multi-confessional roots almost from the very beginning of its statehood. Islam is important for Russia not only because of its sizable Muslim population alone but is essential for Russia from the standpoint of national security, internal security and geopolitics. Islam plays a significant role in shaping Russia's domestic as well as foreign policy.

In the history of Russian civilization and state, relations between Orthodox Christians and Muslims may have been complicated at times, but never hostile. It is a paradox but the truth is that the co-existence of Orthodoxy and Islam continues in Russia from the period of the Golden Horde led by the Tatar-Mongols. Their inter-relations intensified after the incorporation of Khanates of Kazan, Crimea, Siberia and Caucasus into the territory of the Russian state. Islamic cultural influence is vividly seen in Russian architecture. It is particularly evident in the famous St. Basil cathedral in the Red Square in Moscow and the monasteries of the Kremlin palace. Eminent Russian Scholar Lev Gumilev, showing intensity of relations between the Russians and the Tatars, paid particular attention to the fact that Russian historians like Karamzin, poets and writers like Derzhavin, Ogarev, Turgenev, Dostoyevsky, Kuprin, Bulgakov, great scientists such as Mendelyev, Mechnikov, Pavlov, Timiryazev, renowned artists like Anna Pavlova, Galina Ulanova, Skryabin, Tanayev, Shishkin, etc. had Muslim Tatar origins. Living for long in the framework of a single state and territory, its centuries-old spiritual, social, and human links, the collective creation of cultural values and state structure, its collective defense, common destiny— all join to form common attitude to the fate of Russia among the multi-ethnic and poly-confessional people. These lay the foundation for strong traditions of tolerant co-existence while preserving original ethno-confessional culture.

The revival of Islam in post-Soviet Russia and the desire of Russian Muslims to assert their role in cultural, political and public spheres have gained new dynamics to their integration in both the state and the society. Russian state's multi-ethnic and multi-confessional character has been reflected in its federal structure. The country's top leadership perfectly realizes the significance of the "Islamic factor" in the life of the nation and the role of Muslim organizations in preserving and strengthening peace, stability and harmony in the society.

The inter-faith situation in modern Russia largely depends on relations between Orthodox Christian Church and the Muslim Spiritual Boards: Orthodox Christians and Muslims. Today, these relations are healthy, sound, forward-looking and positive. It is widely believed that Russian civilization and spirituality are inalienable from Islam and Muslim culture.

If you look at the population of Russia and India from a confessional point of view, you will find lots of similarities as well as differences. Therefore, our rich common multi-religious heritage is mutually beneficial for the two countries.

This volume is the first attempt in India to make a profound analysis of Islam in Russia, its contribution to the Russian civilization and spirituality. The book offers a wealth of information about Russian Islam and State-Islam interaction in Russia to Indian readers, and provides an insightful account of the ethno-confessional composition of the Russian population, the role of Islam in shaping domestic and foreign policy of the country and the revival of Islam in post-Soviet Russia. The volume provides indispensable expertise and, without any doubt, will be of particular interest for the experts on Russia, foreign policy analysts and the country-research students.

Alexander M. Kadakin
Ambassador of Russia in India

1. History and Demography of Muslims in Russia

Islam's Expansion into Russian Territory

Islam appeared on the territory of Russia as early as in the 8th century, which was obviously linked to Arab expansion. Arab conquerors had reached the main Caucasus mountain-ridge, occupying vast territories in Central Asia including Horesm, Fergana, and Maverannahr etc, which left the Volga region to come under their control. About 120,000 strong troops, led by Mervana, moved close to that territory in the year 737 AD. Present day Tatarstan is situated in this territory. In the year 922 AD Islam was officially declared as the state religion on this territory and people of Volga-Bulgaria were converted into Muslims.

Ali Ahmed ibn Omar ibn Dasta in his essay *Information about Khazars, Burtasas, Madvyaras, Slavs and Rus* (903-912) writes: The Bulgar king Almush practises Islam, large sections of Bulgar practise Islam and there are Masjids and primary schools with Imams in their settlements".[1] Arab writer Ibn Fallan writes about the journey of the ambassador of the Bagdad Khalifa, Zafar al-Muktadir to the Volga region. He noted that there was large number of Muslim communities living there until the arrival of ambassadors in that region. There were many mosques. However, Islam became the state religion in Volga-Bulgaria when its ruler Almush adopted Islam in May 912. The Bulgar king received the name Zafar ibn Abdulla when he was converted to Islam. Chubashia, Mari, Bashkiria and Kama-Bulgaria adopted Islam partially or fully. The famous Tatar historian Shahabuddin Mardzhami talks about the expansion of Islam in the Volga region during the period of the Khalifa al-Ma'mūn (813-833). According to historian R. Farheddinov, infiltration of Islam in the Volga region took place at the end of 7th and beginning of 8th century. What is noteworthy is that Islam came to the Volga region peacefully. This is how the first stage of Islamic expansion in Volga-Bulgaria ended. As a result of this, North-Eurasian forepost of Muslim civilisation was created in the Turkic Volga region. The scientific-philosophical and the literary ideas that were popular in the Islamic world entered this territory along with adoption of Islam. The public life on the territory was gradually shaped on the principles of Islam. The Islamic civilisation in Volga region gradually spread to the neighbouring territory without violence.

According to Russian writers, Bulgar ambassadors proposed to the great Kievan ruler Vladimir, to adopt Islam in his country in the year 986, and for this, three conditions were proposed – that the people avoid eating pork, avoid drinking and stop the tradition of 'cutting'. Vladimir agreed to accept only two conditions but did not accept prohibition on alcohol consumption. After two years he introduced Orthodox Christianity in his country. Orthodox Christianity was chosen as state religion in the interests of the elite of Kievan Rus. It is possible that Vladimir gave priority to a strong Byzantine influence, thus ensured independence of Rus from the East as well as West. That is why Russia is always faced with the dilemma between East and West. The choice of Islam would have meant the choice of the East. The choice of Orthodox Christianity was the choice of a middle path.

Relations between the Rus and the Volga-Bulgar were very uneven, and often had a militant rivalry rather than a peaceful coexistence. Nevertheless, the interaction of the Russian kings with the Muslim world was very strong. Arab, Persian and Khoresm traders brought silk, precious stone, gold, silver, spices, glass utensils, jewellery etc to sell in Rus. Vladimir-Suzdal territory was their major trading partner. Merchants from Rus traded in cloth, leather, fur, honey, wood etc. It is through the traders that Russians got acquainted with Islam. Because of these trading practices, the first mosques in Rus appeared in port-cities like Yaroslav, Kostrama, Tver, Astrakhan etc for meeting the religious needs of the Muslim traders.

The process of interaction between Rus and Bulgaria was very active. The Russian kingdoms established relations with Khoresm, Bulgaria, Persia, and countries of Arabic world. Thus Rus' relations with the Muslim world were very consistent. Russia had maintained sufficiently active contacts with the Polovets. Some historians are of the opinion that the Polovets were subsequently assimilated with the Uzbeks, Kyrgyzs, Tatars, Kazakhs, Bashkirs, Karakalpaks, and Karachaevs. Records are prevalent of the influence of the Polovets in Russia. Rus had similar contacts with the Pechenegs as well.

Volga- Bulgaria prospered till it was conquered by Tatar-Mongols in the 13th century. This opened up a new chapter in the interaction of the Rus with the Muslim world.

After their victory at Kalka, the Mongols turned to Bulgaria. The Bulgars were well-informed about the state of affairs on this front and confronted Mongols in the remote approaches of Samara. The Bulgars could were victorious over the Mongols. It was an important victory over this strong and shrewd enemy. Less than 4,000 soldiers out of the 30,000-strong Mongol troops returned to the South.

Calm reigned for some time after their defeat. People of East Europe looked at Bulgaria with a great deal of hope in the face of a Mongol invasion. However, the Bulgars understood that a shrewd enemy like the Mongols would sooner or later come back. It spurred them on to mobilise all their forces to confront the old enemy. The Mongols launched their second attack in 1229, this time near the Ural Mountains. A 30,000-strong horde of Mongols inflicted heavy losses on the Bulgar forces. However, the Mongols could not muster courage to continue invasion of Bulgarian territory, because of their experience with the strong defence and courageous resistance from the Bulgars.

Though the second attack by Mongols was frustrated, the Bulgars further strengthened their defence in preparation for facing new attacks. They proposed to build a defence alliance with King Yuri 1 of the Principality of Vladimir Suzdal. The Bulgsars even proposed to pay the king for his participation in such an alliance. However Yuri did not understand the significance of this alliance in the face of an imminent Mongol invasion. He instead organised a military campaign by Russian dukes against Bulgaria. Even after the battle of Kalka they did not realise the importance of uniting forces for defending Rus. That is why Batu Khan the Mongol chief could defeat them so easily. However, he took control of Bulgaria before he took Rus.

The Bulgars halted the advance of the Mongols for the third time in the year 1232. However, Mongol troops were concentrated in close proximity to Bulgaria. In 1235, Mongols while discussing their military strategy in the Kurultai, decided to first occupy Bulgaria. Around 200,000-250,000 Mongol troops launched their attack on Bulgaria in 1236. Bulgar forces were badly defeated in the battle, leading to the control of their major city – Bulgar. Thereafter, the Mongol troops moved on to take control of the rest of Bulgaria. In 1237, they took control over western territory of Bulgaria following which they entered into the Russian territory virtually without any resistance. There were mutinies and partisan wars were organised against Mongols in the occupied territory. Mongols movement towards West Europe led to reduction of their forces in Bulgaria, and Bulgars taking advantage of this made a bid to regain their independence and had some success in this. However, Mongol troops returning from West Europe in 1240 re-established their control over Bulgaria.

Volga-Bulgaria was famous in all of Eurasia and the Arab world. The History of Bulgaria, written by historian Iakub ibn Nugmani in the middle of 11th century, played a significant role in the formation of the Islamic civilisation in Volga region. Cultural-spiritual centres like Bulgar, Suvar, Bilyar, and later, Kazan, appeared in this territory. The Sunni form of Islam spread over Bulgaria. Subsequently Sufism, mainly propagated by Bukhara's ascetic Baha-uddina Nakshab and, was practiced by the Bulgarian people. Sufi communities existed not only in the Middle-Volga region but also in Siberia. They were the dominant form of the Islamic world view from the 14th to the 15th centuries.

The Golden Horde (Mongolian khanate) provided a strong impetus for the expansion of Islam (during 13th- 14th century) in Rus. During this period Islam spread into the other Turkic and Turkic- converted regions of West Siberia and East Europe. These people were Hazars, Oguzs, Kipchaks and others. The Golden Horde khans pursued a prudent policy of granting equal rights to all religions. Golden Horde rulers provided protection to preachers of any religion in the event of their being harassed by bureaucrats or military leaders. This policy was effectively implemented particularly during the years of Khan Uzbek (1312-1342). During his rule,the death penalty was imposed on those who abused the religious feelings of others. Apart from this, Christian spiritual leaders were exempted from paying taxes.

The first ruler of Golden Horde was Khan-Muslim–Berke. In 1313, the Golden Horde ruler, Sultan Muhhamed Uzbek declared Islam as his state religion. Because of this, a multitude of Turkic tribes from Crimea to Siberia adopted Islam.[2] Along with this Khan Uzbek protected the Christian spiritual leadership by instructing his subjects not to do any harm to them —and to Orthodox Christians as a whole. His son Zanibek, in continuance of his father's traditions, established very warm relations with the Moscow metro pol it, Aleksei, who had helped in healing his wife, Taidulu. Most likely, this was the time when interfaith dialogue took roots on Russian soil.

The acquaintance of Moscow state with Islam took place through contacts with the visiting Tatar nobility who came to serve the Great Russian kings.[3]

In 1445 the great king of Moscow, Vasily-11, gifted the town of Gorodets-Meschersky to the Kazan prince Kasim for his military assistance—and thus began the history of the Kasimov kingdom on the banks of the Ok River. Muslims coming here to so settle were permitted to live comfortably here; they and built mosques and enjoyed full religious rights. Towns such as Serpukhov, Zvenigorod, Kashira, Yuriyev etc were also gifted to the Tatar Khans at different times. However, their authority was reinforced only in Kasimov.

The Kasimov kingdom is considered by many historians as an accidental phenomenon, and its emergence is explained largely by the desire of the Moscow kings to create a trouble-spot for Kazan, by creating a refuge for the members of aristocracy not satisfied with the Kazan ruler. The Kasimov Khans received their salary from the Moscow government and the Rezan kings. Apart from this, they possessed land on the basis of local laws. When Kasimov ceased to be a threat to Kazan, it turned into an enclave for those Muslims who wanted to serve the Russian kingdom.

Incorporation of khanates of Kazan, Astrakhan, Nagai and Siberia into Russia

- The Kazan khanate was created in 1430s out of part of the territory of the disintegrating Golden Horde. The Golden Horde was defeated by Russia in the year 1380 at the Battle of Kulikovski, le, which was followed by Tamurlane's devastating attack,which resulted in the fall of the Golden Horde. The GoldenHorde gradually weakened further as a result of a massive internal struggle for power— particularly between Tokhtamysh Khan and the Khan of the Trans-Volga Horde, Temir-Kutlu, who was supported by the Siberan Khan Shadibek. Following Tokhtamysh Khan's death in 1406, the power struggle intensified further,with his sons taking part in it. In the year 1411 Jalal al- Din Khan one of the sons of Tokhtamysh, dethroned Temir- Kutlu with the help of the Lithunian king Vitovt.

Jalal al- Din Khan who re-established Tatar control over Russia, forced Moscow king Vasily-11 to pay taxes to the Golden Horde from1412. Russia's dependence on the Golden Horde continued during Jalal al- Din Khan'sson Ulugh - Mohammed's rule also. Russian kings continued to visit the capital of the Golden Horde, Sarai-Berke, for receiving the necessary title to rule.

Ulugh-Mohammed was thrown out of power by Giasuddin; however, he permitted the former to rule over Crimean territory. Subsequently, Ulugh-Mohammed created the Kazan khanate, which was not dependant on the Golden Horde and which included the present-day territory of Tatarstan, Mari-el, Chabasia, Udmurtia and subsequently, it incorporated the present-day territory of Ulyanov, Penza, Saratov, Tambov districts. Ulugh Mohammed was not satisfied with this much territory and wanted to bring all of Rus under its control. He launched several attacks on Rus between 1439 and 1445 and finally took king Vasily -111 as prisoner of war. The Tatars subjected Vasily-111 to inhuman treatment but finally freed him, making Rus as a vassal of Kazan khanate. According to Russian historians, Kazan khanate's yoke over Russia was much worse and even harsher than that of Golden Horde.[4]

Vasily's son, Ivan -111 sincerely wanted to liberate Rus from Tatar yoke, but unfortunately he did not have an adequately strong army to fight the Tatars. Ivan-111 had to face several military set backs at the hand of the Tatars before he could liberate the Novgorod republic and incorporate that into Rus during the period from 1471 to 1478. But he never forgot his duty to get back the historical Russian territory from Tatar occupation. He launched his attack on Kazan in the year 1487, as a result of which, Kazan was captured by Russian troops and Khan's family members were arrested.

However, Ivan-111 did not dismantle the Kazan khanate. The only step that he took, after the Tatar defeat, was that he ceased paying the humiliating tax to the Kazan khanate which had become a Russian protectorate from the year 1487 to 1521. Kazan's khan, Mohammed- Emin, in order to liberate his khanate from Moscow's control, launched several attacks on Russia, but could not achieve any significant success.

Vasily-IV became the new ruler of Russia, following the death of his father Ivan-111 in the year 1505. Kazan's attack on Russian territory continued unabated. In the year 1536, Kazan's khan launched a massive attack on Russian territory, killing thousands of Russians and taking many as prisoners of war. It was only from 1545 that the new Czar, Ivan the Terrible, could really protect Russians from Tatar attacks and looting, by creating a strong army. Armed thus, Ivan the Terrible launched a massive attack on Tatars in the year 1551, which led to the fall of Kazan and liquidation of its khanate. However, serious military action between Russians and Tatars resumed once again in the year 1552, leading to the final defeat of the Tatars, ending their oppression on the Russians. This is how Kazan khanate became part of Rus, under Ivan the Terrible.

Ivan the Terrible understood well that the khanates of Kazan, Siberia, Astrakhan, Crimea and Turkey presented serious threat to Russia's peace, stability and security. The Astrakhan khanate was an independent unit which had broken away from the Golden Horde during the period 1459-1460. Independence of Astrakhan can be discussed only in relative terms, as it was dependant on the Nogai Horde from the east, and heavily dependant on the Crimean khanate from the west. Since the Astrakhan khanate was opposing Moscow, the first military campaign against it was launched by Russia in the year 1554.[5]

Russian troops captured Astrakhan under the military command Prince Yuri Ivanovich Pronsky-Shemyakinand Ignatiy Veshnyakov (My Source: http://www.prlib.ru/en-us/History/Pages/Item.aspx?itemid=580)Since it was useless to enter into peace agreement with Tatars, it was decided to merge Astrakhan with Russian territory.

In the 16th century the Siberian khanate occupied territories of all western Siberia along with the territory between the rivers Ob and Irtysh. However, only 31,000 people belonging to small ethnic groups such as Khanti, Mansi etc lived in this huge territory. The Tatars reached this territory in the 13th century without much resistance. There were no townships except some small settlements along the river banks. Chingi–Tura, what is present-day Tyumen, was the capital of the Siberian khanate. The Siberian khanate it self asked that it remain under the protection of Russia. The khan of the Siberian Khanate, Ediger, himself came as an emissary to Moscow in 1455 to offer greetings to Ivan the Terrible on the occasion of his victory over Kazan and Astrakhan khanates, and requested the Czar to keep his territory and population under his protection. Ivan the Teribile accepted the request, and this is how the Siberia khanate became part of Russia.

After Ediger was killed by the Kazakhs, their representative, Kuchum, became the new Khan, who suppressed the native people and killed the Russian ambassador. About ten years after he became khan Kuchum tried to conquer Russia and attacked the neighbouring territory. The native people,invited the Volga Cossacks, headed by Ermak Timofeyivich, to defend them; then trropsm of Kucham were routed, but Kuchum continued to remain a source of concern for the Russians. Kucham's troops were finally defeated at the hands of Russians in the year 1598, paving the way for Russian control over the territory. Nogai Horde,created towards the end of 15th century, occupied the territory from the left bank of Volgain the west, and Upper Irtysh—its former eastern border. This territory is practically the present-day territory of Orenburg district and Bashkiria. The nomadic people, who numbered almost 300, 000, lived in this massive territory. The Nogai Horde broke up into Greater Nogai, Little Nogai and Altyul territory in 1556. The Greater Nogai, ruled by Ismail and his successors, could maintain its independence till 1606 when the dynasty ceased to exist. Greater Nogai came under the zone of Russian influence voluntarity, starting from 1557. However, part of Nogai came under the control of Kuban and the other part came under the control of the Crimean khanate and Turkey after 1606. This is how Greater Nogai lost its state independence and ceased to be an ally of Russia.[6]

This is how, conquest of Kazan, Astrakhan, Nogai and Siberian khanates in 16th century led to incorporation of great tracts of territories, marked by a predominantly Muslim population, into Russian state. Central Asia and the Caucasus with their huge Muslim population became part of the Russian empire in the second half 19th century through conquest.

RUSSIA'S INTERACTION WITH ITS MUSLIM SUBJECTS

Russian kings were tolerant towards their Muslim subjects and did not take coercive measures to convert them into Christians, encouraging the conversion exclusively through economic measures.[7] However, strict measures were taken against conversion of Christians to Islam.

The reality of the time forced Rus to interact very closely with Islam. There was a significant number of Muslims in Nizhni-Novgorod from 1365 to 1366. Of course, there were large numbers of Muslims in Moscow as well. Beginning from the second half of the 15th century, Tatar settlements appeared in other Russian towns such as Kashir, Serpukhov, Kolomna, Zvenigorod, Podolsk etc. Islamic norms were reflected in the family as well as in the public life of these settlements. However, it must be noted that Christianity and Islamshareda peaceful co-existence in those places. The Golden Horde pursued a right policy in this regard.

The Kazan and Astrakhankhanates were conquered in the second half of the 16th century. Subsequently, the Great Nagai Horde and later western Bashkiria were incorporated into Russia. Gradually the entire Volga region came under the Russian Czars. The Siberian khanate merged with Russia around the end of the 16th century. Russia launched a war to conquer North-

Azerbijan in the 18th century. Nakhicheban, of the Ajeri kingdom was merged with Russia in 1828. Russia conquered Crimea in 1783. The last point of resistance in North Caucasus against Russia was liquidated in 1864. Following this the Central Asian khanates and emirates were merged into the Russian empire. The people of these conquered territories were Muslims.

Russia'sczar, Ivan the Terrible, issued a decree to convert the people living in the conquered territories, to Christianity. In the year 1556 the local populace rebelled against Russian authorities. Those Tatars who had converted to Christianity rose against the rebels and helped the Russian authorities suppress the rebellion. The Czarist authorities no doubt valued this.

The Russian authorities were under the impression that Islam could be uprooted from the Volga region and Siberia. Steps were taken to motivate Muslims materially, in order to convert them to Christianity. Muslims discriminated against Christians to some degree extent. According to a decree of Czar Mikhail Fyodorovich, Muslims could not hire Christians to work for them as servants. Czar Aleksei Mikhailovich confirmed this through a decree that stipulated severe punishment for converting somebody to Islam.[8] Representatives of Orthodox Christianity used any occasion for harassing Muslims. For example, the Orthodox Christian priests in Kazan had set a goal to oust all the Muslims from the city.

The Czarist authorities took away the land from Muslims and gave it to those who had converted to Christianity. Russian rulers, starting from Ivan the Terrible to Elizabeth Petrovna, took all necessary steps to convert the population in the conquered territory to Christianity. However, these steps did not yield the desired results.

Peter the Great brought changes in the hostile policy pursued earlier against the Muslims. The Quran was translated from French into Russian under his personal instructions in 1704 in Pitersburg. Muslims suffered once again under Catherine-II. Tatars and Bashkirs were subjected to harassment for supporting Pugachev's rebellion in 1773-1775. However, their rights were restored in 1784. They were given documents providing permission for engaging in trade.[9]

Catherine-11 issued a decree to set up an Assembly of Mullas belonging to Kazan Tatars in Ufa, headed by a Mufti. Crimea with its Muslim population was incorporated into Russia in 1783. Under the decree issued by Catherine II, the Muslim Spiritual Board was set up in Crimea.

The Centralised Muslim Management Board of Russia's Mohammedan Spiritual Assembly was set up in 1788 in Orenburg through a decree announced by Catherine the Great. In 1878 this Assembly was reorganised as the Spiritual Board of Muslims. The Muslim community in Crimea in 1794 was officially brought under the control of the mufti of Bakhchisarai. All these steps suggest that authorities accorded Islam an officially recognised status. That there were more than 100 mosques in Kazan province towards the end of 18th century bears testimony to this fact. There were schools under the mosques where Arabic as well as Islam were being taught. Under the personal instruction of the Empress, Muslim literature was allowed to be published. The Quran was published in Arabic languages. For this purpose the first Muslim printing press was opened in Kazan in the year 1802. These prudent steps were taken as huge territories with Muslim population like Central Asia, Caucasus, and Criemea were incorporated in the Russian empire which maintained relations with important Islamic states such as Turkey, Persia, and Morocco etc.[10]

Nikolai Krizhanovsky, the Governor-General of Orenburg in his report, drafted in 1865 -66, provided a detailed account of the situation with the Muslims living in his territory and highlighted the importance of the "Mohammedan Question." Krizhanovsky in his report also drew attention to the fact that the activities of the Muslim religious leaders created obstacles in the integration of Muslims with the Russian state and suggested measures to change the attitude of the Muslims towards the government through reform in the Muslim Spiritual Board.[11]

Czar Alexander-11 personally went through the report prepared by governor Krizhanovsky and asked the interior ministry to look into the issue. The governors of Novorossia, Tavria were involved in looking for a solution to this problem. In the year 1870, a special committee was set up in Orenburg to discuss the issue. The issue of Muslim spiritual leadership was discussed, not only for Orenburg and Caucasus but also for Turkestan and the Steppes.[12]

There were many territories with predominantly Muslim population in Russia whose religious affairs were regulated by the local administration. Here the mullas were elected by the local Muslims and confirmed by the regional administration. Thus, the spiritual leadership of Orenburg, Tavria and Caucasus, according to Russian laws, was considered as a *Sosloviye* or special category. Its confessional body was considered a state organ,whereas the central government did not regulate the religious life in other territories inhabited by a large number of Muslims.

Russia's central government, while pursuing a democratic approach towards Muslim spiritual leadership,tried to create conditions for the Muslims which permitted them to reap the benefits from integration with the multi-national state.[13] However, local Muslim spiritual leadership, which did not have much interest in this, was keen to get more material benefits. The spiritual leadership in the Volga region, in Orenburg behaved in this manner and resisted giving lessons in the Russian language in its Muslim educational institutions.

Nevertheless, the Russian interior ministry was of the opinion that the Muslim spiritual leadership did not have any particular political line that would require government attention while selecting higher spiritual leaders.

The Russian interior ministry in 1889 put forth a proposal before the State Council to change the system of election of the appointment of the mufti. A law was adopted by the ministry of interiors, in 1890, which stipulated the procedure of appointment of the mufti by the emperor and the members of the Muslim Spiritual Board.

There were nearly 30 million Muslims living in Russia around the end of the 19th century. Kazan became the fore post of Islamic civilisation in Russia. It turned into a significant centre of Muslim culture. Tatar spiritual leaders played an important role in this by reconciling major Islamic requirements with the politico-economic interests of the times.

There were nearly 50,000 mosques in the Russian empire on the eve of the Great October Revolution, out of which 22,000 mosques were in Russia alone. Large numbers of mosques were in Kazan, Nizhegorod, Orenburg, Ufa and other provinces.

The Muslim Spiritual Board was as rich as Orthodox Christian Church.. For example, 80% of all shops in the bazaar of Bukhara were located in the territory that belonged to the Muslim spiritual organisations. The Muslim spiritual organisations had great tracts of land from which they collected huge rents.

There were a number of mutinies that took place in the territories conquered by the Czar. There was one mutiny in Kazan province in 1878-79 while there was yet an other in the Bukhara khanate in 1888. Mutinies also occurred in Tashkent and Andizan in 1892 and 1898 respectively. The people living in the Caucasus launched a war against the Czarist regime from

1820s till 1864. There was a well-organised war by the local Muslim rebels against the Czarist army for decades. The head of the Imamat, Mulla Gazi Muhhamed was killed in the war. His successor, Mulla Gamzat, was killed in a conspiracy. The third, Mulla Shamil fought against the Russian army for a long time. He received all assistance from Turkey and Iran in his war against the Czarist army. Shamil was captured by the Russian army in 1859 after which the war came to an end, following a brief period of resistance. The Russian government did not plan to get rid of Muslims at that point of time. The Czarist regime tried to influence the Muslims through their spiritual leadership, which well-understood that there is no threat to their life, religion and property.

The Turkestan Governor-General Sergey Dukhovsky, in the year 1899 drafted a report for the government, which once again dealt with the question of the spiritual organisation of Muslims, at the level of the regions as well as the empire as a whole. Much before this,the ministry of internal affairs had proposed not to spread the activities of the Spiritual Board to Turkestan in the year 1880. A decision was taken in 1886 about the administrative system in Turkestan Krai (Governor-Generalship); however, it did not touch the issue of Muslim spiritual leadership. It can be said that the Russian empire did not feel the need to interfere in the religious life of Muslim Turkestan.[14]

The Turkestan Governor –General Sergey Dukhovsky in the year 1898 had proposed to the Ministry of Internal Affairs to set up a Muslim Spiritual Board in Turkestan along the lines of the one in the Caucasus, but without the mufti having to head the organisation. Instead,, it was proposed to appoint a Russian with the knowledge of *Shariat,* and the Turkic and Persian languages as the chairman, to lead the organisation. However, this proposal was rejected by the interior ministry which thought there was need for a higher spiritual body of Muslims, because it could lead to the strengthening of Muslim unity.

Governor General Dukhovsky once again placed the report on 'Islam and Turkestan' before the government in 1899. The report dealt with the Muslim issue not only in Turkestan but also in all the regions predominantly inhabited by Muslims. General Dukhovsky was guided by the thesis that Islam was inimical to Christian state and Islam was more a political force than a religion. This was the reason he proposed dismantling all the Muslim spiritual boards in Russia.[15]

However, General Dukhovsky's proposal was not accepted. Eminent Russian public and political figure Sergey Vitte speaking in this connection said that governor's proposal was a mere reaction to the attack on the Andizan garrison, and argued that there was no need to come to such a conclusion out of an isolated incident.

The Russian government issued a decree in 1904 that proclaimed the principles of inter-faith tolerance, which led to the reviewing of the entire complex of laws regulating Muslim religious life Muslims from different regions reacted sharply to the decree by advancing radical demands such as the election of spiritual leaders, state allocation to meet the expenses of spiritual leadership, equalising the status of Muslim spiritual leadership with that Orthodox Christianity and instituting Muslim spiritual boards in regions that did not have such bodies etc.

In order to deal with the situation, the government set up a commission to look into the questions of procedure of selection or appointment of Muslim spiritual leaders, exemption from military service to certain categories of Muslim spiritual leaders and institution of special spiritual boards for Kyrgyzs, the Muslims of Akmolinski, Semipalatinsky, Ural, districts and also for Muslim communities of North Caucasus, Stavropol province, Turkestan Krai etc.

A. Budilovich, representative of the interior ministry, insisted that knowledge of the Russian language should be made mandatory for all spiritual leaders. He also proposed the formation of Muftiat, not on the basis of nationality but on the basis of territorial principle. Changes were brought into the procedure of law-making in the year 1906, following which the suggestions were sent to the government for review.[16]

The revolutionary situation during the period 1905-06 made the religious movement in the country active. The first all Russia Muslim Congress held in Nizhni Novgorod in 1906 demanded the removal of all government control over the activities of the Muslim spiritual boards, and to create in Russia five muftiat – two in Caucasus, one each in Orenburg, Tavria, and Turkestan. The head of the muftiat was to be elected. All the muftiats were to function under one spiritual leader with the right to place reports about Muslims before the emperor. The Muslim representatives put forth these demands in the newly formed State Duma. However,the government's reformist activities ebbed as the revolutionary situation cooled down in the country.[17]

The government drafted its policy on Muslim spiritual leadership on the principles proposed by the conservative Muslim leaders, as it was really concerned about penetration of liberal ideas into spiritual leadership. In the year 1911, the Ministry of Interior sent out circulars stipulating that Muslims receiving education in certain madrasas could not work as mullas without the certification of the regional administration about their political reliability. The interior ministry imposed a ban on people, who had received their training in Turkey and Egypt, for teaching in madrasas. While appointing a mulla it was required to check that he was not associated with any Islamic movement. Many spiritual Muslim leaders were arrested during 1911-1913 for their reported involvement in pan-Islamism. [18]

The issue of state financing for maintenance of Muslim spiritual leaders remained relevant. State finances were available for maintaining the regional Muslim spiritual leadership and muftis were paid their remuneration by the government.

A special section was set up in the interior ministry for resolving the issue in Volga region. It was difficult to resolve the issue since the Orenburg spiritual assembly was controlled by the Tatars, which helped in spreading the Tatar influence, dominated by 'pan-Tatarism', to Turkestan and Bukhara.

The interior ministry conducted reviews on the activities of spiritual boards of Orenburg and Tavria during the period 1910-1912, which was the first ever revision in the history of Russian Islam. The government commission in its report pointed out the excessive bureaucratic trend, as well as lack of independence by some members of the Assembly. The commission, noting that spiritual assembly was paying attention only to religious schools, concluded that the Assembly had become outdated and met the requirements of neither the state administration nor Muslim community. A similar commission reviewing the activities of the Tavria Assembly came to identical conclusions in 1912.

In the year 1914, an inter-departmental commission was set up in order to look into the Muslim problems and representatives of Muslim spiritual leadership took part in the work of the commission whose main task was to resolve the issue of 'pan-Tatarism'. The interior ministry in its report noted that state created Muslim spiritual leadership as a *sosloviye* (Class) and thus facilitated the emergence of Tatar- Muslim propaganda amongst different ethnic groups in the Volga region, Ural and Siberia,and helped the strengthening of Islam in Russia. The home ministry report argued that the state should not play any role in organising religious-spiritual life of Muslims.

The issue of bringing a unified practice in the system of Muslim management was a controversial question. While a foreign ministry functionary, B. Klemm, drew attention to the diversity among Muslims of Russia, others spoke in favour of bringing a unified practice in Muslim management system. There were two points of view amongst the commission members on the issue. The first viewpoint suggested that measures were required, not against Islam, but against anti-state teachings. The introduction of a unified practice in the management of religious affairs on the entire territory would be helpful in blocking the development of sects. It was believed that the creation of the muftiat on the basis national principles would significantly reduce the dominating role of Tatars.

The second viewpoint noted that Islam is intolerant towards other faiths, and that is why maintaining its 'cleanness' cannot be the state's duty. It was also noted that nationalisation of Muslim spiritual leadership could hardly reduce Tatar influence. Finally, the majority decided to preserve the muftiats in Orenburg and Tavria.

The efforts to find a solution to the Muslim question continued after the February Revolution of 1917. The interior ministry report emphasising the importance of the Muslim question, argued in favour of the need for re-organisation in the spiritual management and cautioned about Muslim agitation for political and cultural self-determination. The ministry proposed to set up a common management system to run religious affairs on the basis of autonomy and this kind of system was proposed to be introduced in all regions with a sizable Muslim population. It was also proposed that some suggestions be made in the Musim congress held at Peterburg in 1914 be taken into consideration while reforming the system of Muslim religious affairs. Thc interior ministry representative, Sergey Rybakov, argued that in the new political situation in the country, state should not provide patronage to any religion, which meant the spiritual management board,should not function as part of the state structure. Rybakov was of the opinion that the bid for cultural – national self-determination does not threat territorial integrity of the state. More than that, he argued that progressive sections of Russian Muslim would facilitate integration with the state.[19]

A prudent policy pursued by Czarist regime yielded its result. Muslims joining the Russian empire did not regret it. Seven years after Samarkand was incorporated into the Russian empire, the Islamic spiritual leadership congratulated General-Governor Kaufman on the occasion of the victory of

Russian weaponry. Muslim spiritual leadership did not support the uprisings against the Czarist government; rather it extended help in establishing order and establishing stability on their territory. When there was an uprising in Kazan province in the 1820s, the head of the local police department Major General Zhitkov reported to the central authorities at Petersburg that the Muslim spiritual leadership was not taking part in the mutiny, and rather demonstrating its loyalty and prudence. Mullas themselves accused the provocators for the disorder.

The Russian Muslim spiritual leadership had always conducted itself very wisely. Moreover, the Czarist regime also pursued a rational and pragmatic policy towards Muslims. For example, the Ufa mufti, Aby Salim Abdurahimov, in his religious-spiritual message to the Muslims in the year 1836 called all of them to be loyal to Allah and Czar Nikolai Pavlovich and obey his orders.[20] While taking the oath the Muslims promised to do so this by putting their hands on the Quran to declare they would serve and obey the Russian Emperor.[21] The authorities were equally strict with Christians and Muslims alike on matters of observing religious rituals, and corresponding decrees were issued in this regard. Muslim loyalty to the Czar was demonstrated by the fact that Muslims conducted prayers and ceremonial meetings during the celebration of 300 years of the Romanov dynasty's rule in Russia.

The turn of 20th century witnessed growing political activities by Muslim representatives. Muslims had organised two national congresses (1905-07) which passed resolutions that demonstrated their loyalty to the Czarist government but advanced many demands.

The factors that promoted political activism were Russia's defeat in the Russo-Japanese war of 1904-05, developments in Muslim countries and the uprisings by workers and peasants. The first Russian Revolution of 1905-07 compelled Czar Nikolas 11 to initiate certain political reforms that created space for the political movement of the Muslims. In the year 1905, the Muslim movement succeeded in building a unified political platform that demanded religious self-determination, fair land reform etc. The building of a common platform was followed by a major initiative to convene the first-ever Congress of the Muslims of Russia (CMR) that appreciated the step for creating the Russian Duma and called for inclusion of Muslims in the reform process. The second congress, held in 1906, took the decision to create a political party, the Union of Muslims (UM), which was liberal and pro-reform without being radical or anti-Russian. The third congress held in Nizhni Novgorod, adopted a programme that was close to that of Constitutional Democrats. This is explained by the fact that members of both parties consisted mainly of the bourgeoisie, intelligentsia, and land -owning nobility. This membership gave the new Muslim party, like the Cadets, a liberal democratic character and placed it in the mainstream of the reform movement; however, as a loose association of influential members of the Muslim elite, Ittifak suffered from a major weakness in that it was not representative of most of Russia's Muslim community.[22]

While Russia's Muslim political leadership developed a Muslim agenda through All Russia Muslim Congress, Ittifak party tried to establish itself in Russia's newly-constituted State Duma. The Muslims had 25 members in the first Duma and 39 members in the second Duma. The Second Duma, despite the rise in the number of Muslim members, witnesses decline of Ittifak party's influence as a result of infighting and factionalism. The dissolution of second Duma by the Czar in 1907 coincided with the virtual break up of Ittifak as an effective party.

Although Ittifak and the All Russia Muslim Congress faded in significance as Czar Nikolas 11 reasserted his imperial authority and revolutionary sentiment declined, their legacy as vehicles for unified Muslim political action remained alive. The moderate bourgeois liberals, who formed the majority of Muslim political activists, abstained from discussing issues of political autonomy and limited themselves to demands for liberal reforms and equal rights regardless of ethnicity or religion.[23]

The fourth congress held in 1914 was almost a non-event with just 30 delegates, and failed in its attempt to revive Ittifak as a viable political party. All though Ittifakand All Russia Muslim Congress lost much of its influence, nevertheless it remained as an united platform championing Muslim cause.

The fall of the Czarist regime and victory of the October Revolution offered plenty of opportunities to obtain greater autonomy in the sphere of culture, religion and politics. Some Muslims even aspired to gain full independence, and some even achieved it for a brief period.

After the fall of the Czarist regime,Muslims emerged as a strong force between the period of February Revolution and October Revolution. The All Russia Muslim Congress got a new lease of life to influence the political developments in the country and its congress held in May 1917 gathered more than 800 delegates from a host of Muslim organisations across the country.

The congress despite differences on a host of issues, took decisions in favour of a unified Russian state and formation of separate Muslim regiments in the army to serve in Muslim-dominated territories. Delegates of the next congress recommended that the Muslims of inner Russia and Siberia should resolve issues concerning their territorial autonomy,religion,culture, education, language etc. The Congress took a decision in favour of setting up a Council, consisting of 12 members, headquartered in Ufa, to take steps for creating a Muslim national-cultural autonomy. There was a strong move to create a Volga-Ural Republic with adequate autonomy.

After the October Revolution, the Bolsheviks offered an opportunity to Russian Muslims to organise themselves politically and promised to provide national self-determination, particularly in the religious and cultural spheres. The Bolshevik government issued a "Decree on the Rights of Peoples of Russia "that stipulated equality and sovereignty of the peoples of Russia and the right of non-Russian peoples to self-determination,including the right of secession. The Bolshevik leadership in its famous "Appeal to All Toiling Muslims of Russia and the East "promised religious, as well as host of other freedoms to Muslims. The Muslims supported the Bolsheviks because they met their aspirations, contrary to the White Guards. During the civil war Muslims on the whole fought on the side of the Bolsheviks. Reformist Muslims were convinced that Muslim revival would be much easier under the Communists than under the reactionary While Guards. The nascent communist government permitted Muslims a certain degree of cultural, religious and national autonomy.[24]

Historically, Muslims had aspired for greater political and cultural freedom and autonomy. The idea to form separate units with the majority of the Muslim population under the federal political system was always strong. There were proposals to form three major political – territorial units with a dominant Muslim population, namely – one in the Volga region, incorporating the Tatars and Bashkirs, the second one in Central Asia and the third one in North Caucasus.

However, there was a radical shift in the policy of the Bolsheviks towards religion as a whole from 1928. While the 1918 constitution had permitted both religious and anti-religious propaganda, Stalin launched a full-fledged onslaught against religion from 1928 from an ideological point of view, in order to achieve the objective to create a"Soviet Man" — forgetting all religious and ethnic differences. The attack against Islam was no exception.

As a result, the country saw a massive closure of hundreds of churches and mosques. This attack on religion affected clergies from both Orthodox Christianity and Islam. The Law on Religious Associations, promulgated in 1929,stipulated that state authority supervise and regulate religious life in the country. All regions, including Islam, suffered as a result of this law which placed severe restrictions on religious practices.

During the Second World War, there was a serious change in the attitude of the government towards religion as it was required using all means to the entire population using all. That is why there was a relaxation of restrictions on religious practices during the war years, and Islam too benefited from this. The more or less relaxed atmosphere, in the case of religion, continued after Stalin's death during Khruschev's period too. The Breznev period did not see excesses in the sphere of religion, though the atheism continued to remain the state religion. The situation in the sphere of religion started improving only during Gorbachev's *perestroika* years.

Russian Intelligentsia and Islam

The Quran was translated into Russian from French in the year 1704, under the instruction of Peter the Great. Russian philosophers and thinkers such as Alexander Khomyakov and Peter Chadayev had made objective assessments about Islam. Khamyakov in his writings highly appreciated the moral values of Islam, the strength of its spirit, and its greatness and reformist's tendencies. Khomyakov wrote that Muslims could not be defeated as long as they maintained moral strength and intellectual might.[25] The Great Russian Philosopher Chadayev, in his philosophical letters wrote, 'Islam is part of Christian teachings'. According to him, Islam combines truth with confusion. However this kind of combination is necessary and useful for universal acceptance of a true and spiritual law. Famous Russian philosophers such as Nikolai Danilovsky, Nikolay Fyodorov and Solovyov also wrote about Islam in the 19th century. Danilovsky was of the opinion that Islam has lost all its potential and was on the verge of complete collapse. He thought Islam was a step backward compared to Christianity. He found its proof in the fact that the Muslim states had failed to develop.

Nikolai Fyodorov, who found the Muslim perception of God to be very harsh, did not accept Islam. According to him,the Muslim god does not have the attributes of God, and that is why it does not share man's sufferings. That is why; 'He' is not the father of all people as it is perceived by Christians.

Solovyov perceived Islam more objectively. In the first stage of his creative evolution Solovyov did not accept Islam at all. He believed that Islam leads to despotism in politics, and in the moral sphere it leads to a huge gap between spiritual and human beginnings. In the first state of his evolution he perceived Islam as an obstacle to the progress of the Muslim community. In the later state, Stag Solovyov had a more balanced assessment of Islam. He acknowledged the significant role of Islam for Pagans.

It is mentioned in the 'Povesti Vremenikh Let' (Chronicles) that contacts between Russichs (Russians) and Muslims of Volga-Bulgar began in the year 985. There was a peace agreement signed between Kievan Rus and Volga-Bulgaria in that year. The Muslims of Volga-Bulgaria sent a special delegation to Kiev for meeting King Vladimir in order to acquaint the Russichs with Islam. Vladimir liked the polygamy permitted under Islam, but thought that the ban on wine and 'cutting' (circumcision) ritual would not be acceptable to his subjects. Vladmir sent a special mission to Volga-Bulgar Bulgaria to get acquainted with Islamic services. However, the emissaries did not like the prayer –ceremony. As a result of the negative report of the mission, Vladimir gave up the idea of adopting Islam in his kingdom–Kievan Rus.

Ethnic Composition of Russia's Muslim Population

According to the census conducted in the year 2002, the total population of ethnic Muslims—citizens and non-citizens of Russia(which includes Tatars, Baskirs, Kazakhs) the people of Central Asia and North Caucasus- constituted 14.4 million people— roughly 10% of the country's total population. Other sources suggest that Muslims constituted a populace of 20 million, out of Russia's total population of 140 million. Official statistics about the Muslim population show less than the actual data, because it takes into account only those who are registered in particular places in the Russian Federation. For example, the Ajeri population in Moscow constituted only 30,000 souls in the year 1996 whereas, according to the Interior ministry figure, there are nearly half a million Ajeris living in Moscow.

All the people belonging to the Turkic language group, with the exception of Chubashi, Yakuts, Hakas and Altai, and also entire population of the North Caucasus, with the exception of Abkhazs, are considered as ethnic Muslims. Because of the problem with the division of ethnos and sub-ethnos, the exact number of Muslims in Russia is not known. The majority of scholars tend to think that there are 300,000 Kryashen and Nagaibaks among the Tatars and 10,000 ethnic orthodox Christians among the Kabardinians. There are around 100,000 Ossetin-Muslims. Almost one third of Azhars have adopted Christianity. According to a sociological survey, one-fourth of the Adigei and Tatars, and upto 10% Kazakhs have adopted Orthodox Christianity over the past 20 years. Russian Muslims represent nearly 30 percent native people of the country.

The All-Russia census conducted in 2002 shows the number of ethnic people belonging to Islam.

ETHNIC COMPOSITION OF RUSSIAN MUSLIMS

Table 1.1: (in thousands)

ABAJIN	37,942
CHECHENS	1,360,253
AVARS	814,473
AGULS	28,297
ADYGEI	128,528
AJERIS	621,840
ARABS	10,630
CENTRAL ASIAN ARABS	181
BALKARS	108,426
BASHKIRS	1,67,3389
BESREMAN	3122
AZHARS	252
DARGINS	510,156
DUNGAN	801
INGUSH	413,016
KABARDIN	519,958
KAZAKHS	653,962
KARAKALPAKS	1609
KARACHEVS	192-182
KYRGYZS	31,808
KUMIKS	422,409
KURDS	19,607

LAKTS	156,545
LEZGIN	411,535
OSSETIN DIGORTS	100,000
PUSHTUNS	9800
TUTULTSI	29,929
TABASARAN	131,785
TAJIKS	120-136
TALLISH	2548
TATARS	5,554,601
CRIMEAN TATAR	4,131
TURKS	92,415
TURK-MESKHETEN	3257
TURKMEN	33,053
UZBEK	12,916
UIGUR	2867
HEMSHIL	1542
TSAKHUR	10,366
CHERKES	60517
SHAPSUTI	3231

Source: All Russia Census conducted in 2002.
Source: Silantiyev, R.A. (2008), *Encyclopedia on Islam in Contemporary Russia* (Энциклопедия ислама в современной России), Moscow: Algoritm

Thus, the largest Muslim community in Russia is the Tatars (5.5 million), Bashkirs (1.6 million), Chechens (1.3 million), Avars (0.8 million), Kazakhs (0.65 million), Ajeris (0.6 million) Dargins (0.51 million), Kabardins (0.52 million), Kumiks (0.42 million) and Ingush (0.41 million).[26]

According to most of the Muslim leaders, Russia's Muslim population could be around 20 million. There are some Muslim scholars who assert that Russia's Muslim population could be 25 to 35 million, or even 45 million. The Russian President,Vladimir Putin, is of the opinion that the country's Muslim population is around 15 million. Most scholars believe that the Muslim population of Russia fluctuates between 12-18 millions.[27] It should be noted that in the 20th century the ratio between Orthodox Christianity and the Muslim population has been constantly fluctuating in favour of the latter. If the ratio was 16:1 in 1926, it became 10:1 in 1999. The fact is that the country's Muslim population is constantly growing.[28] Who can be called a Muslim in Russia? If we go by the perception that a man who regularly observes all the rituals and prohibitions of Islam is a true Muslim, then there number could be between 8-9 million; yet others think this number could be 2-3 million.[29] According to some reports, 90% of those consider themselves as Muslims do not visit Mosques.[30]

Russian Muslims consists of two areal(branches) – Tatar-Bashkir and North-Caucasus. Tatars—consisting of 5.5 million,are settled in Tatarstan and Bashkirstan, and also in some districts of Povolzhya, Southern Ural and Siberia. Bashkirs, consisting of 1.6 million people, constitute the second largest community. It cannot be ruled out that the Ajeris,consisting of 1.5 to 2 million living in Russia, could be the second largest Muslim community in Russia. In certain regions of North, North-West, Far East, Ajeris constitute 25-40 % of the Muslim population.

Chechens constitute the largest Muslim community in Northern Caucasus. Out of the total 1.3 million Chechens, about 800 thousand live in Chechnya itself. The total Muslim population in the North-Caucasus region is estimated at around 6 million people.

Muslims constitute the majority in 7 federal units of the Russian Federation : Ingushetia – 98%, Chechnya – 96%, Dagestan – 94%, Kabardino-Balkaria – 70%, Karachevo-Cherkasia – 63%, Baskortstan – 54,5%, Tatarstan – 54%. The Muslim population in Adygei constitutes 21%, Astrakhan district – 26%, North Assetia – 21%, Orenburg district – 16.7%, Khanti-Mansi autonomous republic – 15%, Ulyanovski oblast – 13%, Chelyabinsk oblast – 12%, Tyumenski oblast – 10,55, Kalmykia – 10%.[31] The 1. 5 million Muslim population of Moscow constitutes 10% of the capital's population. According to Ravil Gainutddin, Chairman of the Council of Mufti of Russia, Moscow's Muslim population has reached 2 million. However, according to the census total true Muslims in the capital constitute 400,000.

Muslims living in Russia can be divided into four groups on an ethnic and territorial basis: the Volga region (Tatar –Bashkir), Caucasus, Central Asia and external. Large Turkic groups of Russia, such as the Tatars, Bashkirs and Kazakhs, form the largest inter-regional Muslim community of Russia —Pavolzskaya Ummas,in terms of population. This community looks like the most mono-ethnic (about two thirds of its members belong to Tatar nationality) and most mono-religious, with an absolute majority of its members belonging to the Sunni faith of Hanifa Mazkhab. About 55% of Russian Muslims (7,890,000) belong to Pavolzhskaya Umma. All the regions of Volga, Ural and Siberian federal districts (except Tyva, Hakasia, Altai and Krasnoyarski krai), Astrakhan and Volgagrad districts of Southern Federal district belong to its Areal. Tatars, Bashkirs and Kazakhs also constitute a majority of the Muslims in regions of central, north-west and Far East districts. However, its share fluctuates from 44% to 60%, which allows for considering these territories as zones convergence of different inter-regional Ummas.

There are three sub-centres in the Middle-Volga—namely Kazan, Ufa and Moscow, to which the majority of its Muslim communities is historically drawn. The Ummas of Central and North –Western districts, except the Komi republic and Nizhgorodski district, are oriented towards Moscow sub-centre. Tatarstan, Udmurtiya, Mordoviya, Marii El, Chubashiaya, Komi, Kirov, Ulyanovski, Samarski and Penza district belong to the zone of influence of the Kazan subcentre. Muslim communities of Bashkortstan, Orenburg, Chelyabinsk, Sverdlovsk and Kurgan districts, and also Permsk Krai are oriented towards the Ufa subcentre. Regions like Saratov, Astrakhan and Volgagrad and Tyumen districts have more independent regional Ummas, which do not have clear ties with any of the sub-centres.

The Muslim community of North Caucasus, dominated by Chechens, Avars, Ajeris, Dargins and Ingush, belongs to the Caucasian inter –regional Umma. This Muslim community looks different from the ethnic and confessional point of view. More than 30 ethnic groups of people belonging to this community practice Sunnism of Sariat Mazkhab (around 65%), 30% practice Sunnism of Khanafit orientation and 5% practice Shiism. A significant part of the people of Dagestan, Chechnya and Ingushetia practice Sufi Tarikat of Nakshbandiya and Kadiria Ansshajiliya. The Muslims of North Caucasus are highly religious. However, their degree of religiousity depends on their ethnic belonging.

About 42% Russian Muslims (6,55,000) belong to the Caucasian Ummas. However, their orientation is limited to only 9 regions of south federal district—namely Dagestan, Chechnya, Ingushetia, Karachaevo-Cherkesia, Kabardino-Balkria, North Ossetia, Adygei, Kalmykei and Stavropolski Krai. However, the Caucasian Ummas very swiftly spreads their influence to new regions, which is conditioned by the high level of birth rate and migration mobility of their members. Over the last several years, the people of North Caucasus have significantly changed the ethnic structure of all large and middle cities of the country, which has questioned the monopoly of the Volga region Ummas in the Far East and Central Asia.

The Central Asian Umma has the third inter-regional Muslim community;primarily Uzbeks, Taziks, Kyrgyzs and Turkmen belong to this community. The vast majority of this community practices Sunnism of the HanifaMazkhab, though, there are many supporters of Wahabism among the Uzbeks and Tajiks and a significant number of Muslims living in the Pamir region also practice Ismailism.

Unlike the people of the Middle-Volga and Caucasus Umma, the ethnic groups constituting Central Asian Ummas do not form regions of compact living in rural areas, preferring instead to settle in cities. Due to their unity and high level of religious feelings, Uzbeks and Tajiks exert significant influence on the life of the urban Muslim community, often occupying leading posts in it. Their migrant status brings them closer to the Muslims of North Caucasus, many of whom have abandoned their native places in search of better life or save themselves from war and political instability. Only 2% of Russian Muslims roughly 310,000 belong to the Central Asian Ummas, who do not dominate in any of the Russian regions. However, their number is 4-6 times higher in Siberian and Far East federal districts.

Arabs, Turks, Kurds, Persians and Pushtuns constitute the smallest group of Russian Muslims and are described as belonging to the community of the External Ummas. This inter-regional Muslim community is quite multi-ethnic. Arabs, belonging to Sunni faith seem to be most active in this group. Their being native Arab speakers and highly religious, has created the impression that among the Russian Muslims they are the teachers of Islam and the Muslim culture. They form a significant part of the madrassa teachers, and in some regions they occupy the position of spiritual leaders. Only 1% of Russian Muslims, comprising of around 1 lakh 40 thousand belong to the External Ummas. Because of their small number, the members of External Umma do not dominate in any region. However, they exerted a strong influence in the life of some regional Muslim communities. For example, the leader of Karelia Umma is a Palestinian Arab.

Despite the existence of four regional Muslim communities in Russian Islam, its destiny is largely determined by two ummas, namely Middle-

Volga and Caucasian umma. Sharp differences between the two major Ummas provide bipolar character to Russian umma and make it difficult to unite Russian Muslims under one leadership. The Middle-Volga centre of Russian Umma is larger and more powerful than the Caucasus Ummas, in terms of number of Muslim population and communities belonging to them and also in terms of the influence of their spiritual leaders on the Russian Islamic process. However, this advantage is not absolute. Muslims of the North Caucasus are more active and energetic than their fellow people in Kazan and Ufa. According to some scholars it is possible that in course of time the situation in Russian Islam might change in favour of the Caucasus centre.

Ethno-Religious Composition of Population:

According to their faith, Russian Muslims are divided into major groups – namely Sunni of the Khanafat orientation,which includes Tatars, Bashkir, Kazakhs, Karachaevs, Balkars, Kabardins, Cherkes, Adygei, Abazin, Nogaits, Islamised Ossetians, and one third of Ajeris and people of Central Asia,except the small group of Tamir Ismails. Chechens, Ingush and the majority of people in Dagestan belong to Sunni of Sharifitski orientation. About 65% and 30 % of Russian Muslims belong to these two groups respectively.

'Sufi Tarikat of Nakshbandiya' and 'Kadiriya Ansshajiliya', popular among the Muslims of Dagestan, Chechnya and Ingushetia, of late have tried to spread their influence beyond these regions. Followers of non-traditional sects, tarikat, particularly the *Nimatullakhii* brotherhood, are seen among the Muslims of large cities like Moscow, St. Petersburg and Kazan. Two thirds of Russian Ajeris practice Shiism of Zafaritorientation, which constitutes 3% Russian Muslims. One can find many Shiite–ismails among Tamir Taziks. Registered Shiite Muslim communities function in Moscow, Astrakhan, Makhachkala and Dervent.

Territorial Structure of Muslim Population:

Russian Muslims are settled in regions very unevenly as they were historically concentrated in several regions. At present, Russian Muslims live in all the regions of the country. However, they have not formed places of Muslim concentration in the cities. Ethnic Muslims constitute a majority in seven federal units of the Russian Federation, namely Chechnya, Ingushetia, Dagestan, Kabardino-Balkaria, Karachaevo-Cherkesia, Bashkortstan and Tatarstan.

As a whole, the share of Muslim population in the 20 most Islamised Russian regions looks like the following:

Table 1.2: Muslim Population in Regions

1	Republic of Ingushetia	98 %
2	Chechnya	96 %
3	Dagestan	94 %
4	Kabardini Balkaria	70 %
5	Karachaevo-Cherkesia	63 %
6	Bashkortstan	54.5 %
7	Tatarstan	54 %
8	Adygei	27 %
9	Astrakhan District	26 %
10	Northern Ossetia	21 %
11	Orenburg district	16.7 %
12	Khanti Manciski region	15 %
13	Ulyanovsk	13 %
14	Chelyabinsk district	12 %
15	Yamalo Nenetski region	11.5 %
16	Tyumen district	10.5 %
17	Kalmikiya	10 %
18	Udmurtiya	7.65 %
19	Altai republic	7.4 %
20	Stavropol Krai	7 %

Source: Silantiyev, R.A. (2008), *Encyclopedia Islam in Contemporary Russia (Энциклопедия ислама в современной России)*, Moscow: Algoritm

Table 1.3: Regions with the Largest Regional Ummas in Terms of Population Look as Follows

1	DAGESTAN	2 million 430 thousand
2	Baskortstan	2 million 234 thousand
3	Tatarstan	2 million 40 thousand
4	Chechnya	1 million 58 thousand
5	Kabardino-Balkarskari ya	5 Lakh 35 thousand

6	Ingushetia	4 lakh 58 thousand
7	Chelyabinsk district	4 lakh 25 thousand
8	Moscow	4 lakh 10 thousand
9	Orenburg district	3 lakh 65 thousand
10	Karachaevo- cherkes republic	2 lakh 76 thousand
11	Astrakhan district	2 lakh 60 thousand
12	Sverdolov district	2 lakh 36 thousand
13	Khanti-mansisk autonomous district	2 lakh 16 thousand
14	Perm krai	1 lakh 92 thousand
15	Stavropol krai	1 lakh 90 thousand
16	Stavropolski district	1 lakh 85 thousand
17	Samara district	1 lakh 83 thousand
18	Ulyanovsk district	1 lakh 80 thousand
19	Northern Ossetia	1 lakh 50 thousand
20	Tyumen district	1 lakh 40 thousand

Source: Silantiyev, R.A. (2008), *Encyclopedia Islam in Contemporary Russia (Энциклопедия ислама в современной России)*, Moscow: Algoritm

It is note-worthy that half of Russian Muslims lives in the three federal districts of Dagestan, Tatarstan, and Bashkortstan. It is their regional Muslim community, along with the Moscow and Chechen Ummas, thatshape the face of Russian Islam.

The other indicators of active Islamic life in the regions are reflected in the data provided by the Ministry of Justice of the Russian Federation,which talks about the share of the registered Muslim community in the total number of registered organisations. In 2007 3783 Muslim organisations were registered in Russia,constituting 16.5% of the total number of registered organisations. This following table shows this ratio in different regions of the country.

Table 1.4: Share of Muslim Organisations in The Total Number of Registered Organisations in Different Regions

1	Republic of Dagestan	96.6%
2	Chechen republic	88%
3	Ingushetia	85%

4	Republic of Tatarstan	74.2%
5	Karachaevo-Cherkesk Republic	70.8%
6	Kabardino-Balkar republic	70.8 %
7	Republic of Bashkortstan	65.7%
8	Ulyanovsk district	44%
9	Tyumen district	36.6%
10	Orenburg district	34.1 %
11	Kurgan district	32.5%
12	Astrakhan district	30.5%
13	ANAO	28%
14	Chelyabinsk district	24.6%
15	Permski Krai	22.2 %
16	XMAO	20%
14	Penzenski district	19.45
18	North Ossetia	18%
19	Omsk district	17.8%
20	Adygei	17%

Source: Silantiyev, R.A. (2008), *Encyclopedia Islam in Contemporary Russia (Энциклопедия ислама в современной России)*, Moscow: Algoritm

Table 1.5: Number Of Muslim Organisations Region-Wise

1	Republic of Tatarstan	1041
2	Republic of Dagestan	658
3	Republic of Baskortstan	499
4	Orenburg district	130
5	kabardino-balkarski republic	121
6	karachaevo-cherkask republic	107
7	Ulyanovsk district	105
8	Permski krai	93
9	Samara district	84
10	Tyumen district	79

Source: Silantiyev, R.A. (2008), *Encyclopedia Islam in Contemporary Russia (Энциклопедия ислама в современной России)*, Moscow: Algoritm

Administrative-Territorial Division of Muslim Community in Russia

The Islamic community of Russia at present is a divided house. In terms of number of Sunni Muslims bearing higher spiritual designation, Russia is ahead of any other country in the world. The number of centralised Muslim organisations is almost equal to number of the eparchy diocese) of the Russian Orthodox Christianity. However, this kind of division did not exist always. The first centralised Muslim organisation appeared in Russia in 1788 when Catherine-11 issued decrees for defining the mulla and other spiritual clerks under Mohammedan law, as also on the establishment of a spiritual assembly in Ufa, on appointment of the mufti etc. Starting from 1805, decrees were issued for bringing order in the life of Muslims of Transcaucasia.

Russia's October Revolution brought unprecedented changes in the situation of Muslim society in the country

At present there are 57 functioning centralised Muslim organisations, some of which are not registered. Out of these 26 belong to the Central Spiritual Board of Muslims, 18- council of muftis of Russia, 8- 'ksmsk' and 5 organisations function independently.

Muslim communities in 17 regions of Russia that include all the republics—the North Caucasus, Altai republic, Marii El, Karelia,Komi, Altai Primorye, Krasnoyarski Krai, Irkutsk and Stavropolski Krai and Hanti-Manski autonomous republic, all function under one regional centralised structure. There is no centralised structure of muftiat in the 20 federal units that include Hakasia, Buryatia, Belgorod, Vladimir, Vologda, Ivanovo, Kaliningrad, Kaluga Kamchatka, Kostrama, Kursk, Leningrad, Murmansk, Orlov, Ryazan, Tambov, Tver, Tula, Chita, and Yaroslav districts. However their Muslim communities have a similar legal status.

Two parallel centralised structures function in 19 Russian regions, which include Tatarstan, Bashkortstan, Mordovia, Chubasia, PermskyKrai, Kurgan, Kemerova, Moscow, Omsk, Orenburg, Penza, Rostov, Sverdlovsk, Tomsk, Tyumen, Chelyabinsk, Ulyanovsk, districts and Yamalo-Nenetski autonomous region. Nine Russian regions that include Republic of Udmurtia, Yakutia, Astrakhan, Volgagrad, Kirov, Nizhegorod, Novosibirsk,Samara districts and St. Pitersburg, have Centralised Muslim organisations and also separate Muslim communities which do not fall under those centralised structures.

Seven federal units, that include Altai, Krasnodar, Stavropol and Havarov Krai, Archangelsk, Magadan and Sakhalin districts, have separate

Muslim communities of varied legal standing. There is no registered Muslim community in 15 regions, that include Tyva, Amur, Bryansk, Voronezh, Lipetsk, Novgorod, Pskovo, Buryat, Ust-Ordinsk Buryatsk, Chukotka and Evenkiski Autonomous Region and Evreisk Autonomous District.

"Muslim Demographic Threat":

Of late, there is lot of talk in Russia about the "Muslim demographic threat", even "imminent Islamisation of Russia." The Russian nationalist political leaders often raise this issue. This discourse gains momentum against the backdrop of the decline of Russia's population by almost one million per annum and the rise of its Muslim population in absolute terms and in terms of percent. The North Causasus region witnessed the highest growth of Muslim population between 1989 and 2003. For example, during this period, the Muslim population of Ingushetia grew by 91%, the Muslim population of Kalmikiya by 52%, population of Dargints by 44%, population of the Avars by 39% and the Kabardins by 34%. The Tatar population increased by 36, 000 during this period.[32] This vividly demonstrates that the assertion about "imminent Islamisation of Russia" is highly exaggerated.

However, if you look at migration from North Caucasus, you find tens of thousands of young Muslims penetrating into the cities of Central Asia and Russia. However, the share of Muslim population is growing more rapidly in regions like greater Moscow, Astrakhan, Volgograd districts, Krasnodar and Stavropol Krai, and this demographic movement is perceived rather negatively by the native population. According to some statistics, the number of migrants has reached 200,000 in Novosibirsk and 300,000 thousand in Orenburg.[33]

According to Russian sociologist Larisa Khoperskaya, about a million migrants have reached Kuban in South Russia over the last ten years,most of them from the Caucasus region and Central Asia.[34] These ethno-Islamic trends in the migration process have created a certain number of problems in those regions. The Russian Muslim community is multi- ethnic and multi-cultural in character, with 38 nationalities of Russia practicing Islam. Each of the two above-mentioned large areals has its own confessional tradition, history— and each of them has a separate relationship with the Centre. According to the chairman of the council of muftis of Russia, the chief Imam of the Moscow Mosque, Ravil Gainuddin, Muslims of Russia can be divided into three groups according to their place of living. They are Siberia and Far

East (situated a great distance from the Centre),the Central region consisting of Povolzhya, Ural, Moscow etc, and the third,the North Caucasus.

The Tatar Muslim community has integrated the most closely with Russian society. The peak of strained relations with the central authority took place in the 16-18 century,whereas the memory of war with the Central Authority in the 19th and 20th centuries remains fresh in the case of the Caucasus Muslims. The mentality of the Tatar and Bashkir Muslims is quite different from that of other Muslims. Looks-wise also they are quite similar to Europeans. One should bear in mind that there appears to be some kind of confrontation between Christianity and Islam in the world, whereas there seems to be no contradiction between Orthodox Christians and Muslims of the ethnic Tatar and Bashkir origin in Russia.

North Caucasus appears to be different in this respect, as its integration into Russian society appears to be incomplete, and feelings of alienation seem to be pretty serious. The eastern part of North Caucasus – Dagestan, Ingushetia, Chechnya are more Islamised,whereas its western part is less Islamised though the influence of Islam is on the rise in that region. Experts divide North-Caucasus into several sub-regions. According to Russian expert Enver Kisriyev, the first sub-region is Dagestan, second- Chechnya, third - Karachaevo- Cherkesiya and Adygea, and the last one is Northern Ossetia.[35] Russia does not have a single unified Muslim community. There are two loosely inter-connected Muslim communities. The Tatar Muslims are not connected with North Caucasus, and Caucasus Muslims do not show their activism in Tatar-controlled mosques. Coordination between the spiritual leaders of two communities is seen only when the secular authorities put some common task before them. This situation seems to be favourable to spiritual leaders of both communities. Religious solidarity between them has a limited character, which was quite noticeable during the first and second Chechen wars.

There is no organisational unity between the spiritual leadership of both communities. The break-up of the Spiritual Administration of Muslims of the European half of Russia and Siberia, (which existed during the period of the Soviet Union—uniting Tatars and Bashkirs) led to formation of more than 40 Muftiyat—which means practically all federal units, with more or less significant Muslim populations, formed their own Muftiyat. Contradictions appeared between the Central Spiritual Administration Muslims Boards, which was the successor to the Spiritual Administration of Muslims of European half of Russia and Siberia, and the Council of Muftiyats of Russia. There is some kind of competition on between the two organisations for representing Muslims before Central Authorities of the country. The council of Muftiyats has an advantage in this competition as it unites 80% of the 6000 of the Muslim communities. Over the last few years, it has been observed that the majority of the muftiyats take a common position on key issues.

Though a Coordination Centre of Muslims of Northern Caucasus had been established in North Caucasus in 1998, the spiritual leadership of the region is oriented towards local secular authority. Except in Dagestan, the national muftiyat in no other republic is in a position to oppose the secular authority and take independent decisions. Administrative and ethnic principle of their formation rules out the creation of a capable centralised structure. If at any time the Federal authority makes an attempt to create "Islamic vertical of authority", it would aggravate relations inside the spiritual establishment, and also between the respected religious leaders and the administration.

Notes

1. Mizun, U.V (2004), Islam and Russia (Ислам и Россия), p.221, Moscow: Veche.
2. Ibid., p.18.
3. Mizun, U.V (2004), *Islam and Russia (*Ислам и Россия), Moscow: Veche.
4. Ibid., p.198.
5. Ibid., p.215.
6. Ibid., p.217.
7. Gilyazov, I.A. (1993), Politics of Christianization of Middle Volga in 16th to 17th Centuries (Политика христианизации Средней Волги в 16 и 17 веков), p.162, Kazan.
8. Hunter, T.S. (1984), *Islam in Russia*, New York: ME Sharpe.
9. Mizun, U.V (2004), *Islam and Russia*, p.224, Moscow: Veche.
10. Ibid., p.224.
11. Ibid., p.242.
12. Ibid., p.243.
13. Ibid., p.247.
14. Ibid., p.250.
15. Ibid., p.251.
16. Ibid., p.253.
17. Ibid.
18. Ibid., p.254.
19. Ibid., p.258.
20. Mizun, U.V (2004), *Islam and Russia*, p.10, Moscow: Veche.

21. Hunter, T.S. (1984), Islam in Russia, New York: ME Sharpe.
22. Ibid., p.18.
23. Ibid., p.20.
24. Ibid.
25. Ibid.
26. Silantiyev, R.A. (2008), *Encyclopedia Islam in Contemporary Russia (*Энциклопедия ислама в современной России), Moscow: Algoritm.
27. Verkhovsky, A. (2007), *Islam in Russian regions* (Ислам в российских регионах): Moscow.
28. Kurbatova, O.L., Pobedonostseva E. et al. (2002), Muslims in Changing Russia (Мусульмане в Изменение Россию), p.155, Moscow: Rosspen.
29. Modestov, S.A. (2003), *Geopolitics of Islam* (Геополитика ислама), p.130, Moscow: Molodaya Gvardiya.
30. Malashenko, A. (2007), *Islam for Russia* (Ислам для России), Moscow: Rosspen.
31. Silantiyev, R.A. (2005), *Modern History of Islamic Community of Russia* (Современная история исламского сообщества России), p.149, Moscow: Ikhtios.
32. Nezavismaya Gazyeta 11 November 2003.
33. Navakhatski S. (2006), *Islamization of Russia* (Исламизация России), p.160, Moscow.
34. Khoperskaya, L. (2003), *Migration processes and political situation in North Caucasus* (Миграционные процессы и политическая ситуация на Северном Кавказе), p.56, Yerevan.
35. Ibid.

2. Revival of Islam in post-Soviet Russia

The process of strengthening the role and place of Islam in Russian society,which began under Gorbachev's Perestroika and further continued after Soviet disintegration, is called the revival of Islam by some experts. Some experts call it the re-Islamisation process. However, some Imams, ideologues of Russian Islam, do not agree with these terminologies, arguing that Islam never died in Russia, and hence it is not correct to call the above process a 'revival of Islam'. They prefer to describe the above process as strengthening of religious foundations in the consciousness of the people, re-establishment of role of Islam in the society or 'legitimisation of Islam'.[1] Differences in the interpretation of the process do not bear any principled character, because talk is about one and the same phenomena.

Emergence of Islamic Parties and Movements of Russia

The emergence of the Muslim political and social movement took its roots in the second half of the 19th century, when the Dzadidism movement was organised— the first was in the sphere of education, and subsequently, spread into the other spheres of life of the Muslim community. By the 1880s Dzadidism emerged as a powerful social-political movement, whose representatives demanded reform in spiritual education, and called for the development of science, enlightenment (prosve sheniye) and book publication. It is the Dzadids who formed the first Muslim party— the liberal-democratic movement —"Ittifak -al - Muslimin, in 1905."

The first All Russia Muslim Congress took place on 15th August 1905 in Nizhny Novgorod, and was attended by 120 delegates. This Congress approved the Tsarist Manifesto, dated 6th August, for convening the Duma, and took the decision for setting up All Russia Organisation of Muslims. The second All Russia Muslim Congress was held secretly in January 1906 at St. Pitersburg, which took the decisions for organising the political party "Ittifak -al-Muslimin and supporting cadets in the election to the first State Duma. The main plank of the platform of this party was the demand to provide the rights to the Muslims for self-determination.[2] The Bolsheviks gave this right to the Muslims after the October Revolution. The third all-Russia Muslim Congress took place in legal conditions, at Nizhny Novgorod in August, 2006: it approved the draft about the general administration (with 13 clauses) of the Muslims of Russia. The October Revolution brought huge changes in the life of the Russian Muslim community. The first decade following October Revolution did not see any harassment or violation of rights of Muslims. Rather, this period witnessed an upsurge of political activities by the Muslims.

Towards end of Gorbachev's Perestroika, the country saw a flurry of religious and political activities by the Muslims. The desire of representatives of underground Muslims to share power was reflected in the attempts to change the leadership in the existing muftiyats, as well as in the creation of alternative or parallel structures, basically in the form of Islamic parties. During the first wave of democratisation, there was a mushrooming of Islamic parties in the country.

Post-Soviet Russia witnessed active participation of the Muslims in the political and social life of the country. During the first wave of the democratisation, there was a great mushrooming of Islamic parties and movements in the country.

However, the experience of post-Soviet elections clearly showed that parties of this kind had little chance to represent the people in the power structure of the country and could only help in protecting the economic and political interests of its functionaries. From 1995 the majority of the Islamic parties, movements and organisations were created for political and financial manipulation—even for covering the criminal activities. Many old parties also chose the same path, thus discrediting the idea of political Islam and doing a great disservice to the cause of Islam. The Islamic parties,by dragging part of the spiritual leadership to the arena of political struggle, turned out to be effective instruments for split The political conditions created by this splitting could not become effective because none of the Islamic parties could unite any significant part of Russia's Muslims.

The First All Tatar Congress,which established the "Peoples Movement in support of perestroika – Tatar Public Centre", was subsequently known as the All Union Tatar Public Centre from February 1991, and then the All Tatar Public Centre from the beginning of 1992. The Congress of Muslim societies of the USSR held in June 1990 at Astrakhan took the decision to form the Islamic Party of Revival, which became the first clear religious party on the territory of former USSR. The All Tatar Public Centre and Islamic Party of Revival existed for a short period and in 1994 quitting the political scene,they became the fertile ground for emergence of more influential Muslim parties in the country.

The founding congress of Tatar Party of national independence "Ittifak" (accord) was held on the basis of radical wing of the All Tater Public Centre, and after few months the youth group "Azatlyk" joined this party. By the end of 1991, more than ten such parties, with similar agendas,emerged in the republic.

Political Islam

Growth of Nationalism and Islamic Revival

Towards end of 1990s, the Muslim political parties tried to form an alternative government –Milli Mezhlis, which took an extreme anti-Russian position. The nationalist movement in the republic grew without any check from the regional authorities (may be even in connivance with them), who saw in the movement a strong bargaining chip in their negotiations with the Federal Centre.

In the beginning,the strategic objective of the Tatar political parties was the revival of Tatar nationality, restoration of independence of the Tatar people through its separation from Russia, and realisation of rights of Tatar people as subjects of international law. Subsequently, nationalist demands were combined with demands of a religious nature, which laid the foundation for conflict between the nationalists and moderate Muslim spiritual leaders, who were reluctant to get involved in political battle.

The Chairman of DUMES, Talgat Tadzhuddin, became the main target of the nationalists. Activists of Tatar Public Centre and "Ittifak" demanded the transfer of the residence of DUMES chairman from Ufa to the Centre of Russian Islam –Kazan. It should be said that these demands fully corresponded to the aspirations of the Tatar President, who dreamt of transforming Kazan into the Volga region Mecca,and strengthen his position in the Islamic community. However, Tadzuddin rejected the ultimatum, after which the nationalists began forming their own Muslim structures. The Imams, unhappy with Tadzuddin, helped the nationalists in this endeavour. The Imam, Gabdul Galiulin,of the Kazan mosque,was first among them to extend a friendly hand to the nationalists.[3]

The Bashkir nationalists, seeing the 'hostile Tatar Muftiat' in DUMES, launched their main attack against it in Bashkortstan. "I have documents confirming that the Bashkir national centre and the Bashkir Peoples Party are directly participating in events around Spiritual Administration", said Talgat Tadzuddin in an interview with Nezavisimaya Gazeta.

The scandal in Naberezhny Chelny sent out the signal to begin an anti-Tadzuddin campaign in the nationalist media of Tatarstan and Bashkortstan. Everything was done with the idea of a decisive move against Tadzuddin. Only a pretext was required, which was provided by Tadzuddin himself, when he publicly rebuked the Ufa Imam, Nurmukhamed Nigmatullin. The conflict could have been amicably resolved but the Bashkir nationalists exerted lot of pressure on Nigmatullin, provoking him to speak against Tadzuddin. An attempt was made to form an alternative Muslim spiritual board. The Bashkir National Centre 'Ural', and the Tatar Public Centre in Bashkortstan issued a joint statement on the situation around DUMES and accused Tadzuddin of madness,authoritarian behaviour, financial bungling and also called for convening the founding congress of the Muslim spiritual board of Bashkortstan. A similar movement began in the neighbouring Tatarstan, for forming a Muslim spiritual board of their own.

The leaders of the nationalist parties took active part in the founding congresses of the Muslim spiritual board of Tatarstan, as well as of Bashkortstan. The chairperson of the "Ittifak" party, Fauzia Bairamova, in the founding congress taking place in Naberzhny Chelny, said that Tadzuddin had been 'stealing money in suitcases' and appealed for the election of Gabdul Galiullin,the imam of the Nurulla Mosque in Kazan. Ultimately, he was made the chairman of the independent Muslim Spiritual Board of Tatarstan, which facilitated the quick politisation of the Muslim spiritual leadership of the republic. Many delegates in the VI congress of DUMES directly accused Ittifak and Milli Mazhlis for instigating ethno-religious separatism.[4]

In October 1992, Galiullin headed the BKTSDUMR, and after its registration in 1994 received the title 'Supreme Mufti of Russia'.Heading the opposition DUMES-TSDUM, which had reached the peak of popularity, Galiullin virtually obtained a national status, which helped him in conducting an independent policy that did not always take the interests of the republican authorities into account. His closeness to nationalists, the opposition to the federal centre and even to the republican president Shamiyev, aggravated the contradictions with the Tatar President.

There was a direct confrontation between President Shamiyev and Galiullin towards the end of 1995, when people from the Tatar muftiyat occupied the building of Kazan madrasas. Galiullin openly challenged Shamiyev, forming a public-political movement —"Muslims of Tatarstan", while aspiring to capture power.[5] The confrontation ended in 1998 with the victory of President Shamiyev, who had put in all efforts to replace Galiullin with a loyal mufti. Ittifak, in putting up a strong defense for Galiullin, had lost most of its influence that did not allow it to split the Muslim Spiritual Board of Tatarstan.

Galiullin for some time maintained a low profile, agreeing to work in the Muslim Spiritual Board of Tatarstan. However, he soon launched an open opposition to President Shamiyev and the new Mufti Gusman Iskhakov. He transformed his movement "Muslims of Tatarstan" to the 'Omet' movement, in an alliance with the left forces, and also launched the anti-President newspaper "Nadezhda-Omet".[6] During the 1999 presidential election, Omet's attempt to join the ruling party—'Unity',did not succeed. His outfit ultimately joined the "Stalinist Block - for USSR". Galiullin subsequently revived relations with the Central Muslim Spiritual Board and joined the movement 'EURASIA', supported by Tadzuddin. The former mufti still enjoys the support from part of the Muslim spiritual leadership and has supporters amongst the left and nationalist forces of Tatarstan.[7] The Islamic Revival Party formed in 1990 launched the process of reforming the Soviet system of spiritual administration and achieved some success in this effort. However, this party achieved significant success in Tazikstan, where its activists subsequently constituted the backbone of the armed opposition and plunged the republic into civil war for a long time. In Russia its activists played a significant role in splitting the Muslim community.[8] Muslim leaders of Soviet Union negatively viewed the emergence of Islamic Revival Party (IRP).

Activists of the IRP, on their part, demonstrated negative attitude towards the Muslim spiritual leadership. According to the press secretary IRP, Valiakhmet Sadur in this connection has said, "IRP in general has negative attitude to the muftis and other Muslim leaders appointed by the government. The position of IRP leaders could be easily explained by the fact that many of them had their first political experience in ousting such odius muftis like Gekkiyev in North Caucasus and junior Babakhanov in Central Asia".[9] Apart from these coups, IRP functioneries also participated in splitting the DUMES.[10] After the dissolution of the IRP its leaders such as Geidar Dzemal, MohamedSalahedin, Shamil Sultanov, Valiakhmed Sadur and Mukkadas Bibarsov, continued their political careers, participating in many inter-regional Islamic parties.

Starting from 1990 the IRP actively worked in Dagestan, calling to create an Islamic State on its territory, and from 1992 onwards it participated in the conflict between the different spiritual boards of Dagestan. The radical activities of the IRP in the region forced the representatives of the official Muslim spiritual leadership to create an alternative organisation –the Islamic Democratic Party, in September 1990. The Chairman of the Muslim Spiritual Board of Dagestan Ahmed Derbishgidzhiev, describing IRP as a "Wahhabi Party", noted that the disrespectful attitude of IRP towards the official Islamic spiritual leaders and my uridism evokes strong protest in the Republic.[11]

The supporters of the integration of Islam took the side of Talgat Tadzuddin in the conflict between DUMES –Central Muslim Spiritual Board and the alternative structure. The participation of political forces in this conflict aggravated it further.. The Chairman of the Muslim Spiritual Board in the Volga region, Mukkadas Bibarsov, became the key figure in spreading political Islam in the opposition. The Union of Muslims of Russia, the most odius organisation amongst the Russian Islamic parties, was formed with his active participation. In fact, the main initiator behind the formation of the Union of Muslims of Russia (UMR) was Aahmed Khalitov, a close associate of the Russian nationalist leader Vladimir Zhirinovsky.[12] Till September 1995, when the first Congress of the movement replaced its leadership, this organisation under the influence of the Liberal Democratic Party of Russia was headed by Zhirinovsky.[13] The political agenda of the Union emphasised the protection of the rights of Russian Muslims in all spheres; from declaring Muslim festivals as national holidays to additional investment in the Muslim regions. In the first congress of Union of Muslims held in September 1995, Ahmed Khalitov was replaced by Mykkadas Bibarasov, chairman of Muslim spiritual board in the Volga region as leader of the organisation. Key posts in the organisation were given to the supporters of General Director of IKTS of Russia, Abdul Vahed Niyazov, who quickly re-oriented the party towards "Our Home Russia", the ruling party and transformed it to a pro-government Party.[14]

In February 1996, as a result of differences between the pro-Yeltsin members of the 'shadow' leadership of the union and functionaries loyal to Niyazov who had the real power with them, Bibarasov had to resign from his post following which Dagestan businessman Nadir Shah Khachilayev became the new leader of the union. Niyazov headed the executive committee of the Union of Muslims of Russia.[15] Khachilayev and Niyazov had sharply different views on supreme mufti Talgat Tadzuddin, who called on the community not to involve Russian Islamists in a political fight. Subsequently Khachilayev took active part in domestic political fight, using his new status as a State Duma member. The activities of Khachilayev in Dagestan provoked several armed conflicts, which became the reason, to deprive him of the immunity enjoyed by parliamentary members, and also to arrest him. In 1998,the Russian Justice Ministry initiated proceedings to declare the party illegal.

The creation of the Union of Muslims not only deepened the split between Central Muslim Spiritual Board and block of alternative muftis but also triggered internal conflict in the block itself. The stand off between the Union and the Movement of Muslims of Russia, combined with the illegal activities by its leadership, dealt a heavy blow to the idea of political Islam. Many leaders of the anti-Tagzuddin opposition hastened to distance themselves from participation in political battles. In this connection, the council of Arab ambassadors in Moscow expressed concern that Islamic Cultural Centre of Russia (ICC) became active only during the election campaign or other political events, and noted that "this is largely linked to the organisation of provocative campaign of forming Islamic political parties or movements.[16]

On the other hand, thanks to the Union of Muslims, its general director, Abdul Vahed Niyazov, obtained the political weight which helped him to become a State Duma member. He successfully played the Muslim card during the presidential election of 1996 and convinced the Kremlin administration that he had made his contribution to the election of Yeltsin as the President of Russia. The collapse of the Union of Muslims did not do much damage to Niyazov's career as he distanced himself from Khachilayev on time.[17]

Only the All Russia Muslim public movement 'Nur', which had a political agenda similar to that of the Union, but because it was led by less radical leaders and loyal to the Central Muslin Spiritual Board, it could take part in 1995 Duma elections, while the Union, on the other hand, was barred from participating in the race on technical grounds. Nur, which received only 0.5% votes, showed the inability of the Islamic parties to come to power independently.

The new wave of political activism by the Russian Muslims began in 1998-1999, before the election to the next State Duma. The electoral block Mejlis, was formed in June by managers of the Oil and Gas Company, Leonard Rafikov and Marat Hairullin along with leaders of Nur, All Russia Muslim Congress and Refak. Leonard Rafikov became the chairman of newly formed party, Medzlis. This block became the largest Muslim political organisation in the history of Russia, thanks to which it had good chances of entering into some popular electoral alliance. However, leaders of the party, blocked with 'Our Home Russia', did not have much chance for success. Niyazov, who founded the movement "Refak" in 1998, also took part in the formation of Medzlis party. However, when Medzlis made an alliance with Our Home Russia, led by the former Prime Minister, Victor Chernomyrdin, he did not show much interest in it. Realising clearly that the new ruling party, Unity,had the maximum chances to win the election, Niyazov's Refak movement made an alliance with it.

As a result of Unity's success in the electoral race, Niyazov managed to procure a seat in the State Duma, thus raising his status among Muslim leaders. That is also how Refak became the leader in Islamic politics, while other parties lost their weight, with the exception of Medzlis, which still enjoyed some support. Nur was barred from registration on technical grounds. Experts interpreted this as Nur's defeat in its long protracted fight with ICC of Russia and its sister organisations.[18]

Niyazov became vice-chairman of one of the committees of the State Duma and started forming his own parliament faction. Some of the State Duma members getting elected to the parliament with his help distanced themselves from Refak. But Niyazov managed to get support from some independent State Duma members. Niyazov's political successes helped him in expanding his support base in some Asian parts of the country and also to receive support from regional governors. Other members of the Council of Muftis of Russia received significant help by Niyazov's membership in the parliament.

At the same time, the success of Niyazov led also to the consolidation of his opponents. The second All Russia Union of Public Organisations Medzlis was held at Moscow in February, 2000, which was attended by many Muslim spiritual leaders,including the entire leadership of CMSB. Niyazov's opponent, Mukkadas Bibarsov, joined Medzlis. The congress did not change the co-relation of forces inside Russian political Islam, but it did demonstrate the decisiveness of Niyazov's opponents to continue the fight on all fronts. The arrest of one of the delegates of the second Kurultai taking place in August 2000, and the subsequent action of Refak, showed the first signs of crisis in the party. The Chief Regional Federal Security Service (FSB) of Omsk district, Victor Mironov, said that the delegates of Kurultai and Refak gathering in Omsk were supporters of radical Islam. Their attempt to come to power using religion could be a serious problem and a matter of serious concern. Refak's situation seriously deteriorated in 2002. By then leaders of CMSB and their allies,having established close contacts with Russian President Putin and his team, had started influencing the Putin government's Islamic policy. Niyazov's active international activities which some times went against the state interest, annoyed the presidential administration and the leadership of the ruling party, 'Unity'.

"Unity" leader, Sergey Shoigu, in the second congress of the ruling party scheduled for October 2000, declared that in the next meeting of the political council of the party he was going to raise the issue of sacking Niyazov from the Duma faction for his support of the Wahhabi-styled opposition Turkic party of, which dealt a heavy blow to the image of the party.[19]

Subsequently, Niyazov was forced to resign from the ruling party, following which Refak was transformed into a national political party—the 'Eurasian Party of Russia'. Niyazov's resignation from Refak seriously weakened its position. Even the transformation of the party into the Eurasian Party of Russia could not save it. As a result of Niyazov's activities, four to five members of the State Duma were elected to the parliament and with its help resigned from Refak, leading to its subsequent collapse.

Refak's collapse led to re-activisation of its opponents. In December 2000,the All Russia public movement, Nur, was transformed into a Democratic Muslim organisation, which in the spring of 2001 was converted into the Islamic Party of Russia (IPR), led by Dagestan businessman Mohmed Razabov. The former leaders of Nur Sadykov and Yarullin occupied the posts of chairman and first vice -chairman, respectively, in the presidium of the party. The Chairman of the Moscow Regional Muslim Spiritual Board and Moscow district, Mahmed Velitov, and former chairman of this organ, Sultan Gulamov, both became members of the general council of the party. Dagestan's Muslim spiritual leadership and Council of Muftis of Russia extended their support to the new Islamic party. IPR was closely linked to Talgat Tadzuddin.

In the spring of 2001, a new political movement, similar to IPR, was born, which claimed to represent the interests of the Central Muslim Spiritual Board. The Advisor to the Duma speaker and famous Russian geopolitical expert, Alexander Dugin initiated the formation of the movement—"Eurasia". Its founding congress, held in April 2001 in Moscow, was attended by all heads of the regional muftiyats Central Muslim spiritual board. Talgatr Tadzuddin and leader of North Caucasus Muslims mufti, Mohamed Albogachiyrv, clearly showed their sympathy to the new movement. The Russian Orthodox Church, the Federation of Jewish Communities of Russia and traditional Buddhist Sangha directly, or indirectly, expressed their support to the "Eurasia" movement.[20]

Dugin's professional team helped the Central Muslim Spiritual Board (CMSB) in public relations. The CMSB and the Eurasia movement jointly organised a conference titled "Threat to Islam", which benefited both the organisations. They also organised some more joint projects.[21]

Niyazov and his supporters' stand on the US operation against the Taliban determined the final of the stand-off between the CMSB and its opponents in the political sphere. The anti-US and pro-Taliban events, organised by the Eurasian Party of Russia, evoked a strong anger against the Kremlin and triggered off rumours that parliamentarian immunity of Niyazov would soon be withdrawn.

This did not bring an end to Niyazov's political career. He launched new global Eurasian projects. The Refak movement was re-organised into the Eurasian Party of Russia which had planned to take part in the subsequent parliament elections independently. However, this party had to face strong competition from Eurasia movement as well as from the Islamic Party of Russia, aiming at Muslim voters. The experienced Niyazov seemed to gain an upper hand in the stiff competition in the Eurasian field. He managed to get important leaders such as Pavel Borodin, Ruslan Aushev, Ioshif Kovzon and Chengiz Aitmatov to his party, which helped him to launch an effective election campaign. The Eurasia movement was forced to concede its defeat in the competition with the Eurasian Party. However the IPR did not retreat from its position, and from time to time continued to launch initiatives. Realising that the religious tone in his party might not help him in getting a large support base; Radzabov renamed his party the "Genuine Patriots of Russia" and thus prompted Niyazov to change the name of his party from the "Eurasian Party –Union of Patriots of Russia" to the "Great Russia -Eurasian Union".

Both parties claimed that they would get as much as 40% of the votes. However; each of them polled not more than 0.2 % votes. The only satisfying factor for them was that contrary to the Nur party of 1995, these two parties found themselves among the top 20 parties and movements of the country. In the next year IPR could not get registered for its multitude of violations during the election campaign. In 2004, two new parties were formed out of IPR – 'Genuine Patriots of Russia for Civil Society' and 'Party of Justice and Development of Russia', which were headed by Mohmed Razabov and his son Zaur respectively.

Somehow, one Muslim candidate became a member of the fourth state Duma. He was, Shamil Sultanov, a former activist of the Islamic Party of Revival and a close supporter of Mukkadas Bibarsov, who got elected on a Motherland party ticket.

By 2005 the disparate opposition to the institute of muftiyat took the decision to get united, forgetting ideological differences. Dagestan Tarikatist, radical psedo-shiite, Tatar nationalists, members of the Wahhabi Zamat were in their ranks. The Umar and Husain Zabraillov brothers, not known for their sympathy for Islam, financed the opposition. The founding congress,held in March 2005, formed the All Russia Public movement "Russian Islamic Heritage" (RIH). The new organisation positioned itself as a hostile opposition to the existing structure of the muftiyat.

Apart from a struggle against the muftiyat, leaders of RIH promised to facilitate the consolidation of society on the basis of a unified civic identity— to consolidate the Russian Islamic Umma as the most important factor of strengthening the unity of the entire Russian society; to preserve and develop the Islamic cultural heritage of the Russian federation as an inseparable part of Russian culture; to fight against any form of political extremism,racial and religious hatred— and to propagate views of Russian Islam Umma in national and global events.[22]

From among the Muslim spiritual leaders, only the supreme mufti Naffigula Ashirov extended support to the RIH, even though he was not invited to be part of the leadership of the new organisation. Famous personalities like philosopher Gaidar Zemal, his supporter journalist Maxim Shevchenko, Dudasyev's foreign minister Shamil Beno and some other prominent people were included in the leadership of RIH. While Husain Zabraliyev became chairman, his brother Umar headed the political council of the movement.

Leaders of the Central Muslim Spiritual Board, the KTSMSK and the Council of Muftis of Russia were indifferent to the new movement. Only the leader of the Muslim Spiritual Board, Mohamed Bibarsocv, publicly expressed his opposition to this movement. Ultimately,the ideologues of the RIH invited Bibarsov to be a member of its Presidium. The movement's leadership concentrated its attack on the Central Muslim Spiritual Board and the KTSMSK. The new movement virtually occupied the niche earlier occupied by the Russian Islamic Party of Revival, the Union of Muslims of Russia and 'Refak'.[23]

The head of the Council of Muftis of Russia, Ravil Gainutdin, assessed the activities of RIH positively. He made an alliance with RIH and became a member of its governing council. However, the alliance did not last for long. In April 2007, its chairman, Husain Zabrailov, was replaced by his assistant Shaukat Avyasov. By this time many of its sponsors and members of Presidium had lost their interest in the movement.

Revival of Islam

The revival of Islam took place in several directions and can be seen in the institutions such as education, media, halal industry etc.

(a) Islamic Education

The establishment of a viable educational system,which could have helped revive the indigenous Islam of Russia and provide an adequate number of qualified leaders for the Muslim communities and institutions, has been proven more problematic than building any physical infrastructure. But this was absolutely necessary from the political point of view of preventing infiltration of extremist elements amongst the poorly educated Muslims. The major hurdles, in creating adequate Islamic educational institutions, have been lack of sufficient funds, inadequate human resources (particularly lack of qualified teachers) and political factors. When local funding is inadequate, foreign funding should be welcomed. However, foreign funding for creating educational institutions has diluted the educational agenda and helped promote extremism and fundamentalism. This has created a serious problem for the country. Given the fact of political considerations, federal as well as regional, authorities have some reservations about the setting up of Islamic educational institutions. This scepticism has grown against the back drop of some Islamic educational institutions serving as breeding grounds for religious extremism, fundamentalism and terrorism.

Incidents, such as that of the Yulduz School in Naberezhnie Chelny, have strengthened these fears. The school was temporarily closed down after being accused of teaching subversive ideas and training volunteers to fight in Chechnya against the federal forces and conduct terrorist acts. One of the ex-students of the school, Dennis Saitakov,was accused of having been involved in the apartment bombings of 1999 in Moscow.[24]

In order to dispel these misgivings, some schools emphasise the fact that their curriculum is based on secular and scientific subjects. The point is that the case of the Russian Islamic University of Kazan, the instruction is evenly divided between secular and religious subjects such as science, languages and computer skills. During the first few years, 75% of the subjects taught there are secular. Later students are taught Islamic philosophy and law based on the Hanafi School. According to school officials, the objective of the school is to 'create a modern personality who understands both secular and religious matters'.

In the pre-revolutionary Russia the Islamic community had a full set of higher and middle level spiritual educational institutions for meeting all its requirements. The level of education at the madrasses in Kazan, Ufa and Orenburg could train high class specialists in theology and theosophy. Those who passed out from more obscure educational institutions could freely speak and write in the literary Arab language. The network of primary schools covered the entire territory mainly inhabited by Muslims, which permitted any Muslim citizen to receive good education. The Muhammadiya madrassa in Kazan was the most famous and most reputed among all the higher schools of learning. Hundreds of members of the Tatar elite received a fairly good education, not only in religious subjects, but also in secular subjects. There were 900 madrasses in Kazan guberni and 344 in Orenburg guberni.[25]

In the beginning of the 20th century some reforms were implemented, which introduced new methods of education. Its proponents were called Zadids, who called for Europeanising the system of education. However, they faced strong opposition from the conservative Imams. Their stand-off came to an end when Soviet authorities closed all Muslim educational institutions of inner Russia.[26]

Till 1989 the Muslims of USSR could receive education only in the Bukhara Madrassa— 'Mir-Arab', in Uzbekistan and Tashkent Higher Islamic

Institute. The quota for Russian Muslim students for these two institutions was not very large. That is why Russia had only a few dozen educated Imams when the Islamic revival started towards the end of Perestroika. Apart from that, several spiritual leaders, such as the future mufti, Talgat Tadzuddin, could receive higher education in Islamic countries friendly towards the Soviet Union.[27]

In 1988 Ismailia Madrassa, which became the first Muslim educational institution in Russian Federation, was opened on the basis of being an Arab language centre under the ageis of the Moscow Cathedral Mosque. Amadrassa, named after mufti Rezayetdin Faqiredin, was opened in Ufa in 1989. Kazan opened a madrassa a year after, which was subsequently known as Kazan Higher Muslim Madrassa which became a full- fledged institution from 1992. Primary and middle madrassas opened in Dagestan and Chechnya till the year 1991.

After the Soviet collapse, Russian Muslims faced a serious problem in training Imams, who were required in hundreds. The existing madrassas could not even meet 5% of the requirement in cadres. Moreover, the Bukhara and Tashkent madrasses now found themselves in independent countries, and hence could not be easily accessible to their former student markets. At this crucial period the Arab countries extended a helping hand by providing free education to Russian students. However, not all of them had good intentions in providing this opportunity. The main sponsors and funding of these educational programmes came with Wahhabi backing, which needed emissaries for successful expansion in territory that was previously closed for them.

A large number of students went abroad for education in 1990-92 and the first degree holder Imams, perceived by Russian Muslims as extremely knowledgeable, started returning to Russia from 1994. They became the initiators of a network of Islamic spiritual educational institutions —madrassas, colleges, institutes, universities —designed to revive the system of Islamic education. About 30 higher and middle level madrassas had registered themselves in the Russian Ministry of Justice by 1996. The legendary Mohamediya madrassa, receiving the status of higher spiritual educational institution, was re-established in Kazan in 1995. Middle level masdrassas opened in Naberezhny Chelny, Almetevsk, Nizhnekamsk, Nurlat, Buinsk, Octyabrsky, Bugurslan, Ulyanovsk, Saratov, Nizhni Novgorod, Tyumen etc.

Inspite of the obstacles in building the educational infrastructure of traditional Russian Islam, institutions of various size and quality have emerged in different parts of the country. According to the SBM of Tatarstan, its Islamic educational system includes the following institutions of higher learning;

1. In Kazan there is the Russian Islamic University, the higher Muslim madrassa 'Mohammadiya' and the higher Muslim madrassa of the 1000thAnniversary of Islam;
2. In Naberezhnie Chelny, there is the intermediate Muslim madrassa 'Yuldu', the intermediate Muslim madrassa 'A Q Mechet' and the Naberezhnie chelny Islamic institute;
3. The intermediate Muslim madrasa of Risalliya lies in the city of Nizhnekamsk;
4. The Intermediate Muslim madrassa of Rizaeddin Fahreddin lies in the town of Almeteyevsk.

Each of these institutions has more than 1000 students and has affiliated primary schools where students are instructed in the basics of the Islamic faith and its rituals.

In Bashkortstan, 419 Muslim institutions provide some kind of Islamic education. There are five madrassas and two institutes, which are operated mostly by major mosques, including one by the Cathedral Mosque, which was opened in 1990 and another by the Lya Lya Tyulpan Mosque. Other major centers of learning are Rizah Fakretdin Islamic Institute and the Maryum Sultanova Islamic Institute, which offers a four-year course.[28]

The Nizhny Novgorod region has two major madrassas—Mahinur and Medina, which is a branch of Mahinur. Mahinur has been operating since 1994. It has eight affiliated institutions, three Sunday schools and five summer schools. This madrassa also organises cultural events and summer camps. Medina trains male Muslims with secondary education for further religious studies at Mahinur. The tenure of education is two years during which students, in addition to religious studies, receive education in secular subjects.[29]

In the North Caucasus, Dagestan has the largest number of Islamic educational institutions. Only nine of these institutions have official licenses for running them. An additional 45 institutions are affiliated with the recognised universities and institutions.

Dagestan saw the mushrooming of madrassas in the Republic in the 1990s. Every city and large village had its higher or intermediate educational institutions by 2000. The most famous among them are Makhachkala North Caucasus Islamic University and the University named after Imam Shafii, Bunakski University, Khasayur Institute etc.

As of December 2001, there were 17 Islamic colleges, all of which were associated with the republic's SBM. Dagestan has 132 intermediate madrassas and 245 primary schools, most of which function under the aegis of the local mosques, and their main goal is to provide elementary religious education to the children of believers. Because of the irregular character of functioning at the primary–level education —and their sporadic formation and dissolution, it is difficult to establish the exact number of these schools. According to Dagestan SBM mouthpiece "Assalam", as of January, 2001 Dagestan had 72 madrassas and more than 1000 primary schools attached to mosques.[30] The Northern Islamic University of Muhhamad Arif, located in Makhachkala, is an examplery institution that provides a curriculum based on secular values, as well as moderate Muslim thoughts. Apart from religious history and law, students are taught Russian and English languages and foreign literature. The women's department provides training in nursing, medicine and designing clothes.[31]

In Ingushetia, most mosques offer primary Islamic education. The highest center of Islamic education in the republic is the King Fahad Islamic Institute, financed by Saudi Arabia.

The Russian Islamic University, opened in Kazan in 1998, was planned to be the best University in the country. Moscow Islamic University (starting from 1999), the successor to the Ismailiya madrassa (1988) and Moscow Higher Islamic College,set up in 1994, became competitors. These institutions received funds not only from the federal authorities, but also from foreign sponsors. The main difference between the Russian Muslim University (RMU) and the Moscow Islamic University (MIU) was in their approach to the system of education. While, students of Moscow State University (MSU) received a bachelor's degree in 'theology and oriental studies', students of RIU till 2002 received training only in religious specialisations. However after 2002, RIU started a Theological faculty,which trained secular specialists in theology, because of which it became the first educational institution in Russia preparing secular experts.[32]

Moscow has several important Islamic educational institutions, including the Moscow Islamic College, which trains Imams. The first group of

Imam- khatibs graduated in 1998 and went on to serve Muslim communities in Yaroslav, Tver, Nizhny Novgorod, Kosroma, Vologda and Moscow. The Moscow Islamic University was opened in 1998 and began admitting students in 1999. The Rasul Al-Akram Islamic College in the Solnechnogorsk district of Moscow oblast provides a four year course. The Islamiya School, which operates from Moscow Catherdal Mosque, was established in 1998 and offers free primary religious education. These institutions are linked to DUMER, which provides funds to students for studying at religious schools in Egypt, Morocco, Syria, Saudi Arabia, Qatar, Turkey and Libya.[33]

In the Astrakhan oblast, the only institution of higher learning is the Islamic Institute of Haji Tarhan in Astrakhan, which in June 2003 celebrated the convocation of the first batch of Imams – a historical event because it was the first batch of Muslim clerics to graduate in Atrakhan oblast in the past one hundred years.[34]

By 2002 it became obvious that RIU and MIU and other Islamic educational institutions could solve the problem of training new cadres for traditional Islam. The level of training in these institutions could prepare only simple Imams. It was felt that there was a need for highly qualified experts who could form part of Muslim elite and professionally join the fight or argument with the Wahhabis and other sects, for defending the foundation of a moderate Islam. The small numbers of professionals in this sphere were trained in foreign countries. Russia could not train them.[35] In spite of the fact that many madrassas and higher educational institutions were opened in the country in the post-Soviet period, the quality of education was not up to the mark,noted Azer Aliyev, the coordinator inter-religious council of CIS.

In the meantime, the situation in the sphere of Islamic education sharply deteriorated because in many madrassas education was imparted according to the methods of non-traditional Islam, and in some cases madrassas became the centres of extremists and terrorists. The incident with the Ioliz Madrassa in Naberezhny Chelny, which came under the control of the extremist organisation 'Taiba' and the incident with the Alfurkan Madrassa, whose graduates had taken part in the most serious terrorist acts, evoked serious concern amongst the authorities. It was required that the state took control of the educational system. Moreover,the leaders of traditional Islam, concerned about the situation, have been asking for this for quite some time.

In order to protect students from becoming unduly influenced by foreign teachers, non-traditional schools of Islam and extremist ideas, the religious leaders of Dagestan in 2001 decided that no student should go abroad for higher education without getting some elementary education at home. This decision reflects the serious concern about Islamic training abroad to the Russian students. This is a response to the practice of the early 1990s when many students could go abroad with ease for receiving education there.

President Putin on 21st May and 16th June 2002 issued two decrees which stipulated drafting measures for extending organisational, material and methodical assistance for development in the sphere of religious education—first, in the field of Muslim education, as well as opening an Islamic University with a secular character, at Moscow. The Ministry of Education was given this responsibility. After long discussions it was decided to open the Academic Centre of Islamic History and Culture in the Institute of Countries of Asia and Africa, at Moscow State University. It was decided that 20 students would be admitted there each year. But this centre was closed as a result of many complaints by professors about the low level of basic education of the students as well as the poor adaptability of the students to the secular life of the institute. Starting from 2005, quotas were reserved for Muslim students in Moscow Linguistic Institute, Nizhni Novgorod University and St. Petersburg University. However, this step did not improve Muslim education system in the country significantly.

In 2006 a host of other measures were contemplated for overcoming the crisis in the Muslim educational system. These steps stipulated opening five universities that would constitute the backbone of Islamic education in the country. These universities were to be opened in Moscow, Kazan, Ufa, Makhachkala and Nalchik — on the basis of the existing educational centres and institutions. Four to seven middle madrassas would be affiliated to these universities, with a total number of madrassa reaching 30, while other Muslim educational institutions were to be closed. A fund for supporting Islamic culture, science and education was formed for implementing this massive programme. If this huge programme would be successfully implemented, Islamic education in Russia would receive a new lease of life and would reach a near world level.

However, the implementation of this programme does not appear to be very satisfactory. There is a tendency to reduce the number of educational institutions. This is happening as a result of the merger of madrassas. In 2007, there were 75 registered middle and higher Muslim educational institutions,whereas their total number in the country was 229 —including 26 higher institutions and 203 middle level institutions.[36]

In general, during President Putin's period, government has taken steps for including the introduction of standardisation in Islamic education through out Russia to maintain some control over Islamic education in the country.

(b)Islamic Media

Since the peak of perestroika in the 1980s and early 1990s there has been sharp increase in the number of publications and radio and TV broadcasting services dealing with Islamic issues. As of 2002 there have been about forty newspapers and journals dealing with Islamic problems in Russia.

Islamic media has a history of 100 years in Russia. The first newspaper that wrote on Islamic mattersin Tatarstan was associated with the activities of Zadids, the first of their recognised leaders— Gaspirinsky, who launched the paper "Tarzhuman"which became a mouthpiece of the Zadids.A slew of Islamic newspapers and journals appeared in Russia in Tatar, Arab, Uzbek and Russian languages after the 1905 revolution. The most popular among these publications were the Zadid newspapers "Tarakki", "Tudzor", "Al-Islakh", "Idle" etc. The future mufti, Rizaetdin Fakhreddinov, founded the progressive journal "Shura" in Orenburg. The journal "Muslmanin" published from Paris from the beginning of 20th century, carried stories about the Russian Umma in the Russian language. Ideological opponents of the Zadids published their own journals. The Mohmmedan Spiritual Assembly in Orenburg launched its paper with a circulation of 800 copies in 2006.[37]

During Soviet times, Muslim periodicals were around till 1928. Some positive developments in the sphere of Islamic media took place after the revival of the Muslim spiritual boards in the mid-940s. The Muslim Spiritual Board of Central Asia and Kazakhstan started publishing the journal "Muslims of Soviet East" from 1947. However, its publication was stopped soon after, only to be revived in 1968. Till 1989, this was the only Muslim periodical in the USSR. The journal "Science and Religion" used to publish articles on Islamic themes.

The first Muslim newspaper started appearing in the USSR on the eve of its collapse. Many of these papers, for example "Taikhid", the mouthpiece of the Islamic Party of Revival Muslim, and 'Vestnik', published by the Saratov Mosque,were radical in nature.

DUMES revived its newspaper in 1990 which was closed after some time because of financial difficulties. Its publication started again in 1997 with the help of Mahmedgalli Khuzin, mufti of Perm district. The Muslim literature publishing house 'Iman' was inaugurated in Kazan in 1991, which also published a newspaper by the same name. The journal "Islam Nuri" started getting published in Kazan from 1993. Islamic Newspapers "Vera 'and "Yakin" were launched in 1994. After the split in DUMES, the break away group of muftis started publishing their own newspaper. The Muslim Spiritual Board of Bashkortstan founded the Russian language paper "Islam and Society" in 1992, and DUMER started publishing its monthly paper "Islam Minbärer" from 1994. Dagestan Muslims too started publishing their own periodicals from the beginning of the 1990s.

By the end of the 1990s, majority of centralised Muslim organisations had their own newspapers. The most regular among them was "Islam Minbäre" published by DUMER, which became the mouthpiece of council of muftis of Russia. Different Muslim communities too tried to publish their own newspapers, which did not have a long life. Apart from Islam Minbäre, Islamic publications in Moscow included Tribuna Islama, published by DUMER since 1994 with a circulation of 10000 copies, Islamsky Mir, Zam-Zam, published by the charity fund and Al Fiqr, a monthly bulletin published by the Islamic congress of Russia.

Tatarstan, Bashkortstan, North Caucasus and other regions with significant Muslim population have the following Muslim publications:

1. Din Va Masgyyshat; a Tatar language publication of the SBM of Tatarstan,
2. Iman both in Tatar and Russian languages.
3. Muslima, a journal for Muslim women.
4. Islam Nuri in Tatar language from Naberezhnie Chelny.
5. Risalyat, a monthly publication by the SBM of Bashkortstan in Bashkir and Russian.
6. Musulmansky Vestnik published from Saratov.
7. Iman, a newspaper published by the religious society of Muslims of Vologda.
8. 'Solntse Islama', published by the SBM of Penza oblast.
9. Kibla, a newspaper published by the religious society of Muslims of Novocherkassk.
10. Azan, a newspaper published from Samara.[38]

The newspaper Ummah started getting published from 2002 in Kazan. This Russian language Muslim paper is published by a charity fund and civic group, Ikhlas.

In the North Caucasus, Dagestan has the largest number of Islamic publications.

There were attempts to publish a national Muslim newspaper on the eve of the State Duma elections in 1999. Vyachislav Polosin, who converted to Islam in 1999, was given the task of publishing the newspaper "Islamic Gazetta" with a circulation of 500,000 on behalf of the Refak movement, which was in charge of this project. The paper that was being circulated free of cost,had virtually turned into the mouthpiece of Refak. After the Duma elections saw five representatives of Refak in the parliament, the paper closed down.

In 2001, Polosin, with the help of Dagestan Muslim Spiritual Board, started publishing a paper "Everything about Islam", which was to be the successor to "Islamic Gazetta". This time the paper continued for two years with a circulation of 35,000 copies but closed down by the end of 2003. The niche for national Islamic newspapers remains vacant ever since.

In January 2002, the first successful attempt was made to publish a national Islamic journal. The Muslim Spiritual Board of Dagestan started publishing the first monthly Islamic journal "Islam", which is still surviving. In the first quarter of 2004 on the initiative of DUMER, the Muslim spiritual boards of Tatarstan, Nizhni Novgorod and Nizhegorod district founded a quarterly journal called "Minaret".

From the early 1990s, the first radio program dedicated to Islam was broadcast. A project by Sergei Markus in Voice of Russia was among those programmes. Subsequently, similar programmes appeared in regional radio stations and have survived till date. There are also two government–owned stations, Voice of Islam and Islamic Wave-length that serve to popularize the activities of DUMER. The radio and television programmes in the Muslim regions of the Russian Federation include Din Va Tormysh, a programme on the local television in Kazan sponsored by the SBM of Tatarstan; Ihlas, a weekly television programme in Ufa; Allau Akbar, a programme for Muslims as part of the Sarotov Tele-Radio centre; "For Unity and Stability" and "Peace to Your House", are two Radio and Television programmes in Dagestan that 'explain federal laws about freedom of conscience and features Muslim clerics'.

There were also programmes dedicated to Islam in Central Television. However, they could not continue for too long due to lack of funds. Starting from 1992, DUMER initially with support of the government, launched a number of radio and TV programmes on Islam that included 'Minaret', 'Now' and 'Ruhi Miras'. However, these programmes could not generate the desired popularity. The Muslim religious programme "Nine" in the first channel, "Thousand and One Night" in the Russian TV and 'All Sura of the Koran' in TV channel Kultura were among the programmes which had little success.

In August 1995 Mufti Ravil Gainutddin sent a letter to Tatar President Mintemir Shamiyev complaining about discrimination against Muslims in TV programmes and citing a fact that the 30 minute-programme 'Minaret' can be seen only in Moscow and Moscow district. Only in February 2002 did the Russia TV channel started broadcasting a 15-minute long programme "Muslims", which enjoyed much popularity among the Russian Muslims.

In May 2007 the Council of Muftis of Russia reached an agreement for cooperation with TV channel "Russia-today–Russia al-Ayum" for broadcasting in the Middle East. The council along with Televideo Company Islamic Mir "founded the site "Islamic Television".[39]

In July 2007, Saudi Arabia with the support from mufti Ravil Gainutddin, declared its intention of broadcasting the Russian language version of "Mecca" with the objective of informing viewers about moral-spiritual and humanitarian goal of Islam, change negative image of Islam and separate the perception of terrorism and extremism from religion.

From 1998 onwards, Muslim media was strengthened by the emergence of web-resources. The electronic version of several issues of "Islam Minbäre" became the first Islamic site. Subsequently there appeared a site on Moscow Memorial Mosque, which was transformed into the official site of DUMER-Council of muftis – www.islam.ru. The first official site of the Central Muslim Spiritual Board appeared in 1999. The notorious site Kavkaz-centre, run by Chechen terrorists, also appeared in the same year. Several sites were launched by the Muslim Spiritual Board of Dagestan in 2001. Thereafter, many sites on Islam emerged.

Almost every one out of the 57 muftiyats had, has or intends to have its own newspaper. About 40% of newspapers of the Russian Muslim spiritual boards are published in regional language—the first in the Tatar language. Large muftiyats have several newspapers and periodicals published by them.

The newspaper 'Assalam', founded by Muslim Spiritual Board of Dagestan, has the highest circulation with 47,000 copies among all the papers launched by the Muslim spiritual boards; it also has an electronic version. Islam Minbäre, published by DUMER, and familiar to non-Muslim leaders, has a circulation of 10,000. This paper is considered as the official mouthpiece of the Council of Muftis of Russia.

The independent Islamic newspaper Nur-ul-Islam, close to the Muslim Spiritual Board of Dagestan, was published in 1997 and has a circulation of 6000 copies.

Practically each Russian region with a significant Muslim population has TV and Radio programmes on Islam on local channels and radio stations. Islamic media works more successfully in regions such as Chechnya, Dagestan, Tatarstan, Karachaevo-Cherkessia, Ingushetia and Orenburg district.

The creation of the Union of Muslim Journalists (UMJ) represents an important stage in the development of Muslim media in Russia. The founding congress of UMJ took place in the conference hall of the Russian Council of Muftis (RCM) in Moscow in May, 2003. The congress was organised by the RCM and the Eurasian Party/ Union of Patriots of Russia— and its delegates included 35 journalists and editors representing various Muslim publications and media outlets. This included notable personalities in the congress such as RCM Chairman, Mufti Ravil Gainutdin; Chairman of Eurasian Party / Union of Patriots of Russia, Abdul Niyazev, Rustam Arifdzhanov, the president of media holding "Soversheno Sekretno" and the chief editor of the newspaper Versiya, Chairman of Union of Journalists of Russia, Vsevolod Bogdanov; translator of Quran and member of Russian Academy of Sciences, Iman Valeria Porokhova. The formation of UMJ signalled an important stage in the life of Muslim media in Russia.

(c) Book Publishing

In the 19th century and in the beginning of the 20th century the Islamic community of Russia was rather advanced in the sphere of publication of Islamic literature,which included the reprinting of high quality Qurans as well as religious essays. The high level of the education of the Russian Muslims enabled them to publish quality literature in Arabic language, in which many periodicals were being published. Kazan was recognised as the centre of Islamic book publication. Ufa, Orenburg and some other cities had publishing houses as well. The famous Tatar public figure, Ismail Gaspirinsky, was an initiator for opening printing presses belonging to Muslims. The publishing house in Bakhchi Sarai was opened in 1881.

All the Muslim publishing houses were closed within 15 years after the October Revolution. A Muslim publishing house, opened in Tashkent during World War II, started publishing Islamic literature in limited quantities. With the decline of Muslim traditions in the former USSR, less and less Muslims could speak in the Arabic language. However, the number of Muslims speaking the Russian language sharply increased. This was a reason for publishing religious Muslim literature in the Russian language.

Towards the end of the 1980s an encyclopedia dictionary was prepared and published with the help of experts on Islam from the Leningrad branch of the Oriental Institute and their colleagues from Moscow. With the end of militant atheism, people from all faiths got the opportunity to publish or import any literature from abroad. The first lot of books that reached Russia was the Quran, which was sold very quickly. An Arab foundation flooded the market with Islamic literature in the Russian language. Russian Muslims also started publishing cheap booklets on Islam in the country.

The Soviet collapse, accompanied by a huge economic crisis, dealt a heavy blow to book publishing in Russia; Islamic literature publication was no exception. Towards end of the 1990s, the book market was full of books published by Iman, which was founded in 1991 as an initiative of Imam Baliulla Yakupov, first deputy mufti of Tatarstan. Iman, propagating traditional Muslim values, published Islamic literature in small quantities, and was available in only local markets. The publishing house Santlady published books which had a huge circulation and were available everywhere.

Text books for learning the Arabic language were available aplenty. At the beginning of the century, four Islamic publishing houses – namely Badr, Ansar, Umma and Harun Yhyia were opened in Moscow. Their publications were available not only in the Mosque shops but in other places as well. The Iman publishing house in Kazan reached a new level in their publishing activities, meeting the increasing demand in the republic. A large publishing house—Medinawas founded by Muslims of Nizhni Novgorod. The publishing houses Ikhlas and Nur-al-Islam published literature for the Muslim Spiritual Board of Dagestan. The printing presses in Ufa and Perm published books to meet the requirements of Central Muslim Spiritual Board. Some educational institutions like the Russian Islamic University and the Buguruslansk madrassa, Al Furkan and even some mosques started their own publishing facilities.

The works directed against polemics with the Wahhabis received a special place in Islamic literature. The Muslims of Dagestan achieved significant success in this sphere. However, the Wahhabi literature outnumbered the works of their opponents.

The spread of extremist religious literature evoked the concern, not only of authorities, but also of traditional Muslim bodies. In 1999, a criminal case was filed against the Moscow-based Badr publishing house for publishing some objectionable literature. The case was closed for lack of evidence in 2003. In May 2007, the Koptevski local court adjudged some 14 books, penned by the Turkic writer Said Nursi, as literature of extremist nature.

In 2004 the Dagestan Muslim Spiritual Board released a list of books published by publishing houses Badr, Umma and others as extremist in nature. In 2005 Council of Ummas of the Central Muslim Spiritual Board also released a list of extremist literature.

(d) Birth of Halal Industry

Halal industry saw its boom in the post-Soviet period. Along with network of shops selling Halal products, special canteens and restaurants serving food made out of halal meat, shariat super markets such as Moscow's Apelsin appeared in different cities. In many meat and chocolate factories opened special lines for producing halal products. Special cosmetics were prepared without the use of spirit. In 2007,Centre for Standardisation and Certification of Halal Products was opened on the initiative of Council of Muftis of Russia.

In 2007, there were negotiations for introducing a halal menu in some trains. However, no adequate demands for this kind of menu were found. Gradually there was a demand for sharia-style restaurants, and a tourist agency under the name Idel –Khaz was set up to meet this requirement by Muslim Spiritual Board of Tatarstan and an insurance company — NASKO Tatarstan. Apart from organising Hajj, these agencies organise accommodation for Muslim in special hotels and help organise the Hajj pilgrimage.

Special facilities were made available for Muslim patients in the sphere of medical services. In 2002, a special association of Muslim doctors was set up to treat alchoholism, narcotics consumption and smoking amongst the Islamic population. Muslim birth centres and family stomatology centres working on the basis of shariat were also set up.

Special garment centres were opened in many cities to sell Muslim dresses. Muslim school uniforms were sold in the markets. Special Muslim dresses were designed for Muslim girl-students in schools, institutes and gymnasiums. However, the special birth centres, shops, medical centres did not enjoy much popularity among Muslims and were subsequently closed or reoriented to meet general requirements.

Russia saw the emergence of the first Islamic bank – the Badr-Forte Bank, which had very ambitious plans for the Russian market. In 2006, this bank, along with the consumer society—Menzil worked out a scheme for providing housing loans. This project could not take off as the Central Bank of Russia withdrew its license. The other contribution of Islam for the financial system of Russia was the introduction of the Hawala system for quick transfer of money. The major users of the hawala system in Russia were immigrant-Muslims remitting money to their families back at home. However, according to Russian banking law, this practice was illegal and could not survive in Russia.

Islamic Cultural Revival

Islamic cultural revival is a major element of Islamic revival in Russia. According to Russian expert Svetlana Chernova, the central components of the Islamic world in contemporary Russian art are—(a) Construction, reconstruction and renovation of mosques along with anew architectural concept of mosques: (b) Epigraph on the modern Muslim burial grounds and coffins: (c) Shamail and tugra, linked with perspectives of development in contemporary graphic and paintings of Arab calligraphy and folk art;(d) the Islamic theme and motive of Islamic moral in traditional realistic expressive art, Muslim avant-grade.

New Muslim literature, cinematography and theatre art should be added to this. The new mosque—Taube, built in Neberezhny Chelny, was the first mosque in the new Russia built in a new style. Mufti Talgat Tazuddin, chairman of DUMES, took active part in this project. The mosque Kul-Sharif, which opened in 2005 in Kazan, is known for its new Muslim architecture. This mosque is famous for its original architecture. The mosques in North Caucasus distinguish themselves by their size and look like the mosques in Turkey and Middle East.

At the beginning of the process of liberalisation under Gorbachev, only 94 mosques operated in the territory of what would become the Russian Federation.[40] However, there were many illegal and semi-legal places of worship. Since then, there has been mushrooming of mosques in Russia. In the table below, Hunter has given an idea of the number of mosques in selected regions in the Russian Federation. According to Sergei Ivanenko and Alexander Shegortsov, the number of officially registered mosques in Russia grew from 870 to 7000 between 1991 and 2000.[41] However, only a limited number of these mosques are cathedral mosques with domes and minarets. The rest are small prayer halls with rather rudimentary outward signs.

Table 2.1: Mosques in Selected Regions of Russia Region Number of Mosques in 2001

REGION	NUMBER OF MOSQUES IN 2001
NORTH WEST REGION	
St. Petersburg	1
CENTRAL REGION	
Moscow	4
VOLGA-VYATKA REGION	
Nizhni Novgorod district	35
VOLGA REGION	
Tatarstan	700
Samara district	41
Ulyanovsk district	50
NORTH CAUCASUS	
Dagestan	1200
Ingushetia	400
Chechnya	400
Kabardino-Balkaria	96
Karachaevo-Cherkessia	91
URAL REGION	
Bashkortstan	490
Orenburg district	75
Perm district	39

Sverdlovsk district	38
Chelyabinsk district	36
WEST SIBERIAN REGION	
Tyumen district	35
EAST SIBERIAN REGION	
Irkutsk	1
FAR EAST REGION	
Norilsk	1
Total	**3733**

Source: Hunter, T.S. (1984), Islam in Russia, p.65, New York: ME Sharpe.

In December 2000, the Russian commission on the affairs of religious organisations conducted a survey in 65 federal units of the Russian Federation with significant Muslim populations. The survey found 4,658 Muslim devotional buildings of different architectural styles, including mosques.[42]

Out of this total number, 2884 structures were built in 1990s, and 68 devotional buildings were under construction. In accordance with the 1995 the Law on the Transfer of Federal Property, of a devotional nature to religious organisations, the process of returning religious property to the communities of believers is continuing in Russia. By the end of 2000, 522 devotional buildings had been transferred to Muslim religious organisations, while transfer of 42 was pending. The commission concluded that there has been a surge in the construction of places of Muslim worship, which in some regions outnumber the Muslim communities that would use them. The contribution of federal funds in the construction of these infrastructures has been insignificant. Local authorities, foreign Islamic funds and private sponsors have been major sources of funding.

The aforesaid study also indicates that North Caucasus accounts for a large part of Muslim devotional buildings, with the number reaching 2255, out of which 1585 are located in Dagestan. According to Russian expert Maxim Shevchenko, there is a surplus of mosques in Dagestan, and many, particularly in remote villages which people are leaving in search of jobs, remain unattended or poorly attended. The distribution of Muslim religious property in other republics of the North Caucasus is as follows: 300 in Chechnya, 130 in Kabardino-Balkaria, 108 in Karachaevo-Cherkassia, 85 in Ingushetia, 28 in Adygea, and 19 in North Ossetia. In the North

Caucasus, 1322 places of worship were built during 1990s, and 39 were under construction at the time of the commission's survey. There are 2403 Muslim religious buildings in the territory of the European part of Russia, the Volga region, and Siberia. From 1990 to 2000, 1562 buildings were built for Islamic religious practices, and 29 were under construction at the time of survey. The government also transferred 31 buildings to Muslim religious organisations.[43]

Tatarstan had the largest number of historic mosques. Apart from renovation of old mosques, many new mosques have been built in the republic. In the 1990s, the industrial city of Naberzhni Chelny emerged as an important centre of Islamic revival, as well as radicalism. Renovation of old mosques and building of new mosques is an ongoing process in the republic. A similar process of restoration of old mosques and construction of new mosques is going on in Bashkortstan and North Caucasus, largely though private initiative.

Reaction to Construction of Mosques

In the 1990s, federal and regional authorities generally had a liberal approach towards the construction of mosques. However, the negative attitude of Orthodox Christian Church and non-Muslims to this process was not uncommon. For example, in 1999 the local population protested against the construction of a mosque which had a height of 24 meters and was to dominate the sky line and become the city's symbol. The local population in Petrozavodsk—the capital of Kamchatka,resisted the attempt to build a mosque by the Muslims. A similar conflict arose in Taganrog when an attempt was made to build a mosque there. The reason for the opposition was that the mosque would increase the threat of Wahhabi radicalism in the concerned regions.

These developments are not surprising, given the sentiments of the region's populace. During a visit to Novocherk ask in June 2000, its deputy mayor claimed that there were 2000 to 3000 Muslims in the area, mostly immigrants from the North and South Caucasus and other Muslim republics of the CIS.[44]

Since late 1999, the attitude of federal as well as regional authorities has become more cautious and less liberal. The opposing of the construction of mosques is palpable in the regions that are not traditional centres of Muslim concentration.

The art of calligraphy is developing along with the development of original Muslim architecture. Other forms of art have also developed during these years;in 2005 the first international Muslim film festival was organised in Kazan to observe 1000 years of city's foundation. About 70 films from 18 countries participated in the festival. Around 91 films took part in the second international Muslim festival. In 2005 the council of muftis of Russia, jointly with the publishing house Umma and the Federal Agency for Media, instituted the literary award "Islamic Breakthrough", named after Russian Muslim Dmitry Muslima Akhtyamov.

Notes

1. Gainutddin, R. (2004), Islam in contemporary Russia (Ислам в современной России), p.71, Moscow.
2. Silantiyev, R.A. (2008), Encyclopedia Islam in Contemporary Russia (Энциклопедия ислама в современной России), p.63, Moscow: Algoritm.
3. Silantiyev, R.A. (2008), Encyclopedia Islam in Contemporary Russia (Энциклопедия ислама в современной России), p.65, Moscow: Algoritm..
4. Express Chronicle, 28 June 1996.
5. New Vecherka, 28 September 1999.
6. Political Zyavlinie, 12 February 2000.
7. Nezavisimaya Gazyeta, 21 May 1992.
8. Nezavismaya Gazyta Religion, 14 November 2001.
9. Nezavisimaya Gazyeta, 8 May 1992.
10. Sympherpolskaya Pravda, 12 March 2002.
11. Silantiyev, R.A. (2008), Encyclopedia Islam in Contemporary Russia (Энциклопедия ислама в современной России), p.67, Moscow: Algoritm.
12. Aganekh, 16 October 1995.
13. New Times, November Issue 1996, "The Program of Russian Socio-Political Movement of Union of Muslims of Russia."
14. New Business, 8 May 1996.
15. Nezavisimaya Gazyeta, 27 September 1997.
16. Russikaya Gazyeta, 15 March 1996.
17. Nizavisimaya Gazyeta, September 1999.
18. Nizavismaya Gazyeta Religion, 26 January 2000.
19. www.refach.ru
20. Vremya-MN, 29 June 2001.
21. Kommersant, 3 December 2001
22. www.islamnasledie.ru
23. Vremya Novasti, 16 February 2006.
24. Hunter, T.S. (1984), Islam in Russia, p.133, New York: ME Sharpe.
25. Hunter, T.S. (1984), Islam in Russia, New York: ME Sharpe.
26. Ibid.
27. Ibid.
28. Ibid.

29. Ibid., p.140.
30. Ibid., p.142.
31. Hunter, T.S. (1984), Islam in Russia, New York: ME Sharpe.
32. Ibid.
33. Ibid.
34. Ibid.
35. Silantiyev, R.A. (2008), Encyclopedia Islam in Contemporary Russia (Энциклопедия ислама в современной России), Moscow: Algoritm.
36. Ibid., p.100.
37. Silantiyev, R.A. (2008), Encyclopedia Islam in Contemporary Russia (Энциклопедия ислама в современной России), Moscow: Algoritm.
38. Hunter, T.S. (1984), Islam in Russia, p.75, New York: ME Sharpe.
39. www.Islamtv.ru
40. Hunter, T.S. (1984), Islam in Russia, New York: ME Sharpe.
41. Ibid.
42. Ibid.
43. Ibid.
44. Ibid.

3. Muslim Identity and Islamic Revival

Muslim Identity and Revival

The process of strengthening the role and place of Islam in Russian society which began under Gorbachev's Perestroika and continued after Soviet disintegration is called 'the Revival of Islam' by some experts. While some experts call it the re-Islamisation process, others are in disagreement, arguing that Islam never disappeared from Russia, and hence it is not correct to call the process the 'Revival of Islam'. They prefer to describe the process as a strengthening of the religious foundations in the consciousness of the people – a re-establishment of the role of Islam in the society, or 'Legalisation of Islam'.[1] Differences in the interpretation of the process do not bear any principled character, because the discussion is about one and the same phenomena, which Russian scholar Vsevolod Malashenko calls establishment of full-fledged Islam. While talking about an Islamic revival,one should not forget that it was launched deliberately by the Soviet intelligentsia and politicians,who were using it for boosting their popularity.[2]

While talking about Islamic revival or legalisation, we should take note of the fact that statistical analysis does not reflect the process. By the beginning of the 1990s, 67% of Tatars living in Russia considered themselves as Muslims; in 1999 the figure rose to 70%. (**Musina, R.N., Shumilova E. (2003),** ***State- Confessional Relations in Contemporary Tatarstan*, Kazan**).

This indicator is close to 100% in North Caucasus.

The sociological survey conducted by the North Caucasus Centre for Socio-Political Research shows that 60% of Chechens, 41% Ingush, 30 % Dargins, 27% Avars, 305 Karachaevs, 20% Kumyks and 17% Balkars believe that religion should determine all spheres of social life. The same survey shows that 21% Chechens, 31 % Ingush, 13% Dargins, 33% Avars, 43% Kumikos 34% Karachaevs and 48% Balkars are of the opinion that religion must exert significant influence on society.[3]

Re-Islamisation is stimulated by aggravation of ethnic consciousness, which is provoked by the contradictions between the federal centre and the periphery. This is typical of Tatarstan, where 1990s nationalist organisations like 'Ittifak' and 'Milli Mejhlis' made appeals to Islam. Milli Mejhlis approved its programme 'Tatar Kanuni' which talked about the necessity of the revival of *shariat* and *zhadidism*. The Ittifak and Milli Mejhlis both sought the help of Islam while formulating national specific path of development.[4]

It is interesting to know whether Islam dominates in the religious consciousness of Russian Muslims or Islam is taken into account in the context of ethnic culture— or even identified with this. Results of opinion polls conducted in the east of North Caucasus suggest that 56% of Avars, 50% Dergins, 43% Chechens, 41% Ingush and 48% of Lezgins consider themselves as 'just Muslims'. For the rest, their association, in particular with the 'Caucasus Muslim'— which means to the shariat or khanifat branch, is important for them. In the western part of the region, 88% Adygs, 94 % of Cherkes, 86% Kabardins and 80% Karachaevs consider themselves as 'just Muslims'.[5]

The picture is somewhat different in Tatarstan. Opinion polls conducted in 1990 show that 44.6% rural population of Tatarstan and 33.5% of the urban population consider that religion helps to be closer with your own people, and 41% of the urban Tatar population considers general Islamic festivals as national festivals.[6]

It is perceived that people who consider themselves 'just Muslims' would show tolerance and understanding to 'other Muslims'. Usually, Muslim identity in general reflects their own ethno-cultural notions, discarding other versions of religion. This is typical of Russian Muslims who have lived in an isolated situation from the rest of the Muslim world for 70 years.

The Islamic revival is reflected in the growing number of Muslim communities and mosques. By 2004 there were 3,537 registered Muslim communities, which constituted 16.3% total registered religious communities, numbering 2,166,427.[7]

It is not possible to give the exact number of mosques in Russia. In reality, the gap comes from a number of registered mosques and those that really exist. Besides, there are prayer halls which Muslims visit on Fridays to offer prayers.

For example, in the year 2000 the then Russian minister on national policy, Vladimir Zorin, said that 7000 mosques have been built in the country. The deputy Prime Minister Ramazan Abdulatifov in the same year said that that 7000 mosques had been built in the country.[8]

The number of mosques in Chechnya is 465 and in Ingushetia it is 300. There are 1100(700) mosques in Tatarstan, 470 in Bashkortstan, 160 in Ulyanosk district,60 in Samara district,80 in Orenburg district, 78 in Perm district, 70 in Penza district, 70 in Tyumen district, 60 in Nizhgorodski district, 57 in Chelyabinsk district, 40 in Sverdolovsk district, 56 in Astrakhan district and 16 in Volgagrad district.[9]

During the past 20 years mosques have become atypical symbol of the socio-cultural panorama of Russia. If you travel through Volga River region, you will find mosques in various architectural styles standing side by side Orthodox Christian churches.

Just as in the rest of the Muslim world, mosques in Russia are not only religious places for prayer but also serve as social and socio-political centres playing a significant role in the social life of the region, or city, where they exist.

Usually huge numbers of people, including a lot of young people, attend the Friday prayer. Politicians, public figures, businessmen too attend the prayer in large numbers, trying to show their love for Islam before the common masses. The people hear the interpretation of events in Middle East, Iraq, Iran, and of Russia's relations with the Muslim world. Heightened feelings of religious identity stimulate the desire to 'Islamise' the atmosphere by opening shops for halal products, boutiques with religious attributes and literature, and even organising fashion demonstrations for popularising Muslim dress. The process of Islamisation is very strong in North Caucasus and the middle Volga region. It is something more than a 'fashion for religion'.

There are Islamic fashion houses and special shops for Islamic dress in different cities. Tatarstan runs courses that provide training in how to become the ideal Muslim wife. Kazan holds international film festivals, as well as Muslim beauty contests, which are essentially different from the conventional beauty contests. Using head scarfs is encouraged by the spiritual leadership. Orthodox Christian Russians show understanding and tolerance towards these changes.

Imams have demanded the closure of saunas and casinos, which contradict Islam, in Dagestan and other regions. Experts believe that very soon there would be Islamic banks in Tatarstan, because there is an accumulation of capital which looks for an Islamic cover. At present there is only one financial structure— the 'Badr –Forte Bank' which has the right to use Islamic economic technology. Very soon there could be more such financial structures. Islam is penetrating into the sphere of insurance as well. Tatarstan has a programme called Idel-Haj, which helps Muslims save money for conducting Haj. There are attempts to establish a Muslim tax system. Scholars believe that Islamic business is prospering in Tatarstan with the production of halal products, stitching of Muslim dresses, functioning of Muslim cafes etc. Kazan's confessionery factory produces sweets according to halal tradition—without alcohol and animal fat. In the year 2006, the Council of Imams in Dagestan and in its capital Makhachkali, there was a black-listing of certain artists who were not allowed to perform in Dagestan. Popular artists and groups famous for their provocative performance, such as Boris Moiseyev, Sergey Penkin, Shura, Valery Leontev, Minet, Blestashie, Agata Kristi Nochniye Snaiperi etc were included this black list.[10] These are attempts to show that Islam is different from other religions.

The next component of the Islamic 'Renaissance' is the formation of the system of religious education. This system was not prevalent in Russia till the Soviet disintegration in 1991, when the need for spiritual and educational cadres was met by the 'Mir –Arab'Madrassa in Bukhara. The formation of this system began in the mid-1990s quite chaotically, and without the control of an institutional spiritual leadership. Hundreds and thousands of groups, centered around Sunday schools started mushrooming for imparting Islamic teachings. Often they were controlled at random by unqualified people. Often Arab students studying in USSR and Russia were employed to teach in these schools and centres. The educational standard of teachers was very poor. Only three Imams had received full higher education.[11] In 1999 only 8 % of the functioning mosques had professional religious leaders. The situation in North Caucasus was still worse. The situation in this sphere has been improving of late. For example, the number of Imams with middle religious education has reached 25% in Tatarstan.

In 1990s thousands of young people travelled to the Middle East, Turkey, and Pakistan, to get receiving religious education. However, young people who have returned to Russia after receiving religious education in foreign countries often became exponents of the "Other Islam".Many educational institutions have been built in Russia under the patronage of Arab organisations where the emphasis was laid on a non-conventional understanding of Islam. The activities of native as well as foreign missionaries have led to strengthening differences within Muslim community.

By the beginning of the year 2000, the Muslim spiritual leadership by and large succeeded in laying the foundation for an Islamic educational system thought here was room for improvement. By 1998 Russia had 108 registered Islamic spiritual educational institutions, the majority of whom imparted middle level education —though formally they were called institutions of higher education.[12]

Moscow's Higher Islamic College admitted 218 students in 2006. The Russian Islamic Institute is functioning in Tatarstan. The Islamic Instate is functioning in Ufa with branches in Astrakhan, Orenburg, Samara, Pernza, and Ulyanovsk districts. Around 200-300 students are studying in the Islamic Institute of Ingushetia.[13]

There are 16 Islamic educational institutes in Dagestan. Makhachkala has an Islamic University named after Imam Shafii. There are 6,000 students studying in these institutes. About 1410 regular madrasses and 324 primary schools have been opened in the republic.[14] This is the primary reason why t the number of students practising Islam has gone up by three times compared to that in the end of the 1980s in Dagestan. The Council of Islamic Education was set up in the republic in 2006 and it contributed to unifying the standard of education which has been formulated. However, the standard of education in these institutions has not reached the desired level. Russian scholars believe that not withstanding the presence of so many Islamic educational systems and more or less unified teaching system, the main task of preventing penetration of non-traditional Islam engaging the youth is afr from being accomplished fully.

Non-Conventional Islam (Muslim diversity)

There are two kinds of Islam competing with each other in Russia. While the first one is traditional, soft, peaceful, non-aggressive, and practiced by a majority of Russian Muslims, the second one is aggressive and politicized and its followers believe that Russian Islam has been distorted and needs to be corrected by re-establishing genuine Islamic norms of behaviour and thinking. The radical fundamentalists argue that the lifestyle of Russian Muslims is incompatible with the real teachings of Islam. They have a very critical attitude towards the Muslim spiritual leadership.

The fundamentalists or Wahhabis, on the other hand, argue that the teachings of fundamentalists are not compatible with traditional Russian

Muslims and contradict the practicing local culture; and that fundamentalists are trying to use Islam for meeting their political ambitions.

At the same time, the Russian Muslim spiritual leadership does not have a unified approach to deal with fundamentalism. While part of the Muslim spiritual leadership is criticising the fundamentalists for their disruptive activities against the state it nevertheless considers that as being part of Islamic religious thoughts; the other part of the leadership sees in the activities of Wahhabis a deviation from the real Islam and call for its ban. The conflict within the Muslim spiritual leadership reflects the contradiction between the two streams of Islam in Russia. While the followers of conventional Islam are loyal to the state authorities,the followers of fundamentalism believe in defying state authority for establishing a 'clean Islam'.

A split in Russian Islam, on the basis of its various interpretations, became the impetus for the aggressive missionary activities of the Salafits, who saw in the dissenting Islam natural pagans, who needed immediate introduction to the values of a 'clean' Islam.

The numerous Salafi groups did not have any single coordination center and were split on the basis of their ideological faith. However, all their followers were called Wahabis. In Russia the Wahabis are perceived as people calling themselves followers of— Salafism, Sufi Islam or 'clean' Islam, Hanbalism, Habashism, Tabligism, Nurism, Islamic Jamats, Militant Shiism and also Hizb Ut-Tahrir and its numerous clans.

Intolerance towards dissenters, other believers, an attempt to create a shariat state,the confidence that they conduct jihad against godless authority, the inclination to use force in missionary activity—are all characteristic traits of such groups. Many Wahhabi groups recognise terrorism as the most effective means for achieving their objectives.

According to some sources Wahhabis constitute 2% to 10% of all Russian Muslims (3 lakh to 15 lakh). Their share is highest among the Muslims of Chechnya, Dagestan, Kabardino- Balkaria, Karachaevo-Cherkesia, StavropolKrai and also among newly converted Muslims.

Apart from the Wahhabis, the new religious movements of Islamic origin such as the Akhmadia sect of the Bahai faith, different new Sufi movements belong to non-traditional Islam in Russia. The followers of these movements are not inclined towards extremism, and that is why they could be related to the moderate wing of non-traditional Muslims. Their number cannot be more than 20,000 and they usually live in large cities.

The contradictions between the traditional and non-traditional Muslims in Russia got further aggravated by conflicts, contradictions among traditionalists. Friction between Sunnis and Shias, Hanafit and Shariat, between different Sufi Tarikat, and also between Tarikat and Muftiat does not permit them to get united against Wahhabis, who have put up a United Front.

Radical Islam, which is called Salafism or 'clean Islam' by scholars, presents serious challenges to the unity of Russian Islam. The history of Salafism began in the 18th century when Hanbalit proponent Mohammed ibn Abl–Vahhab declared that Islam after the death of prophet Mohammed was diluted and deformed and hence it was necessary to return to the roots. This new movement came to be known as Wahhabism. The main characteristic of the new movement was a primitive interpretation of the Quran, which led to the negation of significant Muslim literature and created dogmas and rituals that emerged as prohibitions. The Shia faith and Sufis became main targets of Wahhabism. Wahhabism in spite of all efforts could not penetrate into the USSR. However, the situation radically changed towards the end of 1980s when perestroika weakened the external borders of the country facilitating the penetration of Wahhabism into Russia. The first Wahhabi Emirs from Afghanistan set up their branches in Tajikistan and the Fergana valley.[15] By 1989, the Wahhabis had reached North Caucasus.

Muslim Diversity and State Approach

Traditionally, Russian Muslims belonged to the Hanafi School, based on the teachings of Imam Abu Hanifa, with the exception of Dagestan where Shafei tradition is dominant. The dominance of the Hanafi School can be attributed to the fact that Islamic thoughts and teachings penetrated most of the Muslim-dominated regions of Russia from Central Asia, particularly from Bukhara. Imam Abu Hanifa was a native of Central Asia and developed his thoughts there, whereas Dagestan was influenced by the Islamic teachings which prevailed in the Arab world. Greater tolerance towards pre-Islamic traditions, forming a significant part of Islam, was one of the attractions of the Hanafi School for Central Asians. Some have ascribed this phenomena to Imam Hanifa's Iraninan origins. The Hanafi School is known for its accommodating attitude towards political power and does not condone open rebellion against the state.[16] Some scholars believe that this is one of the reasons why young Muslims are attracted to political Islam, as well as an activist interpretation of Wahhabism.[17]

Mystical traditions of Islam in various forms and schools, otherwise known as Sufism, are very strong. Various shades of Islam, particularly of a radical nature, have penetrated into Russia's Muslim-dominated regions,particularly after Soviet disintegration. Freedom promoted in the post-Soviet democratic Russia opened the doors for greater interaction of Russian Muslims with the outside Islamic world. Some Muslim countries vied with one another for greater influence in Russia's Muslim space. At present, five major trends can be observed within Russian Islam: traditional Hanafism, Sufi traditions, Salafiyya (Wahhabism), Jihadism, and Euro-Islam.[18]

Traditional Hanafism

Hanafism is considered to be the position of the official clergy. Adherants of Hanafism in general maintain a loyal, cooperative attitude towards the state authorities. They strive to receive recognition for Islam as a significant part of Russian cultural heritage. One of the major traits of those belonging to this stream is to maintain harmonious relations between followers of different faiths, particularly between Islam and Orthodox Christianity. The Ufa centre and its leader mufti Talgat Tadzuddin are even more loyal to the government. Both Ufa and Kazan centres stand for maintenance of Russia's sovereignty and territorial integrity, the secular character of the state, and the principle of separation of religion and state. However, there are forces within mainstream Islam who advocate a more assertive role for Islam and increasing ties with the Muslim world. They are more vocal about the 'anti-Islam' statements and attitude of certain sections of Russian society. This attitude sometimes makes them vulnerable to the charges of secretly harbouring sympathy for Wahhabism.

Sufi Traditions

Mainstream Islam in North Caucasus is still dominated by various Sufi trends—Naqshbandya, Qadiriya, and Shaziliya, though the trend of less mystical practices seems to be on the declining path. While a growing number of religious leaders in North Caucasus pleaded in favour of introduction of sharia as the law of the land, particularly during the period between the two Chechen wars, the Dagestan clergy have maintained that any such action should comply with Russian laws. The dominant view about Sufism in Russia is that it is a peaceful faith and hence stands opposed to the rise of extremist trends. However, this perception is not entirely correct as has been demonstrated by history. The history of North Caucasus and Central Asia shows that Sufism can be turned radical. The stiffest resistance to Russian advance into Caucasus was organised by Imam Shamil, a Sufi leader. During anti-religious campaigns in USSR, Sufi brotherhoods were important centres of upholding religious traditions. So the emergence of political version of Sufism can not be ruled out; nor is Sufism entirely apolitical. In fact, it is not unusual to see some Sufi leaders actively involved in republic's politics.

Non-Conventional Islam:

Perestroika opened the doors for penetration of non-traditional, as well as radical Islam, into Muslim-dominated regions of Russia. The most influential among these schools has been Wahhabism, a set of teachings propounded by Muhammad Ibn Abdul Wahhab. The influence of this radical school is particularly strong in North Caucasus. Because adherants of Wahhabism have been involved in terrorist acts and, since Russian authorities have indiscriminately applied the term Wahhabi to describe all those who use violence as a means to achieve the end, some scholars have ceased to use the term Wahhabism; on the other hand the Wahhabis themselves prefer to use a different name for self-identification. Many of these non-traditional Muslims call themselves Salafiyya or Salafi.

Salafiya in its strictest sense, means those who follow only the teachings of the Quran, the prophet, and his companions – Sahaba, the Taibun, and the Taba Taibun –"the righteous ones" and the two or three generations after them.[19]

Jihadism

Muslims who adhere to strict and reductioninst interpretations of Islam and are committed to establishing the rule of Sharia differ in their means and methods for achieving their goal. They come under two categories: 1) those who want to bring about Islamisation through peaceful means and 2) those who believe that these gaols can be achieved by violent means or through waging a holy war (Jihad). The second category of Muslims is called Jihadist. The Jihadist calling spread through Muslim-inhabited regions of Russia very quickly, particularly as a result of the Soviet Union's Afghan war and Russia's two Chechen wars.

Moscow's Afghan war was described as a Jihad by both the Muslim world as well as the West. The Afghan resistance movement came to be known as Muzahideen or holy warriors. Volunteers from Central Asia and Caucasus, along with Muslims from Arab countries, went to fight against Soviet Union. After the Soviet disintegration, followed by outbreak of ethnic conflicts in Caucasus, some Afghan veterans found themselves engaged in the region's bloody conflicts, in particular the Chechen war.

Shahidism

Shahidism is an offshoot of the Jihadist movement which has recently raised its ugly head in Russia, particularly in North Caucasus. The members of the movement consider martyrdom a way of achieving their objectives. The hostage-taking operations in Moscow's Dubrovka theatre, Buinatsk hospital and a host of suicide bombings are examples of the implementation of shahidist ideology.

The growing participation of women in the suicide bombings represents a new trend in the radical Islam practiced in Russia. The Moscow metro explosion that caused dozens of deaths was believed to be perpetrated by Chechen women suicide-bombers. The suicide attacks on the bus in North Ossetia and at the rock concert at Tushino airfield are believed to have been carried out by women. According to Moscow-appointed Chechen Prosecutor General Vladimir Kravchenko, Shamil Basayev had trained thirty female suicide-bombers for carrying out attacks against Russian federal troops stationed in Chechnya and Chechnya's pro-Moscow administration.[20]

Several reasons are attributed to the rise of extremist versions of Islam in Russia. They are institutional-ideological, social and economic, ethno-cultural and political. It appears that Tsarist and Soviet policies led to the serious weakening of traditional and institutional foundations of Russian Islam, resulting in a shortage of Muslim religious institutions and adequately educated clergy. As a result, the Muslim religious revival during *perestroika* and post-*perestroika* period triggered a crisis that saw lack of adequate number of educated Imams, scholarly theologians. This led to the sending of students abroad, particularly to west-Asian countries for receiving higher religious education and an influx of foreign missionaries to Russia. Foreign missionaries chose young boys and sent them abroad for receiving religious education. The missionaries facilitated the spread of extreme ideology among representatives of the youth. The young Russian Muslims studying aboad were exposed to various forms of extremist ideology. When they came back home and started working as Imams or preachers, they spread this extremist ideology among the Muslim youth.

Socio-economic factors in some Muslim regions have contributed to the rise of radical Islam in Russia. The deterioration of the socio-economic situation in Russia's Muslim-dominated regions, following Soviet disintegration,particularly in North Caucasus, has contributed significantly to the spread of radical Islam. Growing poverty and unemployement have led many young people join ranks of terrorist outfits. The disastrous market reforms carried out in the 1990s resulted in a sharp reduction in industrial and agricultural output, throwing many to the streets and depriving them of sources of livelihood. North Caucasus has proportionately more poor people compared to the rest of the Russian regions. The problem of unemployment is very acute in North Caucasus. The unemployed youth and poor peasants in search of livelihood were attracted to the extremist brand of Islam with its condemnation of luxury, self-indulgence and materialistic excesses. Ideas of equality, ethics of brotherhood, and unity of all Muslims in Islamic fundamentalism attracted many people to Islamic extremism and terrorism. Many turned to Islam as an alternative and a way out of the prevailing crisis.

Cultural and Political Factors

Penetration of non-Muslim culture, particularly western culture into Islamic space is a stronger reason for many to turn to Islam. The danger of cultural dilution has led many to Islamic fundamentalism which talks about the true Islam. In order to protect Islam from alien culture, particularly the European influence, many join the ranks of fundamentalists and extremists. The cultural factor seems to be important for those Muslims who are relatively well-off. The ideas of Muslimself-determination, self-rule, creation of Caliphat are attractive to many who resort to radical Islam. Mufti Ravil Gainutdin subscribes to the view that socio-political and cultural factors are mainly responsible for the rise of radical Islam in Russia. He, in this connection, says,"The reason for the emergence of extremists who are in one way or another related to Islam, in my opinion, should be looked for not in Islam, but in the living conditions of Muslims. If we approach this problem from this position, then the threat is real which is constantly growing. And it is understandable. It is precisely among the Muslim youth that unemployment is the highest in the country and the living conditions are the worst. This youth experiences biggest difficulties in adapting to the contemporary conditions. This process is much more difficult for Muslims than for the followers of other religions. The Muslims are experiencing the crisis of traditional values and the life style".[21]

Euro–Islam (Modernity Vs Conservatism)

Conservatism is identified in Russia with neo-traditionalism, reflecting Islam in its ethnic and religious versions. Here it is not very clear which Islam is meant here -pre-revolutionary or Soviet–time Islam. In the central and eastern parts of North Caucasus, it is about the repressed pre-revolutionary Tarikat Islam or the Islam of Mazkhabs, which was permitted under the Communist regime.

Conservatives are working in all the Muslim spiritual boards and dominate in many such boards. They pose as the preachers of the official line of Islam (supported by the state), which is directed not towards adaptation of new life realities, nor towards recognition of generally accepted secular values—freedom of conscience, freedom of choice of world views—but towards realisation of Quranic and Sunniest values in their fundamentalist interpretation.[22]

This strict assessment of the position of Dagestan Muslim spiritual board, revealed by researcher Zaid Abdulagatov, is applicable to the activities of other North-Caucasus muftis. This can be seen among the leaders of Tatarstan Muslim spiritual board as well as among spiritual leaders of some other regions.

Conservatives advocate for re-Islamisation of social norms, for realisation of sharia in socium, including establishing polygamy, observing religious bans. They approve politicisation of Islam. For example, many Islamic political parties were created with the support of the Muslim spiritual boards.

Conservatives criticise Islamists (those who stand for exclusive Muslim state) for their betrayal of traditional Islam. Conservative tendency is linked to return of more detailed study of mazkhabas. Mazkhabasization is practiced in the Volga region and southern parts of Russia.

Neo-traditional tendency is linked to active appearance of the Sufi tarikats—Naksbandiya, Kadiriya and Shazilia. Nakshabandi has been always very popular,enjoying the support of the authorities. Sufis are dead against Wahhabism. However, they show solidarity with the Wahhabis on some issues like the Palestinian issue and the US policy towards Middle East.

According to Russian expert Enwar Kisriyev, the corelation between modernists and conservatives could be 50-50.[23] Modernists dominate in urban areas whereas conservatives dominate in rural areas.

However, number of modernist Muslims in Russia is not large and they virtually belong to secular intelligentsia. The most vocal representative of Muslim modernists is Rafael Hakimov, the former political advisor to Tatarstan President Mintimer Shamiyev. He believes that the reformist ideas of Jadidism, which should have the form of Euro-Islam, could be revived. According to Hakimov, the term Euro-Islam should be understood in the context of contemporary form of Jadidism, which largely reflects the cultural aspect of Islam rather than its ritual part.[24]

Jadidism was part of the greater reformist movement that spread throughout the Islamic world under the influence of figures like Jemaledin al-Afgani. Several Tatar religious and intellectual leaders became part of this movement. The primary objective of the movement was to revitalise Islamic people and free them from foreign domination. To achieve the goal, they believed that Islam must be free of superstition and other static forms of behaviour, and that Muslims should master science and technology.[25]

In the beginning of the 20th century the Jadidists, whose ideologue was the Crimean Tatar Izmail-bei Gaspirinsky, pleaded for the modernisation of Muslim society with the help of modern education. Jadidism, in spite of its temporary success, could not become an influential movement in Tatar Islam.[26]

However, the very emergence of this active movement bears testimony to the existence of reform potential in Russian Islam. This potential did not find its application under the Soviet state. Stalin's hobnobbing with the movement and its famous leader Mirsaid Sultan-Galiyev was nothing but a maneuver that culminated in the destruction of Muslim reform potential and physical elimination of its advocates.

The votaries of modernisation view Islam as a religious ideology that would provide a rational interpretation of social development. The paradox lies in the fact that Tatar neo-Jadidists,as well as fundamentalists, stand for a form of Islam not linked to traditional Hanafism. This provokes opposition from traditionalists. No wonder done does not find supporters of Hakimov among religious preachers, and Hakimov himself has become a subject of severe criticism by the Tatar Muslim spiritual board chief, Gusman Iskhakov, his deputy Valiulla Yagkupov and other Tatar religious leaders.

Some contemporary Tatar intellectuals have offered new interpretations of Jadidism and have tried to give it a more specific Tatar character. For example, Rafael Hakimov says that Jadidists offered a 'western' interpretation of Muslim culture. Or it could be called the 'Oriental' interpretation of European culture, for the Tatar theologicians found in Islam the concepts that were consonant with European trends. He also argues that Tatarstan's special geographic location on the periphery of the Muslim world, and its political conditions reflected in close contacts with Russia, led to the creation of an 'Islamic sub-civilisation' among Tatars— best exemplified by Jadidism. Hakimov maintains that a new vibrant and modern Islam can be developed on the foundations of Jadidism, particularly in Tatarstan. This modern Islam can be emulated by other Muslims. According to him Jadidism's advantage lies in that, "it encourages individualism, has a creative premise and welcomes all sorts of social activities as pleasing to God, it is a stimulus for a transition to a market economy". Reformist Islam does not stand in the way of present-day European norms and values. On the contrary, it permits traditional Tatar and Islamic values to be organically united with the ideas of liberalism and democracy. Hakimov further maintains that Islam will inevitably become Europeanised, by which he implies that it will adapt to the requirements of the modern world and will rid itself of the vestiges of the past, which impedes progress. However, Hakimov's idea of Euro-Islam enjoys support only among some Tatar intellectuals.

There is scepticism among Muslims about a 'blind return to Jadidism', which can not resolve contemporary issues of Islam. Jadidism, or neo-Jadidism, is no more productive and belongs to the past.

The majority of Russian Imams and muftis prefer a middle path between the traditionalists and modernists, avoiding an extreme path and confrontation. This is explained by the fact that the majority of imams and muftis do not want a split within the spiritual leadership and do not wish to be accused of Islamic radicalism. This particular group forms the religious world view of Russian Muslims. They understand that there is no return to the past, but at the same time a review of religious interpretations is inevitable.

The Muslim world in contemporary Russia is a particular socio-cultural, spiritual, ethno-psychological and political reality.[27] The Islamic revival in

Russia is contradictory in nature and varied in consequences. Its main result is that we have to deal with 'new Islam and new Muslims'. According to Ravil Gainutdin, the situation with Islam and Muslim organisations in contemporary Russian society does not have any thing common with Soviet or pre-revolutionary past.[28] A new kind of Muslim has evolved in Russia.[29]

From theological and political point of view, Islam itself is pluralalistic in nature; says Malashenko. It has obtained adversary tendencies towards the authorities. It is closely linked to global Umma he believes.

However, noted scholar Farid Asadullin thinks that the functions of the muftiyats have increased of late and are closely linked to interests of the state in the sphere of civil peace and international accord.[30] This does not contradict the view expressed above, about the loyalty of the spiritual leadership, because Russian Muslims are second to none in defending international and inter-ethnic peace and harmony.

There have been attempts to unite all Russian Muslims in one community. All those attempts have failed,and it is unlikely to happen in near future. The All Russia Public-Poilitical Organisation, set up in 2004, was designed to protect economic, political and religious rights of all national minorities practicing Islam. The Russian Islamic Heritage Foundation was created in 2005, and aimed at strengthening relations between Muslims living in different Russian regions. However, its activities fall short of expectations.

According to Vsevolod Malashenko, the hypothetical destabilisation provokes radicalisation of Islam under religious slogans in Russia.

Pan-Turkism

Pan-Turkism as a movement emerged in Russia in the 1880s. Ismail –Bei – Gasprinsky was the founder of the liberal-cultural movement of Turkic- Tatar Muslim intellegentsia. Gasprinsky outlined a programme for fighting against the backwardness of Russian Muslims. This programme included reform in the Muslim education system of Russia and stipulated the introduction of new methods of education and secular sciences. This programme was aimed at developing Muslim media, as a result of which the first Tatar newspaper edited by Gasprinsky appeared in the country. He gave a clarion call to the Muslims for unity of language, faith and actions. Thanks to his efforts the single Turkic literary language for all people of Turkic origin was formed. Tatar reformer and scientist Kayum Nasiry (1825-1902) was propagating the idea of global Islamismtill Gasprinsky appeared on the stage.

Afterthe February Revolution,,the leaders of Pan-Turkism organised congesses that demanded the right to form Muslim political parties and Muslim committees with real power at the local level. Even the possibility of forming Muslim military units was promoted. Pan-Turkism as a movement became very strong in Turkey. In the year 1910, there was a split in the Pan-Turkic movement in Turkey. While the radicals dreamt of building a global Turkic state, moderates favoured a policy that would take care of the interests of the entire Turkic world, without pleading for a common state. Turkey's famous leader Kemal Ataturk, who was respected by Vladimir Lenin,supported the moderates and followed the policy outlined by them. [31]

Check space Lenin was the one who really gave freedom to the Muslims of Russia, as a result of which Kazakhstan, Uzbekistan, Turkmenistan and Ajerbaizan emerged as independent constituent republics of the USSR and autonomous republics were created in Tatarstan, Bashkortstan, Chabasia, Yakutia, Karachayev, Crimea,[32] Karakalpak, Hakasia etc, with a fair amount of cultural autonomy. People of Turkic origin living in these territories received significant rights and freedom.

According to experts, Pan-Turkism is a source of threat even today, not only for Russia but also for countries like Armenia, Bolgaria, Greeceand Serbia etc. It has roots in many former Soviet republics as well as within the Russian Federation. The Assembly of Turkic People, founded in Kazan in the year 1991, functions in close cooperation with a host of reactionary political parties abroad. Tatarstan has such a political party headed by writer Bairamova, which demandsa separation of Tatarstan from Russia. The 'Justice' Party of Crimean Tatar nationalists also has a similar separatist agenda.

The Turkic –Muslim world borders with Russia's Siberia, Southern Ural and the, Middle and Lower Volga regions as well as the North Caucasus regions etc. The majority of Tatars, Bashkirs, Nogaits, Karachayevs, Bolkhars and Kumiks belong to Turkic –speaking Muslims. Apart from this, there are number of national minorities like Ajeris, Kazaks, Uzbeks, Tajiks, Kyrgyz, Turkmen, Uigurs etc who for various reasons, have settled in Russia.

The first programme of the Assembly of Turkic People (ATP), approved in 1991, had given a call to fight against the emperial policies of the Federal Centre and their vassals in the regions.

The second programme of ATP,adopted in 1993, had set its objective for strengthening the Turkic integration on the basis of the Ankara declaration of six heads of the independent Turkic states (dated 31 October 1992)and Antalia declaration of leaders of 18 Turkic organisations dated 21 March, 1993. The main objective of these declarations was to fight against federal centre and disintegration of Russian state.

Formation of state structures on the basis of a single religion in multi-confessional states like Russia is simply impossible Pan-Turks fail to understand this. Their objective of building a Muslim state in a multi-confessional state like Russia is simply absurd.

Spread of Wahhabism in the Volga Region

Starting from 1992-93 the Salafits actively launched their activities on the territory of the Volga region Umma. Their main partners were members of the muftiati separated from DUMES, many of whom received the assistance provided by the Wahhabis. Apart from construction of mosques, financial assistance was provided for an educational programme that sought to send young people to foreign countries for education, as well as for their education at home. Financial assistance was provided for publishing special literature with sinister intention. For example, the Committee for Muslims of Asia, a foundation named after Ibrahim bin Abdulaziz Ibrahim, the Badr publishing house published more than 200 books and booklets, most of which were distributed freely.[33]

Active propaganda was launched at a lower level with Wahhabi emissaries visiting communities, and offering to their imams and chairman 'selfless help' in exchange for facilitation of their missionary programme. They organised their own parallel communities, deliberately igniting inter-Islam conflict and provoking contradictions between young generation imams and the older generation imams. Such activities could be organised successfully in cities inhabited by Orthodox Christians, where the Muslim communities were distinguished by ethnic pluaralism and absence of traditions.[34]

The results of these activities could be easily seen after a few years. Along with the division at the level of muftiats, multitude of inter-community conflicts were artificially instigated from outside. Hundreds of Zamats were set up in the entire territory of Russia and became a formidable force. Among the Zamats functioning outside North Caucasus, the Astrakhan community set up in 1990 by Ayub Omarov became very famous. Towards 1995 members of this community, mostly Muslims from Dagestan, formed primary branches in most of the regions of the Astrakhan district and expanded their activities beyond the borders of the district. The dramatic rise of 'Clean Islam' in Astrakhan led to serious conflict inside the Dagestan diaspora, reflecting friction between Wahhabis and Terikatis. This conflict, coupled with contradictions between Omarov and leaders of regional DUM of Astrakhan district, led to several deaths and seriously complicated inter-Muslim relations in the region. In 1999-2000 Omarov's community was practically destroyed by the joint efforts of the police forces, Tarikatists and the Astrakhan muftiat. However, its members continued their activities in other regions of Russia.[35]

Radicalisation of Islam reached its peak in Russia towards the end of the 1990s.

Though Islam played a consolidating role in the fight of radical Chechen separatists against Russia, the slogan to build an Islamic State did not find support amongst the majority of Muslims. The propaganda of radical Muslim fundamentalists could not have an impact on most Muslims. Nevertheless, various interpretation of Islam and the fight for its realisation triggered off differences among the Muslims of Caucasus. Differences of this nature can be found among Muslims of other regions of Russia as well. However, these differences are not so sharp among Muslims of Tatarstan, Siberia or Moscow. The issue debated among Muslims of these regions are about how to practice shariat in a secular country, where Muslims constitute the minority.

The rise of radical Islam in Tatarstan, Bashkortstan, Ural region is attributed to its functioning imams and madrassa teachers, who have received their education in Saudi Arabia, Tunisia, Egypt, Morocco etc. There have been reports in the Russian press that militant muzahidins were trained in mosques and madrassas, which were under the control of radical imams,, for taking part in military actions against official Russian troops.

One of the sources of expansion of radical Islam in Russia are the activities of dubious international Muslim organisations functioning in Russia. They spread Muslim fundamentalism and teach non-traditional forms of Islam to Russian Muslims. Muslim missionaries from foreign countries try to spread the concept of a 'Clean Islam', which hugely differs from traditional Islam practiced by Russian Muslims.

In July 1997 Oleg Marushkin, the emissary of Ayub Abuzar, founded a primary cell in the village of Belozarye in Mordovia, which quickly attracted a significant number of rural youth to its activities. The Wahhabis from this village-cell after some time started teaching in many odious madrasses of

Russia. The local spiritual leaders, because of their low level of education, could not effectively prevent penetration of radical Islam into their territory. Worried by the developments, the local law and order department deported Marushkin and his close associates to Astrakhan district.[36]

Leaders of TSDUM considering Mordovia as their zone of jurisdiction were concerned at these undesirable developments that led to physical clashes between local Muslims. Even the visit of the supreme mufti Talgat Tadziddudin could not bring peace to the region.

Tatarstan became the worst affected region by the increasing presence of proponents of 'Clean Islam'. Full-scale penetration of Wahhabism into the republic began in 1993 when the Saudi charity organisation 'Taiba' signed an agreement with the newly formed Naverezhno-Chelno madrassa, 'Ioldyz', for implementing an education programme, which led to the transformation of the madrassa into a training centre for militants.[37]

In the autumn of 1999, Denis Saitakov, a product of the Ioldyz Madrassa became one of the suspects in the terrorist act that took place in Moscow. Subsequently, the involvement of some other students of this madrassa in terrorist acts was proved. It has been also established that Chechen terrorist leaders Basayev and Hattab were imparting military training in this madrassa. Subsequently, this madrassa was closed down by the special commission of the Council of Muftis of Russia and was converted into a female madrassa. However, this did not resolve the issue of the spread of Wahhabism in NaberezhniChelny.[38]

After Naberezhny Chelny, there were reports about active Wahhabism centres in other regions such as Nizhnekamsk, Kukmor, and Almetyevsk etc. There were reports about successful penetration of Wahhabis to the power structures of different regions, even into the leadership of Kazan muftiat.

The Muslim community's unity was disturbed in many regions by the penetration of Wahhabism. There were reports about clashes between traditionalists and Wahhabis in many places including Moscow, Ulyanovsk, Volgograd, Perm, Izhevsk, Petrozavodsk, Ekatirinburg, Tyumen, Omsk and many other cities.[39] While discussing the radical organisations functioning in Russia, special attention should be given to organisations with Turkic origin which propagate ideas of Saed Nursi. Their interests were represented by organisations like 'Tolerance' in the western part of the country, the Toros foundation and the Eflyak firm in North Caucasus, the Sehat firm in the Volga region, and the Ufuk foundation in Ural and Siberia. These organisations were actively engaged in recruiting people for the Nurdzhular sect, which was banned in Turkey for their extremist activities.[40]

The emissaries of Nurdzhular set up many schools and colleges in different parts of the country. These schools, colleges and other educational institutions run by this sect drew the attention of the Law and Order department in 2003 for their propaganda of pan-Turkism in these institutions. In spite of the fact that this sect is banned in Turkey, its representatives could take their students from Russian regions without any problem to that country, where values of Nursism were openly taught. The Neo-Sufi organisation of Turkic origin, Suleman Zhidar and some other organisations like Grey Fox of Bashkiria were engaged in propagating values close to Nursism.[41]

Starting from 2004, most of the arrested Wahhabis were found to be members of Khizbut –Tahrir, which was dominated in the beginning by Uzbek dissidents coming to Russia.[42]

By then the party had its branches in most of the major cities of Russia. However, their presence was particularly strong in Tatarstan, Bashkortstan and Tyumen district. The relative weakness of Hizbut Tahrir in North Caucasus led one to believe that there was some kind of division of the sphere of influence between various Wahhabist groups.[43]

Russian authorities rose to combat the radical Islam since 1999, particularly after President Vladimir Putin came to power. The Russian Government banned the representative offices of the Al-Harmein foundation, the Al Igasa foundation and the Taiba foundation; it closed educational institutions run by the Turkic sect Suleimanzhar and 'Nurdzhular; it prohibited the activities of odious publishing houses and media. Members of Hizbut Tahrir were arrested on amass scale. Certain legal steps were taken to ban Wahhabism.

In February 2003, the Supreme Court of Russia in an open session looked into the case for declaring certain organisations terrorist organisations and banned their activities on Russian territory. According to the verdict of the Supreme Court the following organisations were declared terrorist outfits with all its consequences.

Table 3.1: List of Terrorist Organisations in Russia

1	Higher military Mazlisul Shura of United Forces of Mujaheedins of Caucasus
2	Congress of People of Ichkeria and Dagestan
3	Baza (Al Qaeda)
4	Asbat al Ansar
5	Sacred War Group
6	Al Zihad
7	Islamic Group
8	Muslim Brotherhood
9	Party of Islamic Revival
10	Lashkar i-Taiba
11	Zamat Islam
12	Taliban Movement
13	Islamic Party of Turkeystan
14	Society of social reforms (Zamiat al –Islakh al-Indzhtimai)
15	Society for Revival of Islamic Heritage (Zamiat Ikhya at Turaz al-Islam
16	Al Hara Mein

Source: Silantiyev, R.A. (2008), *Encyclopedia Islam in Contemporary Russia (Энциклопедия ислама в современной России)*, Moscow: Algoritm

However, imperfection in existing laws and the lack of clarity about Wahhabism does not permit check in the rise of radical Islam, which is still actively spreading in Russia. Their activities have assumed dangerous proportions in North Caucasus, Volga region, Ural and Siberia.

Structure and Functioning of Wahhabi Community in Russia

Wahhabi communities, usually called as Zamat by its members, are as not of sizeable proportions big in size. At best, the large Zamats with a membership of 200 to 2000 are found in Chechnya, Dagestan, Kabardino-Balkria and Karachaevo-Cherkesia. Their small numbers makes it easier to manage the communities and make them mobile which is important for partisan war.

Russian Zamats form part of the international structure of extremist and terrorist organisations, which unites different forces on the basis of hatred towards ruling power, other religions and dissenting Islam. Organisations artificially created by intelligence services and different groups of bandits, not controlled by anybody are also found among Wahhabi cells. In such conditions there cannot be unified international centre of terrorists.

New members of Zamat/Jamat are recruited in different ways. Those Wahhabi structures, which are oriented towards Wahhabi jihad, can admit volunteers whereas terrorist structures recruit new members themselves in order to minimise the chances of security services penetrating the organisation. Special attention is given to missionary work among Muslim spiritual circles, bureaucrats, military personnels, advocates and journalists.

Contrary to traditional belief, popularity of Wahhabism is not linked to one's standard of living. Representatives of rich and educated class constitute the backbone of Zamats. Representatives of poorer sections are used as a human shield. That is why it is not correct to think that increase of subsidy to the North-Caucasus republics can weaken the influence of supporters of "Clean Islam".

As a rule, their position gets strengthened from the flow of money.[44] At the beginning of Wahabi expansion, the followers of this movement could be identified by certain external symbols like the long beard, short pants and absence of under garment. Subsequently, Wahhabis tried to conceal their identity, and presently it is not so easy to identify them.

The external activities of Wahhabi communities were reflected in various subversive acts, which were ideological as well as military in nature. In order to discredit their opponents, they resort to all kinds of method such as organising assemblies and spreading of rumours, distribution of special literature and leaflets and organisation of direct provocations.[45] Special attention is devoted to the Internet network where most cities revolving around Muslim life are controlled by Wahhabis and their allies. Foundations, educational institutions, human rights protections are all organised as shields, which drastically increase results of their work.[46]

It is noteworthy that there are more than ten terms meaning 'Wahhabism' and its followers. Many scholars note that the term 'Wahhabism' is not very accurate because it connotes something unpleasant. The followers of this faith do not call themselves by this name. First of all, Wahhabis call themselves Muslims, emphasising that they are true Muslims. Sometimes they are called Puritan Muslims. The terminology Wahhabism created a misunderstanding between Russia and Saudi Arabia, since the official ideology of Saudi Arabia is also known as Wahhabism. However, the attempt to replace the terminology by any other name has not produced any result.[47]

Notes

1. Gainutddin, R. (2004), *Islam in contemporary Russia* (Ислам в современной России), p.14, Moscow.
2. Malashenko, A. (2007), *Islam for Russia* (Ислам для России), p. 14, Moscow:Rosspen.
3. Krivetski K.V. (1997), *Religion and Politics in Contemporary Russia* (Религия и политика в современной России), Moscow.
4. Malashenko, A. (2007), *Islam for Russia* (Ислам для России), Moscow: Rosspen.
5. Krivetski K.V. (1997), *Religion and Politics in Contemporary Russia* (Религия и политика в современной России), Moscow.
6. Mushina R. (2001), *Islam in Eurasia* (Ислам в Евразии)Moscow: Progress- Traditsiya.
7. Data received from Ministry of Justice, Russia on 1 January 2004.
8. Avdulatipov R. (1997), *Islam in Russia: Traditions and Perspectives* (Ислам в России : традиции и перспективы), p. 96, Moscow.
9. Malashenko, A. (2007), *Islam for Russia* (Ислам для России), Moscow: Rosspen.
10. Ibid.
11. Yunusova A.B. (1999), *Islam in Bashkortostan* (Ислам в Башкортостане), p. 299, Ufa.
12. http://Muslim.ru
13. Arapkhanov U.A. (2004), *Islam and Law in Russia* (Ислам и право в России), p. 79, Moscow.
14. Magamadov A.M. (2004), *Basics of Religious Policy in Dagestan* (Основы религиозной политики в Дагестане), p. 131, Moscow.
15. Bagabov M. (2000), *Wahhabism: History and Contemporary Period* (Ваххабизм : история и современность), Makhachkala.
16. Ibid., p. 79.
17. Hunter, T.S. (1984), *Islam in Russia*, New York: ME Sharpe.
18. Ibid., p. 81.
19. Ibid., p. 83.
20. Hunter, T.S. (1984), *Islam in Russia*, New York: ME Sharpe.
21. Hunter, T.S. (1984), *Islam in Russia*, New York: ME Sharpe.
22. Malashenko, A. (2007), *Islam for Russia* (Ислам для России), Moscow: Rosspen.
23. Ibid.
24. http://www.politforums/ru/msain1112770269_0.html.
25. Hunter, T.S. (1984), *Islam in Russia*, New York: ME Sharpe.
26. http://www.kastopravda.ru
27. Islam in Eurasia, p. 101.
28. Gainutddin, R. (2004), *Islam in Contemporary Russia* (Ислам в современной России), p. 54, Moscow.
29. Ibid., p. 87.
30. Asadullin F. (2003), "Muslim Moscow", Moscow.
31. 1-Mizun U.V, (2004), Islam I Rossii, p. 180, Publishing House 'Veche', Moscow.
32. Ibid.
33. Silantiyev, R.A. (2008), *Encyclopedia Islam in Contemporary Russia* (Энциклопедия ислама в современной России), Moscow: Algoritm.
34. 1. Mizun Y.V,(2004) Islam i Rossii,p- 182, Publishing House 'Veche', Moscow.
35. Ibid.
36. Ibid.
37. Ibid.

38. Ibid.
39. Ibid., p. 140.
40. Silantiyev, R.A. (2008), *Encyclopedia Islam in Contemporary Russia* (Энциклопедия ислама в современной России), Moscow: Algoritm.
41. Ibid.
42. Ibid.
43. Ibid.
44. Ibid.
45. Ibid.
46. Ibid.
47. Ibid., p. 148.

4. State and Islam

The Russian state started taking serious note of Islam and dealing with it from the middle of 17th century. According to the Saborni ulozheniye (statute), issued in 1649, Islam received legitimate recognition in Russia. During the 'dark period' of the early 17th century, when Moscow was occupied by Poland Muslim Tatars extended support to the troops led by Minin and Pozarsky for liberating Moscow from foreign occupation. Subsequently, Muslims took part in the 'Zemski' assembly held in 1613 which took a decision about the new Romanov dynasty ruling over Russia. The resolution was approved in the 'Zemski' assembly talks, in which about seven Tatar murz and kings participated actively in the establishment of the Romanov dynasty.[1]

From this moment onwards began the integration process of Muslims with the Orthodox Christian Russian state, which gradually started acquiring the features of orthodox Christian poly-confessional state. Soviet experts on Islam have also recognised the contribution of Muslims in the formation and development of the Russian state.

There was some kind of repression against Muslims by the state. However, this repression was let loose upon certain Muslim communities, whose loyalty was in doubt, rather than against Islam as a whole. For example, the Kasimov Tatars always enjoyed full religious freedom and occupied high-ranking posts in the state apparatus. Representatives of their elite were given diplomatic assignments in Central and South Asia, direct relations with whom could be possible only after the defeat of the influential eastern neighbours of the Russian state. At the outset, Russia exchanged missions with Bukhara and Khiva, and then attempts were made to repeat the route taken by merchant-traveller Afanasi Nikitin to revive contacts with India.

In 1675, Aleksei Mikhailovich sent a mission to India with Mohammed Yusuf Kasimov, a Kasimov Tatar, asking him to establish trade relations with that country. Kasimov had undertaken similar missions in the past. The diplomatic mission of Kasimov was aimed at finding the shortest route to India, liberating Russian prisoners of war and to establish trade ties with the Mughall empire, which however proved to be unsuccessful. What is noteworthy is that in the middle of the 17th century,the Muslim subjects of Russia were being involved in carrying out responsible foreign assignments.

As a result, Russian authorities recognised the loyalty of the Tatars, particularly the Kazan Tatars, whose spiritual leaders were involved in strengthening the Russian position in Caucasus and Central Asia. However, this did not happen at once. The Russian state policy towards its Muslim minority was quite varied.

In the 18th century, there was hardly any change in the situation with Russian Muslims. Peter, the Great took certain steps that discriminated Russian Muslims. Though it is Peter who facilitated the first translation of the Quran in the Russian language in the year 1704, one of Peter's diplomats, Kutly- Mohamed Tebkelev, who was close to him, significantly strengthened the Russian position in Kyrgyzia and signed an agreement with Khan Abdulakhair which was to herald the process of incorporation of contemporary Kazakhstan into Russia. Tabkelev was made a Major General in 1755 for his services to the Russian state.

At the time of Peter reign, the administrative system regarding the Muslims was destroyed and mullas and senior imams with wide powers conducted themselves unpredictably, sometimes making alliance with Russian administration and at times fighting against it. Urgent measures were required for improving this volatile situation.

The first step in this regard was taken in 1730s, by Empress Anna Ionovna. After going through the materials of the expeditions undertaken by Kirrilov and Rumyantsev, Anna Ionovna became aware of the disloyalty of the mullas and Imams from among Kazan Tatars. She issued a decree, dated 11 February 1736, reducing the number of imams to four, each one of whom has to take an oath of loyalty to the Russian state. This decree also stipulated that building of mosques and schools required the permission of local administrations.[2]

Empress Elizabeth Petrovna issued an order recognising mosques and the Muslim treasury, which was permitted to build mosques in Siberia and the Volga region. The Senate order dated 23 September 1756 stipulated rights for construction of new mosques. The orders No. 1736, 1744 and 1756 prepared grounds for subsequent reforms under Ekaterina-II.[3]

Reforms under Czarist Regime

The State's relations towards Muslims, otherwise favourable, significantly improved under the rule of Catherine II. The expansion of the Russian Empire was also a result of the incorporation of territory with large Muslim populations. In this scenario, first of all Crimea required certain regulations over the life of its Muslim population. Coercive conversions into the dominant faith used in many countries was found unsuitable for Russia, and that is why it was abandoned. The Russian authorities adopted a different attitude towards its Muslim subjects.

Under instructions from Queen Catherine,the Russian Orthodox Church Sinoda issued an order for tolerance towards all faiths. This order stipulated the removal of prohibition on the building of mosques and referring of cases related to Muslims to the jurisprudence of secular authorities. It is believed that the Pugachev Rebellion (during 1773-1775) in which many Muslims from the Volga and Ural regions took active part, led to the corrections in the state policy towards Muslims. On the other hand, it is known that many Muslim spiritual leaders were directly supporting the Czar's regime during this rebellion. Subsequently, Catherine issued some more orders to make the life of her Muslim subjects easier. One of the orders stipulated that Muslims who came from a background of Mulim nobility were granted the same rights as members of the Russian nobility. A Number of orders were issued to establish Muslim spiritual bodies, its Secretariate etc.

The relations between the state and Islam have been complex and have passed through several stages. The Russian orthodox Christian state implemented the policy of Christianising the people of other faiths till the end of 17th century. It is Czar Ivan Grozny who had initiated the policy of converting people of other faiths into orthodox Christianity and this policy was followed by other Russian Czars. Three years after Kazan was conquered by Russian troops, led by Ivan Grozny, the Kazan eparchy was set up in 1555 with the major objective of converting the local Muslims to orthodox Christianity. Following the footsteps of Ivan Grozny, Czar Fyodor Ivanovich in 1593 issued a decree aimed at destroying mosques in the country. The Church Statute adopted by Aleksei Mikhailovich in 1649 talks about taking away land from Muslims and not from those who were converted to orthodox Christianity.[4]

The Czar attempted to impose orthodox Christianity over the Bashkirs in 1681. Peter the Great issued a decree in 1713,to deprive the serving Tatars (who refused to adopt orthodox Christianity) of some rights. Empress Anna Ivanovna formed a special commission in 1731 for converting the Muslims and people of other faiths living in Kazan and Nizhegorod. Subsequently this commission, renamed as 'New Christian Contour', achieved the full destruction of mosques.

According to Russian scholars the campaign to convert Muslims into Christians by the authorities ended in a complete fiasco. The campaign to Christianise Russian Muslims came to an end in 1762, when Catherine II came to power. She dissolved the special commission set up to convert Muslims and granted permission to build mosques on the territory of the Middle-Volga and South Ural in 1767. In 1773, the Sacred Sinoda, the highest body of Orthodox Christianity, issued a decree about for tolerance towards all faiths, according to which the construction of stone mosques was permitted;this was done under the observation of Soviet power but not by the Church.[5] The year 1788 heralded a new era when the secular authorities of the empire completely did away with the policy to impose Christianity on Muslims and launched the policy to establish control over Islam and Muslims. The Orenburg Mohammedan Spiritual Assembly —the first body to regulate affairs of Muslims- was set up in 1788 by a decree issued by Catherine-11. This body, through different names, survived the monarchy and Soviet state under which it existed under the name of Spiritual Administration of Muslims of European part of Russia and Siberia. Afterwards it continued its function under the name "Central Spiritual Administration of Muslims."

North Caucasus and Central Asia were incorporated into the Russian empire in the 19th century. This converted Russia into a huge poly-confessional country. Relations towards people of other confessions, particularly Muslims, became one of the major issues of internal consolidation and development of imperial identity.

In order to establish control over the old and new Muslims of the empire,the authorities used three ways – first; exerting direct military – political impact on the Muslims, second; creation of a system of indirect management through loyal spiritual leaders, third; inclusion of Muslim representatives in the Russian elite.

The attempt to formulate the relation between the state and Islam through legislative means was made in 1819, under the initiative of General Ermolov. The work on "Situation on Islamic spiritual community" began in 1831 but could not be complete. In 1849 eight Muslim educational institutions were opened, which trained imams, who were employed in mosques by the state.

The Tavricheski spiritual administration of Muslims was set up in 1832 and the Sunni and Shiite spiritual administration of Muslims of Trans-

Caucasus was organised in 1872. In spite of the sympathy for Christianity, the attitude of secular authorities towards Islam was that of tolerance. According to Ravil Gainnudin, Islam was tolerated rather than understood or supported.[6] Only the Orthodox Christian students attended the class on religion, while Muslim students spent their time with the mullas. The mullas in turn worked in the military divisions with a large number of Muslims.

Islam was tailored to the political life of the empire. In 1905, the State Duma had an international Muslim faction, which sought to defend the rights of Muslims, remove certain restrictions on ethno-confessional basis and formulate a law on equal rights for different confessions.

In the Russian empire, relations between the state and Islam were shaped in such a manner that the authorities ensured equal rights for all faiths, while keeping the Muslims under its control.

Islam was adopted in territories that subsequently got incorporated into the Russian empire through expansion. There were 18 million Muslims living in the Russian empire. The state hoped to gradually convert those who had adopted Islam in the past to the Christian faith, as long as the number of Muslim subjects was less in the country. However, the Muslim spiritual community was opposed to this as they had lost a huge amount of wealth as well as authority in the process. This is the reason why the imperial government abandoned this idea and launched a process of legislative construction of the life of its Muslims as subjects as well as religious people. Thus, from the second half of the 18th century, the Russian government began to construct the 'spiritual life' of Muslims by defining their religious life in the law.

The first step in this sphere was taken by Catherine II who issued the decree through which the Assembly of mullas from 'Kazan Tatars' was instituted in Ufa in September 1788. There were to be only two to three mullas to be led by a mufti, who was in charge of appointing the mullas and conducting examinations for candidates for Muslim spiritual posts.

In essence the state decided to shape the spiritual life of all Muslims living in the Russian empire. Crimea with its Muslim population was incorporated into Russia in the year 1783. An important step by the state in this direction was the creation of a Muslim spiritual administration in Crimea in 1784. The act about the creation of the Tavrichecky Mohammedan spiritual leadership, designed to shape activities of Islamic spiritual administration in Crimea, was issued in 1831. The activities of the mulla Assembly in

Ufa were organised on the basis of resolutions issued at different times, after the proclamation of the first decree issued by Catherine-II. All these resolutions were incorporated in one Statute in 1857, while publishing the 11th volume of compilation of laws of the Russian Empire. This is how the system of management of spiritual affairs was created and was placed under the Ministry of Home Affairs. According to the law, the spiritual leadership was divided into two layers –higher and lower. There were regional centres of management: the Tavrichesky Mohammedan Spiritual Board was located in Simferopol; the Orenburg Mohamedan Spiritual Board was located in Ufa. These administrative bodies were created by representatives from a higher spiritual body. Thus there were two Muslim administrative districts. Tavricheski and Western provinces were under the first district while Orenburg district included all provinces and regions, except Trans-Cacausus and Asian territory inhabitated by Muslims. The spiritual board functioned like a collegium headed by a mufti.

Since there were differences in the laws concerning the Crimean and Orenburg districts, there was an attempt to unify administrative systems in both districts. This issue received an impetus as a result of the report prepared by the Orenburg Governor General Nikolai Krizhanovsky, in 1865-66. The Governor General drew the attention to the fact that Muslim spiritual leadership conducts itself as a secluded layer which exerts huge influence on Muslims. The conduct of the Muslim spiritual leadership does not facilitate integration of Muslims into the Russian state. He proposed certain control over Muslim spiritual leadership.

Czar Alexander-II personally studied the report prepared by Krizhanovski and sent instructions to conduct a futher study on the issue.

A special committee, consisting of the Governor-Generals of Ufa, Orenburg, Ural and Turgaisk, was set up with Governor General of Orenburg at its head, to study the issue in 1870. The committee proposed that the spiritual leaders be elected by the Muslim community which would then be confirmed by the administration. The requirement for Muslim spiritual leaders to have knowledge of the Russian language was dropped. However differences among the Governor Generals on the issue forced the Interior Minister to stall the reforms in order not to irritate the Muslim community.

The issue of the management of the Muslim spiritual leadership in Cacausus, Turkestan and Step Krai was resolved, taking the specific features of those territories into account.

There were some territories with Muslim population that was incorporated into the Russian empire; however, no law was in force for organising life in those places. The spiritual leadership of Orenburg, Crimea, and Transcaucasus districts were recognised as strata, or sosloviye, by law. The law gave it the status of a state administrative body. Simultaneously, a spiritual affair of the Muslims in a significant territory of Russia was not covered by law. Muslim spiritual leaders functioning in this territory did not have an official status.

The Central government of Russia had a very democratic attitude towards the Muslim spiritual leadership. It tried to create conditions for Muslims which permitted them to enjoy the fruits of integration in a multi-national state. However, the local Muslim spiritual leadership was the least concerned about it. It was more concerned about its material benefits and was scared that it might have to share its wealth with others. For the purpose of integration,the government wanted them to learn the Russian language. The Muslim religious leadership of the Volga region conducted itself very aggressively. There were attempts to promote Tatar-Muslim separatism in that territory. Government authorities, reacting to this, had to control those who had influence among the masses.

In Orenburg territory, the religious leaders were opposed to the teaching of the Russian language in Muslim religious institutions. Though mufti Tebkeliyev was in favour of teaching the Russian language, a big chunk of the Muslim religious leadership resisted it.

In 1889, the Ministry of Internal Affairs brought a proposal to the state council for replacing election of the mufti by his appointment. A law was passed in 1890 that stipulated the procedure of the appointment of the Orenburg mufti. The members of the spiritual board were to be appointed by the minister of home affairs. A law was passed in 1886 for running affairs in Turkestan. This did not concern the organisation of Muslim spiritual affairs. By then the state had formally stopped interference in spiritual affairs of the Muslims of Turkestan.

In 1898, the Governor General of Turkestan, Sergey Dukhovsky, sent a proposal to the Minister of Internal Affairs to create a spiritual administration on the lines of Transcaucasus but without a mufti. Instead of a mufti it was proposed to have a chairman, who would be appointed. It was proposed that a Russian, well-acquainted with shariat, and with knowledge of Turkic and Persian languages, should be appointed to this post. This proposal of the Governor General was not accepted.

In 1899, the Governor General sent a report to the government under the title 'Islam in Turkestan', which proposed to find a solution to the issue, not only in Turkestan, but also in other regions of the Russian empire, where a large number of Russians lived. Governor General Dukhovsky considered Islam not as a religious but as a political force. That is why he proposed dismantling all spiritual administrations of Muslims in Russia and to transfer the affairs of the Islamic spiritual leadership to the jurisprudence of the local administration. The Governor General was of the opinion that the existing spiritual administrations united the Muslims in anti-Russian and anti-Christian propaganda. The proposals of the Governor General were not accepted. Eminent Russian statesman Sergey Vitte was particularly opposed to these proposals.

The Government issued an order in 1904 that stipulated the principles of inter-faith tolerance, which was followed by a revision of an entire complex of laws guiding the spiritual life of Russian Muslims. The Muslims reacting to this order advanced radical demands such as election to spiritual posts, allotment of government funds for maintenance of spiritual leadership, equal rights for spiritual leaders of orthodox Church and Islam, creation of spiritual administrations in regions where it is absent etc.

The government council set up for looking into these issues suggested that the lower spiritual leadership should be elected by ordinary Muslims, while the higher spiritual leadership was to be confirmed by the state authority, in consideration of the wishes of voters.

The representative of the education ministry insisted that the knowledge of the Russian language by spiritual leaders should be mandatory. He also proposed that the mufti council should be set up on the basis of territorial principle, rather than on the principle of nationality. The Government council's proposals could not make laws, as the procedure of considering draft laws was changed in 1906.

The revolutionary situation in Russia during the years 1905 to 1906 intensified religious movements. The All Russia Muslim Congress head Nizhni Novgorod, demanded the removal of all government control over activities of Muslim administrations and the transfer of all religious and educational affairs to the hands of spiritual administrations. Muslim members in the State Duma also raised similar demands.

After the failure of the revolution, the government organised its work with the Muslim spiritual administration on the basis of suggestions made by the conservative section of the spiritual leadership. The government was afraid of the penetration of liberal ideas into the Muslim community. It was decided that those who received religious education abroad, would not be permitted to teach in madrassas. While appointing mullas their involvement in Muslim movements was thoroughly scrutinised. State financing of Muslim spiritual bodies and persons remained to be resolved. Some regional spiritual bodies were financed by the state. It must be said, that Muslim spiritual bodies had possessed huge capital and wealth.

The state authorities were seriously concerned about the growing popularity of pan-Turkism among Russian Muslims. Many Muslim spiritual leaders were arrested in 1911-1913 for their alleged involvement in pan-Turkism. The Interior Ministry created a special division for dealing with the issue in the Volga region. An inter-departmental body was set up by the government in 1914 for dealing with the 'Muslim issue', particularly growth of pan-Turkism.

The question of bringing unification in the administrative system of Muslims was a controversial issue. While some advocated in favour of unification, others argued that there is no uniformity among the Muslims of Russia, hence no unification in the system of administration is required. The 'Muslim Question' remained relevant after February Revolution of 1917. The recommendations of the Muslim congresses, held in 1906 and 1914, were taken into account while forming a state policy towards Muslims.

Summing up it must be said that the state started pursuing policies for organising Muslim spiritual life in the country. Laws were promulgated to shape the spiritual administration in different regions. The Orenburg assembly was set up in 1788, while the Crimean administration was organised in 1831. Two Caucasus administrations were set up in 1872. As a result, Muslim spiritual leadership was included in the structure of state administration. The legal life of Muslims was guided by shariat. The territory with Muslim population had different regulations, which was justified.

Post-Revolution Period and Islam

The Bolsheviks, capturing power in 1917, treated the Muslims as their allies and perceived Islam as a revolutionary force,in contrast to orthodox Christianity, which was perceived as an enemy of the revolutionary transformations. In the first decade, following the October Revolution, the Bolsheviks used terminologies like 'krasny mulla', 'krasni shariat' and slogans like 'For Soviet

Power' or 'For Shariat'. The Muslim religious leaders did not pay taxes till 1928. The Muslim spiritual leadership during this period actively helped in conducting Soviet foreign policy.[7] The year 1929 witnessed a change in Soviet policy towards Islam. This of course took place in the framework of Soviet policy towards religion as a whole. Any religion was treated as enemy by the state; Islam was no exception. The Communists looked at the situation in Central Asia with concern. The state assigned special role to Islam in this region recognising it as a regulator of social relations there.

Mosques, like the Churches, were destroyed across the country. Out of the 12,000 mosques functioning in 1917, only 70 were left in the Russian federation by 1990. At least 8 Muslim religious leaders had to undergo repression; Muslim religious rituals were banned. Maintaining religious identity in the 20th century was more difficult than in the 16th -17th centuries.

There were certain improvements in the situation during the Great Patriotic War. The Reopening of Spiritual Administration of Muslims of European Part and Siberia (DUMES), and creation of Spiritual Administration of Muslims of North Caucasus, was under strict control of the authorities and served as an instrument for keeping a watch over the situation in Muslim communities.

Control over the Muslim community and keeping watch over their activities remained part of state policy towards Muslims till the Perestroika period. Significant improvements took place in the late –perestroika period.

State Policy towards Islam in the post-Soviet Period

In his evaluation of State-Muslim relations in Russia, Sergey Filatov high lights the fact that the perceived success of "sovereign democracy" is conditioned not by the support of any Muslims, but rather the ones who fit within the state's ideological framework.[8]

The state caters for the needs of its Muslim subjects, respects their rights and provides legal recognition of modern Islam. In return, Muslim citizens are expected to fulfil their obligations of staying loyal to the national interests and the development of tolerant Islam.[9]

This is perceived as a process of meeting the requirements of Muslim minorities within the broad framework of the national interests of the country. State efforts to develop Russian Islam present an attempt to 'appropriate' the Islamic faith by removing its foreign influence and integrating it with set of national values.

The State's engagement with Muslim citizens rests on four pillars such as — 'our money', 'our people', 'our institutions' and 'our values'. Our money concept channels state funds for building mosques, subsidising moderate Muslim initiatives and provides funds for Muslim education. While "Our people concept" stipulates training of home-grown imams, "Our Institution Concept" envisages state support to Muslim representative bodies, such as Muslim spiritual boards etc. The fourth pillar stands to promote a more inclusive sense of national belonging by stressing what it means to be a Russian Muslim. All these four pillars imply the state's greater role in Muslim affairs.

Laws Regulating Religious Affairs

First of all, the state adopts a set of laws that guide the religious affairs of the country as a whole. According to the Russian constitution 'Islam is one of the traditional religions of Russia'.

The post-Soviet Russia declared the secular character of the state, equality of all religions, and observation of rights of the religious communities. The Russian constitution declares Islam along side Orthodox Christianity as one of the four conventional faiths of Russia. Formal constitutional separation of religion from state does not contradict close interaction between religious and secular institutions. According to famous scholar Farid Asadullin, in Russia, starting from Catherine's period, it has so happened that the interests of Muslims, before the state, were defended by special Islamic administrative structures, and creation of Muslim spiritual board (muftiyat) in the pattern of Holy Sinoda.[10]

The 28th article of Russian constitution stipulates the right to freedom of conscience, religious freedom, right to practice any religion or not practice any religion, freely select, posses and spread religious convictions and function according to it. This constitutional provision was further developed in the federal law on freedom of conscience and religious organisations, dated 26th September 1997. It should be noted that the law is not prohibitive, and largely consists of clauses providing concessions to religious organisations. The law is designed to translate the provisions of the constitution into reality and to ensure genuine freedom of conscience.[11]

The law confirms the rights of every citizen for freedom of conscience and freedom for practising any religion and provides for equality before law notwithstanding ones' relation to religion and conviction. It is important to note that the freedom of conscience in the context of law, in accordance with international norms, means right to freedom of choice for any concrete religion and to religion as a whole. Freedom to practice any religion is interpreted as 'human right' for freely pursuing ones own religious convictions, fulfil related rituals, traditions and declare one's faith.

It should be stressed that this law is the result of the demands of religious organisations. Representatives of leading religious confessions in Russia took active part in all stages of drafting of the law. Because of this, the Preamble of the Constitution talks about "Special role of Orthodox Church in the history of Russia and its formation and development of its spirituality and culture." And Islam, along with Buddhism and Judaism, is included in the religions "constituting inseparable part of historical legacy of peoples of Russia". As a result of this definition the terminology of 'traditional religions',that includes Islam, became part of religious and social discourse in the country.

There is no unity among scholars about the essence of the term 'traditional religion'.According to some scholars 'mentioning of traditional religions' in the law gives it a legal status. There are scholars who do not share this. According to other experts this term bears a 'cultural-historical character' while yet others believe that it does not have 'independent normative significance' and does not bear legislative function.[12]

Thus the situation with Muslims and Muslim organisations in the contemporary Russian society does not have anything common with the Soviet or pre-revolutionary past. Let us have look at the most significant features of Islam in Russia in the contemporary period. First of all; the situation with Islam and its role in the life of society became different in principle. The Russian constitution adopted in 1993, on the basis of a nation-wide referendum, envisages that the Russian Federation is a secular state. This means that no religion or atheist ideology is established as the basis of state power; religious organisations are separate from the state, do not form part of bodies of state power in the sphere of local self-administration; judicial system of the state does not stipulate creation of confessional courts, establishment of secular character in state and municipality educational institutions, the state does not finance religious activities while facilitating development of charitable, culturally and socially important activities of traditional religions etc. It should be emphasised that in contrast to the Soviet period, 'secular character of state does not stipulate isolation of religious organisations from social life, from social processes, particularly in the sphere of culture, education, healthcare, social protection'.[13]

The Chairman of the State Duma Committee on public organisations and religious organisations communist V. Zorkaltsev, talking about the law, says that the law harmonises relations between traditional confessions and religions in Russia. Status of Orthodox Christianity, Islam, Buddhism and Judaism- the traditional religions of Russia- has been defined for the first time in the law. The law on traditional religions talks about social partnership between state and traditional religions. Who else other than traditional religions can establish partnership with the state? This is indeed the backbone of a civil society.

We can assert that Muslim organisations in Russia are functioning in qualitatively new and unprecedented situation in the history of Russia. This new socio-political situation became the foundation for revival of Islam in the country. In accordance with the fundamental laws and practices of their religion, Muslim organisations received certain privileges and rights, which they never had in their history.

The existing laws in the country permit Muslim organisations to actively participate in drafting, approving and realising important documents concerning issues of religious organisations and believers. This is ensured at the national as well as local levels.

The country's highest leadership well-understands the significance of 'Islamic factor' in the life of the nation, the role of Muslim organisations in preservation and strengthening of stability, peace and accord in the society. President Putin believes that Russia is a Muslim country; the people practicing Islam are not migrants but its native population.[14]

The mufti council preserves its significance in the 21st century. Moreover,the post-Soviet Muslim spiritual board expressed its readiness to cooperate with these structures under simultaneous control over them. The Muslim spiritual elite strives to cooperate with the state under different levels, appealing to it while resolving its problems. In spite of the principle of separation of state from religion, the state should not ignore the spiritual requirements of the society; says Ravil Gainutdin.[15] Russia's entire Muslim religious elite agrees with the statement. For example, Dagestan Mufti Ahmed Hazi Abdulayev in this connection pleads for 'cooperation and joint efforts with the state for spiritual recovery of the society. The Head of Coordination Centre of Muslims of North Caucasus, Ismail Bardiyev has repeatedly emphasised that, "without close interaction with the state, it is not possible to fight against Wahhabism and terrorism."[16]

Muslims approve the state's paternalistic approach towards their community. They need state support for the following reasons.

1. In Russia only the state can ensure confessional rights of the Muslim minority, which is more relevant in conditions of growing Islamophobia.
2. The inter-faith dialogue, particularly between orthodoxy and Islam, takes place under state patronage.
3. State often provides subsidies for construction of Muslim religious and educational institutions through regional administrations.
4. State pays wages to the religious preachers in many regions.
5. Imams and muftis can fight back the radical elements of Islam only with the help of the state.

This does not mean the Muslim elite sees eye to eye with the state on all issues. On certain issues,they express their views, which contradict the official position. All muftis do not share the government view on Wahhabism. During the Yugoslavia crisis, many Russian Muslim religious leaders supported the Bosnian and Albanian Muslims while the government had a different policy supporting the orthodox Christian Serbs. Tatar president Mintimer Shamiyev did not support the official stand of Russian government on Yugoslovia crisis.

Apart from foreign policy issues, Muslims and their clergy have been demonstrating their differences with the state on domestic issues concerning religious and moral problems. For example, the regional Muslim clergy in Dagestan was unhappy when the State Duma rejected the amendment to Law on advertisement.[17]

Separation of state from religion does not obstruct intense interaction between the state and religion. According to some scholars, state policy towards Islam comprises of following elements;

1. Demand for loyalty to the state
2. Reporting by the spiritual leadership
3. Monitoring over the activities of all religious and religious-political organisations including religious educational institutions
4. Control over foreign contacts with the objective of neutralising external influence.

What is the model of relations between Russian state and Islam? What is the role of state;is it a role of a director, architect, defender, engineer and partner? The State is recognised rather as an architect who after the construction of the building is turned into a kind of music director. In order to control the Muslim community, the authorities had to define how much was it interested in their organisational unity. Secondly, the authorities had to clarify if there was need of a special body through which they can assess the mood of the Muslims and contact their leaders. Thirdly, authorities had to find the method for practical politisation of Islamand create political parties and movements on a religious-political basis.[18]

Moreover, the authorities had to formulate their policy as regards 'non-traditional Islam', referring to radical Islam that openly challenged the state, even declared war against it in Caucasus.

While reminding the architect of policy towards Islam, the state initiated a partnership with Islam. Vladimir Zorin, Russian Minister for National Policy spoke in favour of 'state's active interaction with religious organisations'. Of course, there are spheres where interaction between state and the religious organisations, including Muslim organisations, can produce enormous results. These areas include fighting drugs consumption, providing assistance to AIDS patients and protecting homeless children.

Sometimes, the state assigns very delicate tasks to religious leaders. For example, in the beginning of first Chechen war, in December 1994,the Russian presidential administration deputed the St. Petersburg mufti, Zafar Panchayev and Talgat Tazudin, for negotiating with Chechen separatists. Subsequently many famous religious leaders on their own,or on the Kremlin's behalf, conducted peace negotiations in North Caucasus and made efforts to establish contact between the authorities and separatists through the mediation of religious leaders continued, though it did not produce tangible result.

It is natural that authorities would want unity in the Muslim community as that would help them in managing the society. However, unity in the community can also create a reverse effect. The apprehension persists that a united community may try to act independently. Eminent Russian Muslim leader Talgat Tazudin actively lobbied for bringing organisational unity, hoping to revive the Soviet time DUMES, which he himself intended to head. Tazudin really had the chance to occupy this post. He was always loyal to the secular authorities and Russian orthodox Christianity. He often said that right of the community and society is higher than individual rights, which corresponds to official secular ideology and position of orthodox Christianity as well. Though he was popular among Tatars and Bashkirs, his influence was very limited among the spiritual leaders of North Caucasus.

Consolidation on a confessional basis is usual for a religious minority, particularly when they perceive some threat to their rights and status. On the other hand, indivisibility amongst the Muslim community provides additional stimuli for strengthening confessional identity. Russian Muslims have three full identities– civilian, ethnic and confessional. Balance between these identities does not have a permanent character and depends on many factors, including the level of tension in the sphere of ethno-confessional relations.

At the same time, absence of inter-confessional unity makes it easy for the state to implement its policy. This happened during the Chechen war when Russian Muslims, irritated by the military conflict and its anti-Muslim projections in the media, nevertheless as a whole did not support radical Islam. It is not difficult to imagine what kind of disaster Chechen conflict would have brought if Islam solidarity would have worked in the entire country.

Authorities must be feeling satisfied that Tatar and Bashkir Muslims treat the Muslims from North Caucasus living in their territory almost as strangers. The treatment of Muslims of North Caucasus by Tatars and Bashkirs is no different from the treatment meted out by Orthodox Christians.[19]

President Vladimir Putin, just like his predecessor Boris Yeltsin, faces the dilemma of choosing his favourite mufti when all of them declare their loyalty to the state. It is interesting to draw a parallel with the state's attitude towards Islam during Czarist Russia, when the former tried to establish some kind of "Russian Islamic Church" similar to orthodox Christianity. The State is strictly against the legal existence of an Islamic opposition or radical Islam, and any political protest on the basis of religion is usually severely dealt with.

Vladimir Putin came to power armed with a tough policy towards Chechen separatists and terrorists, and his firm determination to stamp out Islamic militancy in North Caucasus at the beginning of the century. However, he has been very careful to distinguish between Muslims and extremists. Putin's views on Islam are hardly different from those held by other Russian political leaders, who have been maintaining that Islam is one of the traditional religions of Russia and, as such, has a place in Russian society, and that there has been peace and harmony between Christians and Muslims in the country for centuries. Emphasizing the commonality between Russian orthodoxy and Islam, Putin had once said in an interview that, "in Russia the majority of the population are Orthodox Christians, which is eastern Christianity, and we have a great deal in common with Islam."[20] Putin also stressed, in the same interview, that Islam as a traditional Russian religion merits the support of the state. Russian state policy towards Islam is a combination of elements like co-option of the Muslim population, suppression of Muslim extremism and, control over Muslim institutions.

The Kremlin clearly understood that given the irreconcilable contradictions between Tatar and Caucasian communities, it is not possible to determine the chief mufti of Russia. It was not prudent to create a united structure for Tatar and Bashkir Muslims with single chief. Authorities thought it appropriate to pursue a policy of equi-distance from all Muslim centres of influence.

Preference to any mufti by the state can have undesirable consequences. That is why authorities are very careful about this. For example, in the Global Summit of religious leaders held in Moscow in 2006, patriarch Russia Aleksei-11 sat to the right hand side of President Putin whereas to the left hand side of the Russian President sat Sheikh ul-Islam Passha-zade, head of Muslims of Southern Caucasus,a guest from Ajerbaijan but not any of the muftis of Russia so that it should not look that the Russian state gives preference to any of them.

In spite of the loyalty of all muftis to the state, there can be differences in their positions on certain important issues, for example on Chechnya and radical Islam. While Tatar Muslims appealed for a quick end to the bloodshed in Chechnya, representatives of North Caucasus Muslims insisted on the necessity to eliminate the separatists in the council of muftis of Russia, organised by Ravil Gainuddin in 1999. This can be explained by the fact that except representatives of North Caucasus,Muslim spiritual leaders in other parts of Russia do not perceive any serious threat from Wahhabism.

The uncompromising position of Caucasian spiritual leaders evokes great sympathy for the Russian President, who sees strong supporters in them on his Caucasus policy.[21] Notwithstanding a different degree of personal sympathy for the muftis, the Kremlin finally gave up the idea in 2000 to create a single all-Russia muftiyat, and preferred to communicate with the Muslim "leadership, consisting of Ravil Gainuddin, Talgat Tazuddin and Islam Berdiyev", head of the coordination centre of Muslims of North Caucasus. These three leaders in May 2004 created the "United Council of spiritual administration of Muslims to combat extremism and terrorism". Though the effectiveness of the body was not significant, the very fact of its existence spelt the end of open contradictions between Russian muftis and the recognition of polycentrism in the leadership of Muslim communities of Russia.

Refusal to have a single controlling body, which was the Council on Religious Affairs under the government at the federal level, is a significant departure of Russian state policy on religion from that of Soviet policy in this sphere. However, new authorities quickly understood the necessity of a body, though not for control, but to keep a watch over the activities of Muslim communities. A dire need of a new body in place of the old one of the bygone years was strongly felt.

A Coordination Commission on religious matters worked from 1992 to 1994 under the leadership of Deputy Prime Minister Alexander Shokhin. In 1994, the then Prime Minister Victor Chernomyrdin set up a commission on matters of religious organisations under the government with Segei Shakhrai at its head. The Commission had following functions: - to resolve issues of property that was taken away during Soviet rule; coordination of activities for reconstruction of Churches mosques, and other religious buildings; collection of information about religious communities.

This information could be obtained from the Ministry of Justice, looking after religious organisations. The Ministry of Justice also issued instructions regarding religious property. However, there was no single mechanism to regulate this issue, which was necessary.

In 1995 the Council for Interaction with Religious Organisations was formed under the Russian President. Famous Muslim religious leaders like Ravil Gainudin, Talgat Tazudin, Dagestan mufti Saed Abybakarov etc became members of this council. The status and functions of this Council were not very clear. This council was given the task to formulate the concept of interaction between state and religious organisations. However, by the beginning of 2000, it became clear that the Kremlin was the only place where the concepts were formulated. The Kremlin did not feel the necessity of a special institution in this regard.[22]

However, the regional authorities felt the need of a central body that would organise links between the state and religion. As a result,18 federal units formed a mechanism on their own for maintaining contact between the state and religious organisations. There are combined structures comprising representatives of authorities and religious leaders in 23 federal units. There are special bureaucrats for dealing with religious organisations in 20 regions. Nine republics and districts including Tatarstan, Udmurtia, Nizgegorod and Sverdolov districts have expert councils for interaction with religious organisations; seven federal units have councils on religious matters; four federal units have commissions for interaction with religious organisations.[23]

Talgat Tazudin, head of the Central Spiritual administration of Muslims located in Ufa admits that, "We go to the republic committee with our problems and find there understanding and support".[24]

The 6th clause of Dagestan's Law on freedom of religion and religious organisations envisages a special body, which is the committee of the republican government on religious matters.

All these committees and commissions and other authorised bodies make every effort for ensuring normal relations between the state and religious communities, trying to play the role of an arbiter in conflict situations. Their employees should be credited for the work they do to collect information about the activities of religious organisations. However, the Russian Orthodox Church does not recognise these institutions and directly approaches the local leadership bypassing these committees.

Muslim organisations and influential Muslim leaders also behave in the same manner in those regions with a Muslim majority or where the Muslim minority is well-organised and has influential leaders.

According to the opinion of many scholars and state bureaucrats, a centralised body could coordinate the activities of federal structures responsible for implementation of state policy on religion. This body can maintain regular contacts with religious organisations and make preparatory work and provide expertise on draft laws for ensuring freedom of religion. This organ can also manage structures on religious matters in regions and can conduct state expertise on religious matters.[25]

It looks unlikely that committee on religious affairs at the federal level would be re-established. The Russian Orthodox Church is opposed to this idea, as it feared that an inter-mediatory body between religion and state would weaken its authority. The situation around Islam also prevents revival or re-emergence of this body, because the law and order department is already looking after this issue. Even if this body is re-established, it is unlikely to get the responsibility of watching the activities of Islamic opposition, since the law and order department is already dealing with the issue.

State and Muslim Officialdom

Muslim Spiritual Boards are the via via-media through which state and Islam interact in Russia. The vertical arrangement of state-Islam relations allows the Spiritual Board to defend Muslim interests while protecting the state interest as well. Although certain sections of the Muslim community resent the extra loyalty of the Spiritual Board to the state, the mechanism is effective, though far from perfect.

The Russian Council of Muftis (RCM), the highest Muslim body in the country, adopted a document under the title 'The Fundamental Principles of the Social Programme of Russia's Muslims (MSP)' in May 2001, which became an important stage in the process of articulating the views of a substantial part of Russian Muslims on significant socio-political issues, including state, citizenship and Muslim relations, with the followers of other confessions. The significance of the document lies in the fact that it outlines the Muslim stand on important issues. By formulating a social and political platform for Russian Muslims, it serves as a starting point for constructive dialogue between the Muslim community and Russian government at both federal and local levels.[26] What is more important is that the MSP provides explanations about Islam's basic tenets and main aspects of the Muslim understanding of contemporary issues to average Russian citizens.

The MSP articulates Muslim views on issues such as role of social accord, secular authority, war and peace etc. The concept of social accord incorporates the formula for concluding agreements with non-Muslim groups and states with the purpose of maximum protection of rights and freedom of Muslims. The document says, "The state and its laws are viewed as a form of social contract, in which the most viable compromise is achieved equilibrium among interests of various social groups and religious organisations is established".[27]

The document further says that "the attitude of Muslims towards the state is based on the rational principles that defend freedom, support justice, and encourage law –abiding behaviour. Muslims view the state and state laws as the result of an agreement among all social groups on general norms of coexistence within a defined territory and within one legal and economic system. Therefore the state and state laws are a means of guaranteeing natural and basic rights and freedom of all citizens".[28] When state laws are made to protect basic human rights and freedom of all citizens, it is not only a civil but also a religious duty for Muslims to follow the laws of their country, as they represent the highest accord among citizens. The MSP condemns the failure to comply with state laws by stating that 'the failure to fufill civil duties and calls for civil disobedience and rebellion on behalf of believers and religious communities are inadmissible in Islam'. However, in case of any differences with the laws Muslims need to resolve them, exclusively in the framework of the existing legislation.[29]

According to MSP the contemporary legal system of Russia is the most favourable for Muslims in the history of the country because 'for the first time it guarantees freedom of religion and the legal equality of Islam with other religions. The document talks about the fulfilment of mutual responsibilities of the state and the Muslim establishment towards each other. The state has to guarantee religious freedom and equality of all religions under state laws; prohibit discrimination against citizens based on their religion and invite representatives of religious organisations to participate in the discussions related to legislative and other governmental initiatives that would affect the interests of the believers.[30]

Muslim organisations are required to honour the legitimacy of laws in the country; demonstrate loyalty to the legally elected state authorities, promote patriotic feelings among Muslims towards their motherland, strengthen spirituality, high moral standards, religious tolerance and fraternal relations among various nationalities, resolve conflicts and disputes only through legal means and avoid interfering in governmental activities on both federal and local levels.[31]

One of the central elements of this arrangement, in accordance with the Russian law on freedom of conscience and religious associations, is that the state would honour internal regulations and charters of religious organisations as long as they do not contradict federal laws.[32]

The document clearly says that Russian Muslims do not cooperate with radical Islamic organisations with terrorist and extremist orientation. The MSP emphasises the idea of forming a comprehensive social partnership between Russian council of muftis and the federal government as means of defending national interests of Russia in relation to Islam both inside the country and form a geopolitical perspective. The realisation of this ambitious objective would ensure the Russian council of muftis a dominant role in guaranteeing 'effective interaction between the secular state and the believers'.[33]

Forms of Interaction between Muslim Community and State Authorities

There are two major models of interaction between state and Islam in the world. They are eastern and western models. In the eastern model of interaction, Islam is virtually state religion and its leaders are closely linked with state structures. This kind of model works in Muslim countries like Iran and Saudi Arabia etc, where the law defends Muslims not only from religious threats but even from other forms of intervention.

The second model of interaction works in countries of West Europe and USwhere Islam does not have any place of priority. Here, the Muslim community evolves into a community not controlled and not managed by any organisation. These communities live according to their own laws and do not have unified leadership oriented towards several centralised organisations. This complicates the relations between state and religion as well as creates conflicting situations in which the authorities do not know with whom to conduct dialogue.

Russia follows a mixed model, in which the state does not interfere in the internal affairs of the Muslim community. For example, President Putin twice declared that he does not have any intention to unite all of Russia's Muslims under the leadership of a unified muftiyat. The state does not defend traditional Muslims from the expansion of non-traditional Islam if the latter functions within the framework of law and also the state do not have special programmes for funding existing Muslim structures.[34]

On the other hand, the authorities pursue a clear pro-Islam foreign policy, strengthening ties with OIC; help in building Muslim educational system; finance construction of mosques; facilitate pilgrimage to Mecca through a special council on Hajj under the government.[35]

The Russian regions have both eastern and western models with several variations. In 17 regions of Russia all the Muslim communities function under one regional centralised structure. There is no centralised structure at the level of the muftiyat in 20 regions. However, all their Muslim communities function under a single jurisdiction. There are a minimum of two centralised Muslim structures in 19 regions. There are centralised structures as well as communities living outside their jurisdiction in nine regions. Separate Muslim communities under different jurisdictions function in seven regions. In 15 regions there are no registered Muslim communities.[36]

Regional authorities in Dagestan, Chechnya, Ingushetia and Tatarstan put in the maximum effort to protect traditional Muslims defending their unity. In 1999, a special law was passed in Tatarstan which confirmed that the Muslim Spiritual Board of Tatarstan is the only legitimate centralised Muslim organisation in the Republic. Dagestan and Ingushetia have passed laws that ban Wahhabism, declaring it as form of extremism. Muslim structures of these regions receive regular funds; most of their educational institutions are directly financed by the regional budgets; imams receive salary just like government employees.

Islam has received a most favoured status in Chechnya under President Ramzan Kadyrov. He has prohibited casinos, gambling,alcohol sales during Ramadanand even banned functioning of restaurants and cafes during Ramadan.Kadyrov has instructed local televisions to actively propagate traditional Islamic values. Kadyrov known for his anti-Wahhabist statements expressed his readiness to eliminate the followers of this faith in North Caucasus.[37]

In Karachaevo-Cherkassia, Kabardino-Balkaria, Adygea, Udmurtia, Krasnodarski Krai and some other regions, authorities practice a more moderate variant of the 'eastern model' that encourages mild form of protection from existing single muftiyats of the republics. In Moscow, St.Petersburg, Chubashia, Permsk Krai and Chelyabinsk district, authorities have reconciled with the existence of alternative muftiyats but give priority to only one of them. A similar situation prevails in Yakutia and Novosibirsk district, where separate Muslim communities with varied jurisdiction have been registered. However, authorities chose one of them as their preferred partners.

Authorities in Bashkortstan, Mordovia, Penza and Ulyanov districts practice the western model of interaction with Muslim communities. There regional authorities tolerate co-existence of alternative muftiyats without giving preference to any one of them. Similar situation prevails in Kemerova and Tomsk districts. In this situation providing state support to muftiyat is very difficult. It is difficult to determine who should receive how much financial help. Also,a mistake in this sphere can lead to serious problems.

There are Muslim communities functioning under a minimum of four jurisdictions in Stavropol, which makes it a difficult situation for the authorities. That is why the regional government is trying to create an independent Muslim Spiritual Board of the krai. It should be mentioned that Dagestan succeeded in uniting all its Muslim communities under single leadership in 1994, and this could be achieved in Tatarstan in 1998 under President Shaimiyev.

Regional Executive Heads and Islam

Russia has two categories of federal units in terms of Muslim population. The first category federal units have Muslim majority or closely living significant Muslim minority. The second category of federal units does not have very large Muslim population, which is spread all over the territory of the region. While Tatarstan, Bashkortstan, Muslim republics of North Caucasus except North Caucasus belong to the first category, rest of the federal units belong to the second category. Adygei is a special case where Muslim minority occupies dominant role in the ruling elite.

When any political decision is taken at the local level in Volga region or any instruction is issued by the federal centre for implementation at the regional level the specific nature of the mentality of the native population has to be taken into account.

According to Russian scholar Vsevolod Malashenko, appeal to the Islam by the regional administration is inevitable and compulsory in the Muslim regions of the Russian Federation; firstly, because of the traditional nature of the society; secondly, consequence of requirement of the authorities in additional religious legitimisation, particularly when this authority suffers from inadequate reputation. Of course, there are differences between Muslim republics. According to Malashenko, in Tatarstan and Bashkortstan the secular authorities manage to manipulate Islam and control the religious situation on their territory using administrative resources where as in Dagestan and Ingushetia authorities need Islam as an ally. Keeping Islam under total control in those regions is not possible absolutely. The regional administration virtually maintains solidarity with the Federal authorities in Volga region whereas the conduct of the regional authorities is linked to the traditions in North Caucasus.[38]

This is reflected in many ways such as active participation in religious festivals,periodic demonstration of loyalty to Islam, use of Islamic levers in the political struggle, search of support from various religious forces. Thus secular leaders often present themselves as religious authority, though state is separated from religion according to Russian constitution.

Friday is virtually a holiday in some Muslim republics. Muslim festival Kurban Bairam is an official holiday. There was a ban on alcohol sales and smoking in public places during Ramadan in some regions. Ruslan Aushev, an Afghan veteran and President of Ingushetia in 1990s not only pleaded but also issued a decree permitting polygamy, which was subsequently annulled. Chechen Premier Minister Ramazan Kadyrov, who too pleaded in favour of polygamy, was supported by Chechen parliament leader Z. Tashmirova. The issue of polygamy was raised in parliaments of Tatarstan and Bashkortstan. An inadequate number of male population was advanced as an argument for introducing polygamy. Chechen Prime Minister Ramazan Kadyrov argued and encouraged the use of head scarfs by working women and girl students. He also advocated teaching Islam in schools.

Chechen leader Kadyrov, the key figure in religious festivals, buys camels for sacrifice. He leads the prayer which is shown in the local as well as federal television channels. Part of the Kremlin elite, scared by Kadyrov's excessive Islamic orientation, tries to prevent his rise in the political hierarchy arguing that this is one step away from separatism.[39]

There is restriction and in certain cases ban on the entertainment business that contradicts Islamic moral values. However, Islam-oriented authorities in the neighbouring Dagestan, oppose closure of saunas and casinos which provide significant sum to the republican budget. According to some commentators, contrary to Chechnya,where entertainment business does not form part of the sphere of economic interests of the ruling elite, owners of entertainment business in Dagestan are influential members of the Republic's ruling elite.

With the active participation of secular authorities, the process of incorporation of traditional values of the society, incorporation of Islam into the sphere of administrative activities and norms of day to day life continues in North Caucasus. Shariat judicial system was working in Ingushetia, even at the republican level. Subsequently, it was transformed into constitutional body for individuals. In two years it had to look into nearly 1000 cases and 90% of those who had filed the complaints were satisfied.[40] Shariat judicial system functions in Dagestan, however, it is practiced only in Wahhabi communities.

In the Volga region, the local authorities have to take the Muslim majority of the territory into account and make laws accordingly. Islam is used by the secular authorities as a regulator of relations in the society. The Tatar constitution for example permits the local Muslims to perform the rituals in the factories, offices and other work places. Religious organisations have the right to create special enterprises and institutions for serving the people according to the religious cannons. For example, there are shops for selling halal products and perform 'cutting rituals'. Similar provisions are there in laws functioning in North Caucasus. Thus, Islamic tradition emerges as one of the real sources of law and a sort of guarantee for legitimisation of the law.

Secular authorities still have a lot of influence in the Muslim regions. For example, during the rule of Valery Kokov in Kabardino – Balkaria, authorities could sack imams, elected by the devotees and gave mosques to the secular authorities for management. There were incidents when girl students were called to the law and order department for questioning for reading Quran in the University auditorium. There were incidents in Adygei when the police did not permit the devotees to visit some mosques where sermons were read by imams not liked by the authorities. There were incidents in some regions when Muslim communities were denied re-registration. The mosque is strictly controlled even in Chechnya. Legal polygamy, introduced by Ingush president Ruslan Aushev, was subsequently changed by Murat Zyazikov, who replaced him in the post of president as it contradicted the federal constitution.

Inclination towards traditional values finds understanding at the federal level. The Commission of the public chamber of Russia on tolerance and freedom of conscience in 2006 launched an initiative to revamp traditional institutes for the sake of stability and modernisation of the society.

Some Russian scholars are of the opinion that the introduction of Islamic law, particularly concerning family, heritage and day to day life,should be permissible in regions predominantly inhabited by Muslims. For example,legal expert Leonid Syukiyainen thinks that inclusion of Shariat into the legal system could be possible, which should be viewed not as an inevitable evil, but as a natural process of revival of serious legal culture.[41] This stand is true in the case of Islam in the Volga region and North Caucasus where one of the major elements of revival is rejuvenation of the legal system. However, it should be kept in mind that Islamic norms should not contradict the Russian constitution.

Application of Islamic norms creates many difficulties both for the supporters and opponents of the idea. One of the obstacles for the application of the idea is the ambivalent attitude of many secular politicians, who, while supporting Islam are also scared of its excessive rise, which might weaken their influence. That is why their tactic is…that while demonstrating loyalty to religious traditions, they also call for upholding the secular character of Russian state. Here it is worth-recalling the statement of the then president of Tatarstan, Mintimer Shamiyev, who once said, "We have our own system, which is more secular". [42]Politicians well understand that in the Islamic field they become dependent on religious establishment and consequently face defeat from Islamic opposition that consistently advocates for social justice.

Muslim Establishment and the State

The revival of Islam in post-Soviet Russia and the desire of Russian Muslims to assert themselves in cultural, political and public spheres, have created new dynamics in their interactions with the state and society. The Russian Muslims who strive to gain more recognition and become an integral part of the Russian society have been hampered by number of factors. First of all, intra-Muslim conflict and contradictions have weakened their bargaining capacity with the state and subsequently damaged their position in the society. Secondly, the strengthening of radical Islam, rise of terrorism and separatism in Muslim –dominated regions have dealt a serious blow to the status and prestige of Islam as a whole across Russia.

As a result of fragmentation and decentralisation of Muslim officialdom, coupled with growing diversity in Muslim community, has led to the rise of differences, even acute rivalry within the Muslim spiritual leadership and consequently in the rank and file at the regional as well as federal levels. These rivalries have resulted from differences on a number of religious and secular issues and further led to significant damage to the interests of the Muslim community and affected the relations between the state and the Muslim community. This has indeed provided ammunition to the secular authorities to exercise control over Muslim communities, though in various degree in different regions. This is reflected by the statement made at the conference of 'The Islamic Factor in Russian Politics', held in Nizhny Novgorod in 2001 by Segei Kiriyenko, the Presidential representative to the Volga Federal district. Kiriyenko said, "Changing realities of life necessitate changes in relations between the state and the traditional religious denominations. I am deeply convinced that we are now at the new stage of the formation of these interactions because the existing system of relations does not satisfy either side".[43]

The problem with this strategy is that it is likely to cause further erosion of the confidence of the Muslims in official organisations, already undermined by intra-Muslim disunity and personality clashes within the Muslim religious leadership. These divisions have led to the emergence of 'parallel' or 'alternative' Muslim organisations. The most serious and potentially most damaging intra-Muslim rivalry stems from differences between the spiritual administration under the RCM, headed by Mufti Ravil Gainutdin, and CSBM of Mufti Talgat Tazdzuddin. This intense competition for the leadership of Russia's Muslims is characterised by mutual accusations of adherence to Wahhabi orientation, which the Russian media has made synonymous with "religious fundamentalism" and "extremism", and competition for Moscow's attention.[44]

Contradictions between Ufa and Kazan

The ruling establishment in Tatarstan and Bashkortstan from time to time raised the idea of having the 'capital' of Russian Islam in their territory. The natural choice for this was obviously Kazan, which, in the words of mufti of Tatarstan, would receive the image of influential Islamic centre in the wide Eurasian region.[45] When the spiritual administration of Muslims of Tatarstan was formed in 1992, it was conceived as the main Islamic centre of Russia by the Tatar leaders. Moreover, leaders of Tatar Public Centre, getting strengthened at that time, proposed to transfer spiritual administration of Muslims of European part of Russia to Kazan.

On the other hand, the Bashkir establishment thought that the only body which can really unite all of Russia's Muslims remained the Central Spiritual Administration of Muslims, located in Ufa. While the leaders of Tatarstan and Bashkortstan were talking about the location of the main Islamic centre of Russia, they did not have North Caucasus in their mind. Regarding North Caucasus, it should be stressed that there is no single republic including Dagestan which can aspire to be the consolidating centre there.

The muftiat of Tatarstan, which is virtually a state body, was set up with direct participation and support of republican authorities. All through the 1990s there was a fight on the issue of formation of local religious structure, in which the secular authorities of Tatarstan, including the President took active part. As a result, the Spiritual Board of Muslims of the republic virtually became part of the administrative system of the republic. Strict monitoring by the authorities over Islam is explained by the fact that high level of influence of religion on the society and also inter-faith harmony is one of the major triumph cards in the hands of republican leaders in their rather uneasy relations with Federal authorities.

In the year 2000, the leadership of Bashkortstan, tired of frictions between republican Muslim board and central Muslim board, made an attempt to unite both the spiritual boards. However, both the muftiats rejected the idea. The board of muftis of Russia also opposed the idea of passing a resolution that suggested that some government bodies of Bashkortstan are trying to violate the rights of Muslims. Presidents of republics located in the central and western parts of North Caucasus have more or less maintained control over their spiritual leadership.

Ingushetia's president Ruslan Aushev strongly supported the idea for revival of DUMSK. The Coordination centre of Muslims of North Caucasus was set up in 1998. However, uniting Muslim administrative boards and communities in North Caucasus is not an easy task. The government is not capable of keeping complete watch on the activities of tarikats, in which emphasis on social problems is increasingly visible.

The reverse link when politicians are more dependent on spiritual leaders is important,particularly in Dagestan. For example, the former Prime Minister of Dagestan Hijri Shikhsaidov paid deep respect to Sheikh Said – Afandi Chirkeiski, who was enjoying a lot of popularity in the republic. The bureaucrats working in the state apparatus consider themselves as myriads of different sheikhs.

The Muslim spiritual leadership and tarikats are in need of some administrative resources, otherwise it is difficult to oppose radical Islam on their own. Thus there is a natural alliance between the authorities and Muslim spiritual leadership to confront the common enemy of radical Islam or fundamentalist Islam in Dagestan.

The situation in regions with Muslim minority is not so tense. Influential Muslim Spiritual Boards do not exist there. The issue of relations between authorities and Muslim community finds itself in the periphery of religious and public life. The issue of observing Muslim rituals is not acute there. However, the authorities face conflicts on ethno-confessional basis in those regions. Those regions also face conflicts between different Muslim religious leaders. In some regions, the two regional Muslim boards –one representing Central Muslim administrative board and the other Council of muftis of Russia, find themselves in a hostile relationship.

Regional governors have to intervene in order to defuse the tension and resolve the conflict between the hostile Muslim leaders. For example, in 2001 the Orenburg governor Alksei Chernyshev had to mediate between regional Muslim board and central spiritual board. The regional governors had to intervene to resolve similar conflicts in Penza and Perm districts.

The Ministry of Internal Affairs and the intelligence services have been keeping a watch over the activities of Muslim communities, particularly to detect the presence of radical or fundamentalist Islam.

Muslim Factor and Military Policy

Political developments in Russia and other parts of former Soviet space during the past two-decades following Soviet disintegration bear testimony to the fact that when Islamic revival takes place in the form of Islamism and when religious revival is replaced by creation of political organisations under Islamic banner, the secular states face not only political but also military confrontation. It is quite evident by the developments in North Caucasus and Central Asia.

There is no clarity about Russia's policy so far in case the Taliban penetrates into Central Asia. Nobody knows if Russia would use military forces if the Taliban movement spreads into Central Asia. Is Russia ready to use forces in another region when Chechenya is still in conflict? This is yet to be resolved fully. These issues fall within the ambit of a defence policy that would be determined by the form, level and mechanism of influence of Islamic factor on it. The very issue of the impact of Islamic factor on shaping defense policy evokes debate and is not even acceptable in many circles. The Muslim Spiritual Board (DUM) so far has been distancing itself from the debate on military-political issues. For example mufti Tazuddin considers that traditional Muslim spiritual leadership cannot counter Wahhabism with its militants, and that is why special agencies should be engaged to fight the menace. Some experts like A. Ignatenko taking a strong position on the issue, believe that since Islamism is challenging the secular authority, secular Russia has to take all measures, including military, to counter the menace.[46]

Despite the debate, the Russian secular state is taking steps to face the scourge of Islamic militant terrorism through pursual of anti-terrorist policy, opening of anti-terrorist centres of CSTO and SCO, setting of committee of heads of border forces of CIAs, formation of Rapid Reaction Force, unification of national laws for providing concessions in military-technical cooperation, removal of obstacles in troops movements etc.[47]

Political parties and religious institutions actively using religion and participating in the state-Islam relations are the subjects that exert influence on the defence policy of Russia. These organisations can be categorised in three groups.

1. Islamic states, their coalition, international government and non-governmental organisations.
2. Formal Muslim structures like the Muslim Spiritual Board, Mufti Council, Muslim Community, Muslim political parties, movements and associations.
3. Illegal armed forces and their leaders banned international Muslim organisations with extremist and terrorist orientation, Islamic terrorists.

All pursue different kinds of objectives. Islamic states and international government and non-government organisations, impacting on Russian policy set objectives, often not different from objectives of Islamic states. For example, Iran and Russia are strategic partners. Such level of relations cannot but have engagements in the military- political sphere and defence cooperation.

The Russian justice ministry has registered seven international Islamic organisations that function in Russia and they have a 'Russian fund named after Ibrahim ben Abd al Aziz al Ibrahim' (Saudi Arabia), International Islamic Salvation Organisation, International Humanitarian Appeal (United Arab Emirates), Commission on scientific symbols in Quran and Sunna, Islamic Agency for Assistance and Salvation, Islamic Relief, League of Islamic World (Saudi Arabia) etc. They are usually engaged in providing information about the life of the Muslims of the world and engage in charity and humanitarian assistance. They do not have any possibility of influencing Russia's defence policy.

The Muslim spiritual boards of Russia officially maintain a distance from influencing defence policies. Nevertheless, a large number of Muslims in the Russian armed forces,the role of the Orthodox Church in the armed forces and the military operation in Chechnya virtually cannot but involve Muslim leaders in active policy-making.

The Russian mufti council finds it difficult to formulate its position on military-political issues. First of all, Russian Muslims were deprived of the opportunity to study Islamic thoughts on military issues for along time, leading to the formation of a vacuum in the sphere. Secondly, the Muslim spiritual boards need military and political experts, capable of producing qualified expertise on the concerned issues. Thirdly, the Russian mufti council tries to define parity directions of its activities which are seen as normal from security point of view by the government.

The Muslim spiritual leaders so far have not been able to formulate a unified position on military-political questions, and express their views on these issues very rarely.

The objectives of non-formal Muslim organisations include realisation of an Islamic project through violation of law, order and stability—tearing away a portion of the territory and creation of parallel organs of authority and capturing power through the use of armed forces. Since all this would threaten national interests, the state has to take steps to prevent this. The use of terror and creation of illegal armed forces compel the state to keep its armed forces ready for combating these forces.

The Muslim spiritual boards do not have opportunities for directly influencing Russia's defence policies. However, there are some levers through which Muslim spiritual boards exert their influence on the state's defence policy. The Muslim spiritual bards try to influence defence policy through central and regional elite, through their own as well as the secular press and their lobby in both the houses of Russian parliament. The Muslim spiritual boards actively use parliament group 'Refak', whose council of spiritual leaders is headed by mufti council chairman Ravil Gainnutddin. In spite of steps taken in 2000 to curb the political power of regional heads of administration, they continue to remain political heavy weights. They actively participate on issues such as location of arsenals in the regions, military academies, helping the commanders in providing military training, troops welfare etc. In Chechnya, federal authorities discuss the issue of appointment of chief commander not only with the military leadership but also regional administration. On the other hand, those who enjoy the army's support become regional leaders.

According to the Russian constitution, transfer of troops to foreign countries is possible only with the consent of the Federation Council,. the upper house of the Russian parliament. The situation in Kosovo, Makedonia, does not keep the Russian senators indifferent, as the Russian peace-keeping forces are located in the Balkans predominantly in Islamic environs. Russia always had its interests in Balkans, where the threat emanates from Kosovo-Albanians, making no secret of their Islamic sympathy and separatist bid.

The Islamic factor influences the formation of the military doctrine, military-political plans and decisions in the country. A significant influence of the Islamic factor is evident in the contents of the concept of national security, military doctrine, and foreign policy doctrine of Russia. The military doctrine of the Russian Federation says that 'activities of extremist nationalist, religious, separatist, terrorist movements, organisations and structures' render a destabilising influence on military security of Russia. Major external threats include creation, arming and training of armed units and groups on the territory of other states with the objective of sending them to act on the territory of Russia and its allies. According to the doctrine the major internal threats include illegal activities of extremist nationalist, religious, separatist and terrorist movements, organisations and structure, directed against unity and territorial integrity of Russian federation, destabilising domestic atmosphere,creation, arming and training and functioning of armed formations, organised crime and terrorism.

Military-political plans and related issues also take into account the Islamic factor. Here it concerns military law, military conflicts with the participation of armed forces of Russia, plans of future wars and military conflicts, understanding of character and forms of future wars.

The law in the military sphere is corrected under the influence of the Islamic factor. For example, the federal law on the fight against terrorism was adopted in 1998, clearly under the influence of the Islamic factor. The law on fight against terrorism for the first time in the history of the country gave a definition to counter-terrorist operation, named the ministry of defence along with the government,federal bodies of executive authority, FSB, Ministry of internal affairs,foreign intelligence service, federal security service as the subjects of counter-terrorist operation. At least 12 clauses of the criminal code are meant for fighting against terrorism, which means it could be used against Islamic formations and Islamists. These are clause No 205 on 'terrorism', No 206 on 'capturing of hostage', No 212 'on mass disorder', No 277 on 'attack on state or public figure, 278 'forcible capture or forcible capture of power, No 279 'armed rebellion', No 281 'diversion', No 282 'inciting nationalist, racial, or religious enmity', No 322 'illegal crossing of state borders', No 323 'illegal change of state border', No 357 'genocide' etc.[48]

Experience in the Afghan conflict and the two Chechen wars, in which the Russian army took part, is taken into account while making military-political plans. Experience of military actions against Islamic militants has been taken into account by the defence ministry and interior ministry, and the results of their research have been conveyed to troops. All these conclusions have been used while drafting military doctrine and foreign policy doctrine etc.

The Islamic factor influences plans of military actions against Islamic organisations in Russian territory. It changes the understanding about the nature and forms of future war. The emergence of Muslim subjects in the international arena, who have no links with national and state formations help this process. They do not have strong military forces like the states. However their military structures are very mobile.

It may so happen that Russian forces have to be engaged in order to resolve conflicts in different parts of the Islamic world or Muslim-dominated areas of Russia. It may also happen that Muslims would be opponents or allies of Russia, depending on the situation. Unusual collisions might take place. For example, Russian peace-keeping forces were more sympathetic to orthodox Christians than to Muslims in the former Yugoslavia.

It is worth recalling that in 1999, in the beginning of the second Chechen war,the State Council of Tatarstan approved a resolution to stop recruitment on the territory of Tatarstan for serving in the Russian army. The objective of this resolution was to get back Tatar soldiers from Dagestan where they were fighting against their own fellow believers from Caucasus. A ban was imposed to recruit volunteers from the territory of Tatarstan for fighting in North Caucasus.[49]

The coalition element of Russian defence policy is prompted by Islamic factor. Russian president is on record that Russia is a state that would prevent proliferation of Islamic fundamentalism into Europe and seek partners and allies in combating Islamic terrorism.

The Islamic factor influences many aspects of military planning and decisions related to it. Freedom of conscience in the armed forces,recruitment of soldiers from Islam-oriented regions, fight against illegal military formations, training of specialists on Islam for troops, development of coalitions, territorial location of troops, arsenal, countering influence of religious organisations in the armed forces, countering discredition campaign against armed forces, participation in anti-terrorist operations,use of experience of military action against Islamic militants – all these issues are influenced by the Islamic factor.[50]

The situation regarding freedom of conscience in the armed forces of Russia is fundamentally different from that of Soviet armed forces. Sociological surveys conducted in the armed forces suggested that a number of believers in the armed forces has increased drastically, which compels military leadership to maintain contact with the leadership of related confessions. A change in the system of value-orientation of the servicemen has to be taken into account while providing military training. The growth in the number of believers in the armed forces increases the conflict potential within the forces on the basis of religion. The issue of religious harmony among servicemen belonging to different confessions, first of all of orthodox Christianity and Islam, is becoming increasingly important. It seems that necessary conditions have not been created for ensuring the rights of servicemen for freedom of conscience and faith.

The presence of a large number of Muslims in the ranks of the Russian army requires special attention to them from the military leadership, and understanding of the significance of Islam for them,in turn, requires knowledge about Islam. This helps in eradicating conflict within the ranks and facilitates the strengthening of combat readiness.

According to sociological surveys, Islamophobic views are not popular within the rank and file of the army. Results of the surveys suggest that only 3.2% have a negative attitude towards Muslims. However, 34.2 % of those participating in the survey showed negative attitude towards Chechens, 30% towards Dagestanis, 21.3% towards Azeris. As a whole 24.3% entertain negative attitude towards people with Caucasus origin.[51]

It is hotly debated in Russia about the presence of Muslim spiritual representatives in the army units. The Russian defence ministry has signed an agreement with the Russian Orthodox Christian Church for having its priests present in army units. A lot of arguments have been made in favour of similar agreement with the Muslim spiritual board. However, Russian Muslim community does not have a centralised leadership like the Orthodox Church, which makes it difficult for signing such an agreement. That is why, perhaps,the army leadership has to interact with the muftis at the level of military districts.

The central element in the agreement between the Ministry of Defence and religious structures is the presence of priests in military units. It can be said that priests have replaced the political sections of the Soviet army (*politotdel*). However, so far it looks like the Orthodox Church priests, present in army units, read sermons, conduct discussions on religious themes and sometimes perform religious rituals during launching of new missiles, ships, submarines etc.

The Muslim spiritual leadership when demanding some kind of parity with Orthodox Christianity asks permission for the mullas to meet Muslim soldiers and organise the Friday prayer in army units where their number is significant. They demand special rooms for prayers for Muslim soldiers. In the Volga- Ural region, where local Muslim youths go to serve in the army, the imams conduct Friday prayers and meet the believers.

Some Muslim spiritual leaders think that observation of fasts in the army units would improve the mood and morale of the believers. This proposal is rather debatable against the backdrop of army experience in Arab countries.

The armed forces and other military structures, in which a significant number of Muslims serve, are engaged in a battle against religious extremism and separatism. The number of people serving in the army from Muslim-dominated republics, where the population is significantly younger, is constantly growing. The percentage of people refusing to serve in the army is less in Muslim-dominated republics compared to Russia as a whole.

Surveys have shown that Muslims constitute 9% in the armed forces of Russia. People traditionally practising Islam demonstrate their confessional identification more strongly than people belonging to Orthodox Christianity. Representatives of Turkic origin from the Volga region constitute 43% of believer- servicemen and from North Caucasus, 61% servicemen who practise Islam.

Religious differences so far have not created any tension in the armed forces. However, as the religious consciousness of servicemen grows, founding of a basis for growth of tension cannot be ruled out. Growth of the influence of Orthodox Christianity in the army may lead to escalation of tension in the armed forces. The only religion that opposes this tendency of growth of influence in the armed forces is Islam.

The Islamic factor influences the recruitment process for the armed forces in the Muslim-dominated regions. Sociological surveys suggest that understanding of religion by Muslim servicemen is based on national traditions. This explains why the number of believers is higher among the inhabitants of Volga-Ural region and North-Caucasus. That is why the growth of believer-servicemen is possible in units that are formed by recruitment from these regions.

The issue of increasing the number of Muslim servicemen cannot be resolved even by the change of principle of recruitment for the troops. If the recruitment takes place on a voluntary basis in future, the Russian army would still remain multi-national— but it would be more Russian, as the proportion between different ethnic groups would change in favour of ethnic Russians. This would increasingly discourage ethnic Muslims from service in the Russian army. If such a scenario does not become dangerous for Russia, it is because the main threat to her military security stems from the South. If such a threat stems from the West or East, the state would face serious difficulty. Either the multi-ethnic character of the Russian society has to be taken into account in the defence policy by creating poly-ethnic military units, or, create units through recruitment of representatives of non-Russian nationality, which happens in Chechnya. Federal authorities are compelled to declare information about the beginning of the recruitment from this republic and that the personal structure of the forces is formed by its inhabitants, which means by ethnic Chechen Muslims.

Islam acts as a leading factor in the post-Soviet space in determining the possible opponent, which compels the armed forces of Russia to continue to get ready and fight against illegal armed formations often functioning under Islamic banner and military-political views of Islam.

There is a debate in Russian society about the identity of the enemy against whom the Russian army is fighting. The Russian media reports suggest that there are three categories of people who are fighting against federal forces in Chechnya – foreign mercenaries, people coming from all over Russia to 'defend Islam', and 'soldiers of destiny' trying to make a living by participating in the military actions. According to Russian reports, most of the people from the second and third categories come from Tatarstan, Bashkortstan and some regions of CIS. Before joining the insurgent groups they go through education camps of Islamists where they learn the Quran and receive military training.

Of late coalition-building is gaining ground in Russia's military policy. The CSTO committee of national security secretaries has emphasised that this body organises its work in three directions: Western, Caucasian and Central Asian, and the last direction is considered as the most important for CIS. Russia is playing a pivotal role in the CSTO Rapid Reaction Force and anti-terrorist centre, set up to counter Islamic terrorism. Similar anti-Terrorist centre is functioning within the SCO too. Moreover, the SCO has set up a contact group to handle the Afghan issue, a possible breeding ground for Islamic terrorism and extremism.

Currently the United Anti-Air Defence System is considered to be most developed and effective in the military structures of Russia-led CIS. However, its presence is not as important as Islamic militants do not have military aircrafts, rockets, missiles etc.

These are certain tenets of evolution of Russian military policy under the influence of the Islamic factor. According to Russian expert, Professor Malashenko significance of the 'Islamic factor' for military policy would only grow in future. This is linked to a demographic situation with acute inter-ethnic and inter-faith relations. Religious radicalism is likely to remain a serious threat to security in Russian military doctrine, which means Islamic factor would remain important in the military policy of the country.

Federalism and the Muslim Factor

Russia is historically a multi-ethnic and multi-confessional country. Its multi-confessionalism is reflected in its federal structure. Bolsheviks after giving the right to self-determination to minorities quickly launched a serious campaign for re-uniting the territory of the former Russian empire. Collapse of central power, the fall of the Czar's regime and ensuing civil war led to fragmentation of the empire and elicited demands for national self-determination from non-Russian nationalities, including from empire's Muslim subjects, though in varying degrees. Taking advantage of the collapse of the empire and lack of central power, several ethnic territories declared their independence, while others proclaimed formation of self-ruled autonomous territories. The Bolsheviks had propounded self-determination for non-Russian ethnic people. After capturing power they issued the Declaration of Rights of the peoples of Russia, which guaranteed national self-determination for non-Russian ethnic groups and the appeal to toiling Muslims of the East, which proclaimed Islamic beliefs, practices and cultural and national institutions to be sacrosanct.[52] After consolidating their power in Moscow and St. Petersburg, the Bolsheviks succeeded in establishing their control over the former empire's territory and gave autonomy in varying degrees to different non-Russian ethnic groups.

According to the Soviet constitution, the USSR became a federal state that provided territorial autonomy to the non-Russian ethnic groups thus providing a significant degree of self-determination and autonomy. The legal basis for this federal system was provided by the Union Treaty signed in December 1922 that led to the formation of voluntary union of sovereign, ethnically defined republics. Within the constituent republics, different kinds of federal administrative units were established, with varying degrees of autonomy. While Autonomous Republics were given the highest level of autonomy;the constituent Union Republics, autonomous regions, districts had less autonomy. The lower-level autonomous territories were carved out for ethnic minorities who lived in territories falling within the constituent Union Republics.

The Bolsheviks began developing a constitutional system of governing relations between the federal centre and the regions even before the formation of the USSR in 1922. The first constitution of the country promulgated in 1918 declared that the Russian Soviet Republic is established on the principle of a free union of free nations, as a federation of Soviet national republics. The second constitution adopted in 1924 declared that the Soviet Union is a voluntary association of sovereign republics with the right to secede from the union and the right to adopt their own constitution. One of the first acts of Soviet state was the appeal of Council of Peoples Komissars of Russian Soviet Federative Socialist Republic(RSFSR) "To all the toiling Muslims of Russia and the East" dated 20 November 1917, which said 'from today onwards your faith and traditions, your national and cultural institutions are declared as free and cannot be touched. Build your national life freely and without any obstacle. Be aware that your rights just like rights of all people of Russia are defended with all the force of revolution and its organs -Council of workers, soldiers and peasants deputies.[53]

This appeal along with practical measures for its implementation played a significant role in winning the political sympathy of Muslims towards the new authorities, and its reinforcement in regions of traditional Muslim habitats. However, subsequently Soviet policy towards religion, including Islam, passed through many changes. In particular, the 1930s witnessed a serious change in the Soviet government's attitude towards religion. The major elements of the anti-religion policy of the Soviet state were reflected in the following directions;

1. Political - Harassment of spiritual leaders as representatives of the dominant class and confessional associations as political organisation.
2. Legal -New political and legal status of the Church, removal of civil rights, absence of guarantee of freedom of conscience
3. Economic- Subversion of organisational and economic foundation of religious activities
5. Ideological -Giving status of state ideology to atheism and exposing religious views as a Bourgeois view.[54]

The Soviet political system, formally structured as multinational federation but operating as a unitary state, in essence reflected the Soviet approach to national and cultural identity. This indeed promoted local nationalism and socialist internationalism. The Soviet state in the early years of its existence clearly promoted the development of non-Russian identities and cultures. This strategy reflected the international ideology of Bolsheviks and granted equality to all ethnic groups. Throughout the Soviet period, the state pursued more or less an anti-religious policy, with varying degrees of intensity at different periods.

This policy by and large continued till Mikhail Gorbachev's Perestroika and Glasnost revolution in the second half of 1980s, with certain relaxations during the years of Second World War and some changes in the subsequent period. The decisions of the 19th conference of CPSU, held in 1988, opened flood gates for political reforms in the country. These ill-timed political reforms encouraged national-separatist movements across the USSR from Baltic to Caucasus. The first republic to declare its independence from Moscow was Lithuania. The parade of sovereignty, starting with Estonia's declaration of sovereignty in 1988,continued throughout the country encompassing all the constituent republics of the USSR. However, the most serious blow to the Soviet federal government, and the most powerful impetus to the disintegration process, came when the Russian Federation with Boris Yeltsin at its helm of affairs declared the Russian Federation's sovereignty in June 1990. All the three Baltic republics had declared their independence before the end of 1990.

The power struggle between Mikhail Gorbachev and Boris Yeltsin, and within the ruling establishment, strengthened the hands of nationalist and separatist forces in the country. While Gorbachev's chief advisor Alexander Yakovlyov virtually encouraged the separatist movement by dubbing it a democratic movement, Boris Yeltsin too used this movement to strengthen his position in his power struggle against Gorbachev. Finally, the USSR ceased to exist after Russian leader Boris Yeltsin, Ukranian leader Leonid Kravchuk and Belorussian leader Shuskevich, signed the Belovezhski agreement declaring that "the Union of Soviet Socialist Republics, as a subject of international law and geopolitical reality, hereby ceases to exist."

By the time the USSR got dissolved and Russia emerged as a separate independent state, the centrifugal forces inside Russia had become quite strong. Russia was threatened by demands of national self-determination and regional self-rule. Boris Yeltsin's call to the regions to take as much sovereignty 'as you can swallow', provided a strong impetus to centrifugal forces inside Russia. Various ethnic groups within RSFSR started demanding national and cultural self-determination. By the end of 1990, encouraged by Russian republic's own declaration of sovereignty, fourteen autonomous republics and three autonomous districts within Russian federation declared themselves as sovereign republics.[55]

Trying to strengthen his political base and weaken Gorbachev, Yeltsin on the one hand played with Russian nationalism, and on the other hand, made concessions to non-Russian ethnic groups of Russian Federation such as incorporating into the RSFSR's declaration of sovereignty a provision guaranteeing the right of 'every people to self-determination in their chosen national state and national cultural form.' In 1991, his administration altered the Russian Federation's administrative structure and elevated all autonomous republics and four autonomous districts to the status of constituent republics of the larger Russian republic.[56]

These concessions might have strengthened Yeltsin's position in his struggle against Gorbachev, but it provided a strong impetus to the disintegration process within the Russian federation, with some ethnic regions demanding right to sovereignty and others —greater autonomy.

The disintegration process taking roots in RSFSR was carried over to the post-Soviet period and the independent Russian Federation, which retained a dual system of federalism characterised by 57 non-ethnically defined regions and 32 national homelands for ethnic minorities. According to the Ministry of Justice of Russia, 19 of Russia's ethnic republics adopted constitutions that violated provisions of the federal constitution. The constitution of Muslim-dominated Ingushetia declared the federal laws valid on its territory, if only it did not contradict the republic's sovereignty, while the constitution of Sakha stipulated that federal laws must be approved by the Republic's parliament before it become valid in the Republic.

Ethnic Muslims constitute a majority in seven federal units of Russian Federation —they are: Chechnya, Ingushetia, Dagestan, Kabardino-Balkaria, Karachaevo- Cherkesia, Baskortstan and Tatarstan. The centrifugal tendencies were very strong in these federal units.

Table 4.1: Muslim Population in Federal Units (in %)

Ingushetia	98%
Chechnya	96%
Dagestan	94%
Kabardino-Balkaria	70%
Karachaevo-Cherkesia	63%
Bashkortstan	54.5%
Tatarstan	54%

In another 13 federal subjects the Muslim population constitutes from 27 % to 7%.
Source: p-15 Silantiyev, R.A. (2008), *Encyclopedia Islam in Contemporary Russia* (Энциклопедия ислама в современной России), Moscow: Algoritm

In the aftermath of the Soviet disintegration, some of Russia's Muslim nationalities were among those who fought for greater autonomy and even for sovereignty. In most cases, territories dominated by Muslim population demanded greater cultural and administrative autonomy rather than outright independence. The President of Ingushetia, for example, demanded legalisation on polygamy for men and abduction of women by their prospective bridegrooms. The Republic of Adygea adopted a constitution that stipulated that the Republic's President must speak the local language, and that 50% of the posts in the Republic's administrative bodies must be reserved for ethnic Adygei, though the titular nationality constituted only 22% of the Republic's population. This was a clear violation of Russian constitution. All eight Muslim republics of the Russian federation declared various levels of sovereignty, emulating the actions of constituent republics of

USSR and encouraged by Boris Yeltsin's slogan-- "Take as much sovereignty as you can swallow".

In Baskortstan, intra-Muslim ethnic rivalries between the Tatars and Bashkirs facilitated the rise of nationalism. Starting from 1989, several Tatar nationalist groups emerged in the republic, including the Tatar Social Center, Tatar Democratic Party 'Idel-Ural' and the Bashkortstan branch of the Tatar Youth Movement Aztliq. Largely in response to Tatar activism, the Bashkir People's Center 'Ural' held its founding congress in December 1989 and demanded that Bashkortstan be elevated to the status of a Union Republic in the USSR. Allied groups such as the Bashkir People's Assembly, the Bashkir People's Party and the Bashkir Youth League advocated the creation of an independent Baskortstan, while Bashkir extremists called for expulsion of non-Bashkirs in order to ensure a Bashkir majority in the Republic.[57]

Bashkortstan, under President Murtaza Rakhimov, taking advantage of these rising nationalist sentiments tried to enhance the republic's administrative autonomy. Bashkortstan ratified a constitution that proclaimed the republic's sovereignty and required the president to speak Bashkir. In August 1994, Bashkortstan gained recognition of its sovereignty in an agreement negotiated with the federal centre.

In certain cases, the Muslim nationalist movement advocated more drastic measures to secure their national rights. In the dual–ethnic republics of Kabardino-Balkaria and Karachaevo-Cherkesia, the nationalist movement tried to divide the republics into separate national homelands. Several nationalist movements arose to represent different ethnic groups in the multi-ethnic republic of Dagestan; most notably, a Lezgin nationalist movement advocated the creation of an independent Lezginstan on traditional Lezgin territory in Dagestan and neighbouring Azerbaijan. Movements sprang up in support of the creation of larger multi-ethnic homelands, including Adygea Khase,which sought to unify the Circassian peoples of the North Caucasus, and the Confederation of Peoples of the Caucasus, which supported the formation of an independent multi-national Caucasian republic.

During the final years of the USSR, and throughout the decade of Yeltsin's presidency, national awakening in Russia was dominated by the rise of nationalism in the Muslim Republics of Chechnya and Tatarstan. An enhancement of Islamic awareness – a principal component of collective identity among Tatars and Chechens, especially those seeking to assert their distinction from the surrounding Russian culture – accompanied this rise with growing religious consciousness, and the response of federal authorities played determining roles in the evolution of Russian federalism throughout Boris Yeltsin's rule and defined some of the most important issues in centre-periphery relations faced by his successor.[58]

Tatar Separatism

Under Gorbachev's Perestroika the nationalist movement in Tatarstan gathered momentum. The formation of All Tatar Public Center (ATPC) in 1989 at Kazan, attended by Tatar representatives from across the USSR, provided an impetus to the Tatar nationalist movement. The forum demanded reduction in ethnic Russian immigration into the republic and designation of Tatar as Tatarstan's official language. ATPC also demanded the raising of Tatarstan's status from that of an Autonomous Republic to a full Union Republic of the Soviet Union, following which the republic was to seek full independence. In 1990 several nationalist organisations like Azatlig and the Sovereignty Committee joined ATPC. Subsequently the most anti-Russian Ittifaq party emerged in Tatarstan. In early 1991, the radical segments of the nationalist movement organised the Kurultai (congress in Kazan), which was attended by Tatar representatives from across the USSR. The congress declared Tatarstan's independence and elected the Milli Mejlis (National Parliament), consisting of 75 members.[59]

The Milli Mujlis in its first meeting declared itself as the supreme legislative body of all Tatars and proclaimed that it had the authority to abrogate acts of Tatarstan's government that contravened the interests of Tatar people. Freedom Square, in front of Tatarstan's parliament,denounced and condemned Ivan Grozny's conquest of Kazan. Violence erupted when a large number of demonstrators attempted to storm the republican parliament after it refused to adopt a Declaration of Independence.

It must be said that it is not religion that played a significant role in fomenting these protests and organising nationalist movements. However, as a central element of Tatar identity, Islam did play the role of unifying cultural symbol even for secular nationalists. ATPC in its political programme glorified the virtues of Jadidism, a reformist Islamic movement, as a modernising force and included the revival of Jadidism among Tatars as one of its principal objectives. ATPC also demanded that the republic should have its own Muslim religious board with its headquarters at Kazan.

ATPC later reiterated its commitment to Islam as a part of Tatar national culture in an official document that said that "the history of tatar culture and enlightenment, the entire way of life, is closely connected to Islam. Therefore, Islam cannot be separated from national policy or from the national movement, and is closely connected to and cooperate with them". The Islamic Democratic Party of Tatarstan, a nationalist party founded in 1991 to build a secular independent state, also stressed Tatars desire to reassert their Islamic heritage.

There were other nationalist movements,such as Iman, which drew much stronger associations between Islam and Tatar nationalism.

The Ittifaq party, led by Bairamova and the Milli Mejlis, espoused an equally radical, although still secular, view of Islam as an instrument to distance the Tatars from the Russians. They issued a joint resolution that proclaimed, "The ancient culture, the entire life of the Tatar people are in an intimate way connected to Islam. And in the complex modern situation, religion must defend the nation, and the nation must defend religion".

As nationalism lost its attraction in the second half of 1990s, Ittifaq and Milli Mejlis adopted a more radical pan- Islamic stand, in order to provide a boost to their declining movement. Ittifaq's fourth party congress in 1997 issued a statement that said, "We declare that the national liberation struggle we are waging against the Russian empire to be henceforth known as jihad aimed at liberation from the infidels' slavery. We Muslim nationalists are launching a struggle for the creation of an Islamic state in Tatarstan". Meanwhile, the Milli Mejlis also adopted a more Islam-oriented position and in January 1996 approved a new unofficial Tatar constitution that included the objective of reviving Sharia as envisioned by Jadidism in the Republic. In June 1996 both organisations participated in setting up "Muslims of Tatarstan"- a socio-political organisation, with former Tatar mufti Gabdulla Galiullin as its leader.

The rise of Tatar nationalism without religious overtones towards the twilight years of the Soviet Union, was evident in the policies adopted by Tatarstan's government. In August 1990, Tatarstan's parliament declared the republic's sovereignty and renamed it as the Tatar Soviet Socialist Republic –Republic of Tatarstan that implied equal status with the constituent union republics of Soviet Union. Mintimer Shamiyev, chairman of Supreme Soviet of Tatarstan, signed the declaration and resigned from the CPSU. Just two days after the so-called coup in August 1991, Tatarstan's parliament, at

Shamiyev's behest, adopted the Declaration of State Independence of the Republic of Tatarstan

Authorising a future referendum on the nature of sovereignty for Tatarstan, it must be said here that Tatar leadership was enjoying tacit support from the federal centre in its bid for the status of Union Republic in the framework of Gorbachev–Yeltsin power struggle. While Yeltsin was supporting nationalist movements in Union Republics for their independence in order to deliver a blow to the federal centre, Gorbachev was supporting a nationalist movement in the autonomous republics of **the** RSFSR, in an attempt to weaken Yeltsin's position. Nationalists in Union Republics as well as within RSFSR took full advantage of this power struggle between Gorbachev and Yeltsin.

In March 1992, for months after Soviet disintegration, Tatarstan held a referendum, which asked the voters, "Do you agree that the Republic of Taterstan is a sovereign state, a subject of international law, building its relations with Russia and other republics and states on the basis of equitable treaties?"Despite threats from Yeltsin's regime to bring criminal charges against officials conducting the referendum, Tatarstan's residents responded positively by a huge margin: 61.4 % out of the 81.6% those participated, voting in favour of sovereignty. On 1st November 1992, Tatarstan's parliament ratified a new constitution reiterating Tatarstan's status as 'a sovereign state, subject to international law'. However, the constitution, without directly declaring Tatarstan's independence, implied that the republic was outside the legal jurisdiction of the Russian Federal government, pending the negotiation of a treaty delineating Tatarstan's status, if any, within the Russian Federation.

Chechnya's Declaration of Independence

Chechnya became another region where the rise of nationalism and separatism posed serious challenges to Russia's federal centre and subsequently territorial integrity. In November 1990, at the peak of nationalist movements across Russia, a self-proclaimed Chechen national congress was organised in its capital Grozny and elected Soviet general Dzakhar Dudayev as chairman of its executive committee and commander of a newly formed Chechen national guard. It must be said that Chechen nationalist movement could not have been so strong without tacit support from the Russian Federation President Boris Yeltsin and his coterie, who used the nationalist movement as a tool against his arch-rival Gorbachev and to weaken the federal centre, without realising the serious consequences that it would have later.Dudayev, the first and only Chechen general serving in the Soviet armed forces was brought by Yeltsin's establishment from Talin to Grozny, in order to lead the separatist movement in the Muslim dominated republic. Understanding that the Republic's legal executive and the legislature were in favour of federal centre headed by Gorbachev, Yeltsin started using the nationalist movement to weaken the central authority and supported the 'independence' movement there. After the so-called coup attempt in August 1991, which was virtually supported by Chechnya's ruling communist establishment, the National Congress of Chechen people (NCCP), led by General Dudayev, forcibly dissolved the Republic'sSupreme Soviet and declared its executive committee as the ruling authority of Chechnya.After the Soviet disintegration, the military garrison located in the republic was left to the separatists and nationalists by the Yeltsin-Gaidar led government. Little did Yeltsin and his coterie realise that very soon separatists would use these very weapons against Yeltsin's army that would try and restore constitutional order in the republic.

Under pressure from Yeltsin's establishment and Dudayev's forces, the communist- dominated ruling body subsequently voted to dissolve itself and surrender power to a provisional Supreme Soviet, which would rule the republic until elections were held. Very soon the Dudayev- led NCCP dissolved the provisional government and captured the government buildings across the Republic, including the regional headquarters of State Security Committee (KGB). Dudayev captured power in Chechnya very much the same way Yeltsin had captured power in Russia, with the exception that Yeltsin was an elected leader whereas Dudayev was installed by Yeltsin. Though Dudayev's regime was installed with Yeltsin's blessings, very soon the Russian president discovered to his dismay that the Chechen leader was in no mood to remain under Moscow's control. Despite warnings from federal authorities that results of any illegitimate elections would be annulled, Dudayev held elections for a president and parliament for a new Chechen republic. Dudayev won decisively in the presidential election held in October 1991, following which, he issued his first presidential decree that explicitly said 'the will of the citizens of the Chechen republic, expressed by direct and general elections, the state sovereignty of the Chechen republic is hereby declared', which was ratified by the parliament next day.

Just like in Tatarstan, at the outset Islam did not play the most important role in Chechnya's bid for greater autonomy and sovereignty from Moscow. Dudayev apparently tried to revive the traditional clan structure and religious community's characteristic of Chechnya's version of Sufi Islam and restored the Council of Elders and other Islamic institutions and traditions of pre-Soviet Chechnya. According to some experts, it is only after Russian military intervention in 1994 that Dudayev linked the fate of his republic directly to Islam. As hostilities between him and the federal authorities grew, he began to use the religious sentiments of the people and even support from external Islam in order to consolidate his power and position

In November 1991, Yeltsin declared a state of emergency in Chechnya and his troops landed in Grozny to arrest Dudayev. Russian forces were surrounded by the Chechen national guards as soon as they landed in Grozny airport. Subsequently, the Russian parliament withdrew Yeltsin's decree imposing state of emergency in Chechnya. Following this, Russian and Chechen forces signed an agreement for Russian withdrawal from Grozny, ending Yeltsin's adventure to curb ethnic nationalism and separatism by force. In the subsequent months the Gaidar government virtually permitted the Chechen troops to take control of the Russian army's formidable arsenal, which included tanks, armoured personal carriers and other sophisticated armaments. Yeltsin gradually became victim of his own nationalist policy which he was using against the federal centre led by Soviet President Mikhail Gorbachev. His own Russian nationalist policy, coupled with his slogan--'take as much sovereignty as you can', played a cruel joke on him subsequently. The separatist movement in some republics, particularly Muslim-dominated Tatarstan and Chechnya, went out of control. Yeltsin tried to pursue a policy to curb separatism and assert central authority. This policy, though not very cohesive, had the following elements: 1) direct appointment of regional officials 2) negotiation of a comprehensive treaty defining relations between the Federal centre and the republics; 3)ratification of a new constitution increasing the federal government's authority; 4) negotiation of bilateral power-sharing treaties with individual provinces; and 5) use of military force.

Yeltsin made a new effort to set the limits of regional autonomy after the Soviet break up. In early 1992, he started talks with regional governments on a federation treaty to provide a legal basis for relations between the federal centre and federal units. In March 1992 federal centre reached agreements with 86 federal subjects, excluding Tatarstan and the then united Chechnya-

Ingushetia, on the provisions of the treaty. The Federation Treaty did not recognise the right of ethnic republics to secede and stipulated that republican laws and constitutions could not violate laws and constitution of the federal state. However, the new treaty defined the ethnic republics as sovereign and granted them significant autonomy, including the right to conduct independent foreign and international trade policies, to assert ownership over land and natural resources of their territories and determine their own administrative structures. By contrast, other federal subjects were not defined as sovereign and were denied the right to have their own constitution or to determine the structure of their administrative organs. President Yeltsin agreed to a formal treaty creating a federal structure that granted the republics substantial autonomy, largely to neutralise the radical nationalists among the non-Russian ethnic groups, in the same manner that he sought to win support of ethnic minorities during his struggle with Gorbachev.

In spite of the concessions granted by Yeltsin,the separatist movement did not subside in the Muslim republics of Tatarstan and Chechnya. Leaders of both republics refused to participate in talks on the Federation Treaty and declined to sign the final document. Almost around the same time when the Federation Treaty was signed, Tatarstan organised its own referendum on sovereignty and the Chechen parliament ratified a new constitution for the self-proclaimed Republic of Chechnya. In December 1993, although the republican leader Shamiyev allowed Tatarstan's citizens to vote during the referendum on the proposed Russian constitution, his government actively discouraged voters to participate in the referendum and thus managed to keep the turnout in the republic to less than 15% of eligible voters. In Chechnya, Dudayev government did not permit voting on the referandum. Thus these two Muslim republics posed a serious challenge to Yeltsin's central authority. Yeltsin in order to overcome the challenge used two divergent strategies: negotiation with Tatarstan, and military action in Chechnya.

Yeltsin adopted a policy of negotiations with regional leaders for the division of power between the federal centre and the federal subjects. In the early 1990s, despite the continuing dispute regarding Tatarstan's status in Russian federation, central authorities and Shamiyev's government had been engaged in serious negotiations throughout in order to find a mutually acceptable solution to power- sharing ever since March 1992 till the end of 1993. Moscow and Kazan concluded a number of accords covering topics like ownership of oil fields and defense industries in the republic, education system, customs regulation etc. Yeltsin's consolidation of power and ratification of the 1993 constitution led to expand these agreements to reach a comprehensive accord on Tatarstan's relations with the federal centre, resulting in the emergence of the first power-sharing treaty, signed in February 1994 between the federal centre and a federal subject.

In order to secure this agreement, Shamiyev agreed that Tatarstan would be a subject of the federation and accepted the language in the treaty that referred to Tatarstan as a state 'united with the Russian Federation' instead of the formulation 'associated with Russia' as mentioned in Tatarstan's constitution. Neither sovereignty nor the right to secession found any mention in the document. The treaty did not define the republic as a subject of international law, as did Tatarstan's constitution and declaration of sovereignty. In return, Tatarstan received powers reserved in the Russian constitution for the federal government or for joint federal-Republican jurisdiction, including the right to engage in foreign and international trade relations, to determine the Republic's budget and tax policies, and to establish forms of alternative civil service for citizens of Tatarstan eligible to substitute such activity for service in the Russian army.[60]

Shamiyev's willingness to make concessions on the nature of Tatarstan's sovereignty largely reflected geographic and demographic weaknesses. Despite its size, Tatarstan is a territory falling within the territory of Russian Federation and has no external borders. Moreover, at the time of signing of the power-sharing treaty, Tatars- Tatarstan's titular nationality, constituted 48% while Russian constituted nearly 43% of republic's total population. Most importantly, just like Yeltsin, Tatarstan's former communist leader Shamiyev simply used the nationalist card in order to consolidate his power and limit federal centre's interference in the affairs of his republic. The power–sharing treaty between Tatarstan and the federal centre served as a model for resolving issues with other republics with similar demands such as sovereignty and greater autonomy. President Yeltsin's power-sharing diplomacy brought an element of stability to the relations between the federal centre and the periphery. However, since most power-sharing treaties were negotiated on a bilateral basis, the content varied from case to case and provided different levels of autonomy for different federal subjects, at times violating the federal law and federal constitution.

These treaties provided uneven devolution of power. For example, the agreement reached with Bashkortstan mentioned the republic as a sovereign state within the Russian federation, the only example of a republic being described as sovereign in any of the 42 treaties, while the agreement with North Ossetia described the republic simply as 'full subject of the Russian federation', and the treaty with Udmurtia referred to the republic merely as a 'republic' and stated that Udmurtia's relations with the federal centre were regulated by the Russian constitution. Similar disparities were found among agreements with ethnic Russian regions.

Military Option in Chechnya

Despite Yeltsin's success in reaching negotiated treaties with the break-away republics, particularly with Muslim Tatarstan, he resorted to a military option for quelling the separatist movement in Muslim Chechnya. Some experts suggest that there were fairly good chances of resolving the Chechen separatist issue through negotions: however, part of Yeltsin's establishment was not keen in negotiating and wanted to fish in the troubled waters there with continued anarchy. One of Yeltsin's spokespersons is on record that Dudayev had presented a sword to Yeltsin on which he had expressed desire for a negotiated settlement of the tangle. However, Yeltsin chose the military option because he wanted to have demonstrative victory in a short war with the rebellious republic, in order to bolster his sagging popularity and restore federal authority there. Yeltsin also chose the wrong people with a dubious track record, to handle Chechnya. For example, he appointed the notorious oligarch, Boris Berizovsky as deputy secretary of national security to handle the Chechnya issue. Berezovsky was widely believed to be hand-in -glove with Chechen separatists and terrorists.

Of course the historical memories of the long Caucasus war in 19th century, Russian atrocities, and Stalin's deportation of Chechen people during the Second World War, must have contributed to the growing antagonism and tough Chechen resistance that culminated in military intervention in the rebellious republic.

Chechnya's proximity to and influence on other Muslim republics and ethnic groups of the North Caucasus also raised concerns about a 'domino effect' that could boost anti-Russian nationalism as well as pan-Muslim and pan-Caucasian separatist sentiments. Russian fears were intensified when Dudayev in one of the interviews to a Turkish newspaper clearly stated, "my plan envisaged the creation of a Union of Caucasus States; directed against Russian imperialism. Our main objective was the achievement of independence and liberation, acting together with the Caucasus republics, which have been oppressed by Russia over the course of 300 years".

Despite hurdles to peaceful settlement, Russia and Chechnya began talks immediately after the failure of Yeltsin's first attempt to forcibly oust Dudayev in November 1991. The talks resulted in a draft power-sharing agreement. However, during the talks, Yeltsin's representative apparently tried to isolate Dudayev, in order to deny him enhanced legitimacy and public sympathy. Instead, Kremlin representatives dealt with other members of the separatist Chechen government, including Dudayev's political rivals Yusuf Soslambekov, chairman of Chechen parliament's committee on foreign affairs, and Yaraghi Mamodayev, Chechnya's acting prime minister and head of the confederation of peoples of Caucasus with respect. Is response, Dudayev dismissed the December 1992 draft treaty, describing it as a private affair. In January 1993, Dudayev's security people turned away Russia's chief negotiators, Sergey Shakhrai and Ramazan Abdulatipov, when they arrived in Grozny to discuss the treaty with members of the Chechen parliament.

In January 1994, Dudayev issued a decree declaring the formation of independent Chechen Republic of Ichkeria, a name derived from the republic's mountainous Shatoi and Vedeno districts. This act aimed at consolidating the support and solidarity of Chechnya's mountain people, which has been historically opposed to Moscow's rule. In the following month, during a speech to the Russian parliament, Yeltsin declared the Dudayev regime illegitimate and ruled out Chechen independence. As a result, the negotiation option virtually came to an end, and Russia and Chechnya moved towards a war scenario.

The Russia-Chechnya conflict triggered the rise of Islamic extremism in Chechnya and other parts of North-Caucasus, intensified anti-Muslim sentiments and the fear of Islamic threat to Russia, and also increased support for re-assertion of federal authority in rebellious regions. Though the Islamic factor was relatively insignificant prior to Russian military intervention in Chechnya, in 1994 the launching of the war drove Dudayev to use the Islamic factor to mobilise support and public opinion for independence within Chechnya and outside of the republic. Subsequently Islam was firmly entrenched in Chechnya's internal politics, and Islamic extremism, abetted by abject poverty and unemployment and financed from abroad, spread to other parts of North Caucasus. By the mid-1990s the Islamic brand of the extremist and separatist virus had seriously affected Dagestan, Karachaevo-Cherkesia,

Kabardino-Balkaria, the Muslim areas of Savropol Krai and Tatarstan, apart from Chechnya-Ingushetia, a hot bed of Islamic terrorism in North Caucasus.

In 1999, the rise of radical Islam culminated in the incursion of several thousand Muslim militants from Chechnya into Dagestan with the objective of creating an Islamic state in the region. Several villages in Dagestan were completely under the control of Wahabbis, creating the impression that federal centre would lose control over the entire region very soon. The apartment building blasts in Moscow and other Russian cities in the autumn of 1999 provoked strong anti-Muslim, anti-Chechen and anti-Caucasus sentiments in Russia, leading to the resumption of military actions against the break-away republic.

In the changed situation, Russia's new Prime Minister Vladimir Putin launched an initiative to reassert federal control, using Chechnya as a testing ground for his policies. Putin launched a counter offensive to restore order in North Caucasus. Russian military action in Dagestan forced the Muslim militants to flee the republic which helped Putin re-establish state authority in the Muslim- dominated Dagestani villages of Chabanmakhi, Kadar and Karamakhi. After repelling Muslim militants from Dagestan, Putin launched military action in Chechnya, which enjoyed support from Russian people, in contrast to similar military operation in 1994-96. Russian troops captured Chechen capital Grozny in February 2000 after a prolonged war that caused huge losses. By the spring of 2000, Russian troops forced the rebellious regime, headed by Maskhadov, underground and established control over most part of the separatist republic.

Kadyrev Regime

President Putin's re-integration drive and bid to establish federal control and constitutional authority through the length and breadth of Russia, yielded some quick results. Despite its participation in some lawsuit against Putin's federal reforms, Adygea amended its constitution to fall in line with the federal constitution. Similarly, Kabardino –Balkaria adopted a new constitution in July 2001, removing provisions in republic's previous constitution that violated federal constitution, including clauses proclaiming republic's sovereignty and stating that republican laws takes precedence over federal laws. Ingushetia President General Aushev did not resist when the courts ordered removing provisions that violated federal law, and soon after resigned from his post.

In Checnya,the remnants of Maskhadov's ousted government remained defiant, despite loss of its capital Grozny and most of the territory of the republic. Russian forces dismantled Maskhadov's separatist regime, reducing it to a terrorist organisation with no governing capacity and a questionable hold over the Chechen population. A new pro-Moscow government with Chechen mufti Ahmed Kadyrev, a former ally of Maskhadov, was installed in the republic.

Dagestan's case was somewhat different. Moscow permitted Dagestan to maintain a political system in the republic that flouted the federal constitution. The system aimed at securing parity between republic's largest ethnic groups, stipulated proportional ethnic representation in the executive and legislative branches of the republic. Any attempt to change the system for corresponding to the federal laws would have destabilised the republic. Against the backdrop of the ethnic power-sharing arrangement that facilitated maintaining stability, Moscow hesitated to challenge the constitutionality of the prevailing system that was approved through three referandums. This ensured the republic's loyalty to the federal centre. Dagestan became one of the few republics to delete the autonomy clause from its constitution.Dagestan also surrendered several attributes of self-rule, including the authority to suspend federal laws that flouted republic's sovereignty, to participate independently in international relations and to unilaterally change republic's status within Russian federation. However, in July 2003 Moscow forced the republic to adopt a constitution that complied with the federal constitution.

While the regions of North Caucasus succumbed to Moscow's pressure to comply with federal laws, Tatarstan and Bashkortstan in Volga-Ural region for sometime challenged Kremlin's efforts to curb ethnic separatism. However, finally both the republics attempted to have compromise-solutions on the disputes with the federal government over their respective republican constitutions. Under pressure from Kremlin they amended their constitutions to reduce their degree of autonomy. Nevertheless, their constitutions retained the language that asserted their sovereign status and claimed some of the federal powers. Bashkortstan's new constitution approved in 2000 stipulated that the republic has the right to enter into international treaties, assert ownership over natural resources located in the republic's territory, and establish an independent republican citizenship. The new constitution incorporated the text of the 1994 power-sharing treaty between Bahkortstan and Federal centre, a document that proclaimed the republic to be a sovereign state. According to Russia's prosecutor General, eighty provisions of the republican constitution violated federal laws.[61]

Tatarstan, following in the footsteps of Bashkortstan, adopted a new constitution which surrendered few elements of autonomy but retained the republic's right to engage in international relations, to claim ownership over resources located on its territory and maintain separate republican citizenship. The new constitution described Tatarstan as a 'state united with the Russian federation' and maintained that the republican president is 'guarantor of sovereignty' of the republic. The constitution also incorporated the 1994 power-sharing treaty between Moscow and Kazan into the Tatar legal system and declared that the treaty, along with Tatar and Russian constitutions, to be defining determinants of Tatarstan's status within the larger federation. These provisions implied that Tatarstan maintained a separate statehood and was bound to Russia on a voluntary basis. The Russian Prosecutor General's office claimed that fifty provisions in the constitution violated the federal law.[62] President Putin seemed determined to initiate measures to establish constitutional authority on the entire territory of Russian Federation.

Along with continued military action in Chechnya, the Kremlin administration attempted to create a new ruling elite in the republics loyal to Moscow and build a loyal interior force consisting of primarily ethnic Chechens to ensure domestic security. Chechen mufti Ahmad Kadyrev, a former ally of Maskhadov, was appointed as head of Republic's administration. By choosing Kadyrov as head of the Republican administration,the Kremlin tried to capitalize on his status as Muslim religious leader and provide legitimacy to the local government. This tactics worked well for Moscow.

In order to further enhance the legitimacy of the Chechen government, Moscow announced that it would conduct a referendum in the republic in the spring of 2003 on a proposed law that would provide legal basis for electing a new Chechen government and creating a new constitution. This was planned to deligitimise Maskhadov, Chechnya's last elected president and curtail support for Islamic separatist forces. The proposed constitution offered an alternative to the Islamist constitution adopted under Maskhadov government in 1999, while providing Chechen people some degree of participation in forming a regional government to subsequently replace Kadyrov's administration installed by Moscow.

The draft constitution rejecting separatism declared, "The territory of Chechen republic shall be united and indivisible and shall be an inalienable part of the territory of the Russian federation." The draft further said, "The Chechen Republic is a secular state. No religion can be established as a state or compulsory religion."

Despite the separatists call to boycott the referendum held in March 2003, Chechens voted overwhelmingly in favour of both new constitution and legislation on electing a new regional government. The result reflected the mass mood for security and stability and lack of support for militant Chechen separatists and their Islamic goals.

Moscow adopted a two-pronged policy to establish its control over Chechnya. On the one hand, it continued its military campaign against the militant separatists, on the other it took steps to ensure Kadyrov stayed in power. Kadyrov won the presidential race thus ensuring federal authority in Chechnya.

In the Volga-Ural region, Moscow adopted a number of legal steps to neutralise assertions of national autonomy in Bashkortstan and Tatarstan. In April 2001, Moscow used the Russian Supreme Court's ruling that the federal government has the right to take legal action against republics that declined to remove sovereignty declaration clauses from their constitutions. This ruling empowered federal authorities to initiate legal procedures to dismiss republican presidents and dissolve local legislatures for not complying with federal constitution. The Russian Supreme Court further ruled that 37 articles of the Bashkir constitution flouted federal law and were henceforth invalid.[63]

A few months later the Bashkortstan authorities, succumbing to federal pressure, adopted a new constitution that had no mention of 'sovereignty' and did not retain the 1994 power- sharing treaty between Moscow and Ufa. Kremlin took a number of steps to establish federal authority in Tatarstan.

Putin procured support from the Russian State Duma, the lower house of the Russian parliament, in his bid to suppress challenges from Tatarstan and Bashkortstan within the policy of establishing Power Vertical in the disintegrating country. The State Duma adopted a bill that ended an attempt to legalize clauses in the constitutions of Tatarstan and Bashkortstan that allowed for separate republican citizenship.

The challenges posed by the rise of the separatist movements in Russia's Muslim-dominated regions, particularly in Chechnya—where militants fought for independence under the banner of Islam, influenced the evolution of federalism in post-soviet Russia. President Putin launched his campaign to re-establish federal control, abruptly ending Russia's ill-conceived experiment with asymmetrical and decentralised federalism.

After a decade of chaos and uncertainty, as Russia defines relations between the federal centre and the periphery, the attitude towards Islam and Russia's predominantly Muslim ethnic groups will serve as an important yardstick of whether the re-assertion of federal authority degenerates into intolerance and suppression of national minority rights.

Notes

1. Silantiyev, R.A. (2008), *Encyclopedia Islam in Contemporary Russia* (Энциклопедия ислама в современной России), Moscow: Algoritm.
2. Ibid.
3. Ibid.
4. Arapov D. (2001), *Islam in Russian Empire: Laws, Descriptions and Statistics* (Ислам в Российской империи : Законы, Описания и статистика), p. 40, Moscow.
5. Arapov D. (2001), *Islam in Russian Empire: Laws, Descriptions and Statistics* (Ислам в Российской империи : Законы, Описания и статистика), p. 45, Moscow.
6. Melkov S.A. (2003), Military-Sociological Survey: Collected Articles No. 4 (Военно-социологическое исследование : Сборник статей число 4), p. 37, Moscow.
7. Romanenko V.S. (2005), Cooperation between Soviet Diplomacy and Muslim Spiritual Community in the USSR in Twenties of the 20th Century, Novgorod.
8. I.S.Filatov, Traditsioniye religii,' russkaya tsivilizatsiya i suverenaya demokratiya,' in A.Malashenko's and S.Filatov eds, *religiya i konflikt*, Moscow: Carnegie Endowment, 2007, p. 42.
9. Ibid.
10. Malashenko, A. (2007), *Islam for Russia* (Ислам для России), Moscow: Rosspen.
11. Gainutddin, R. (2004), *Islam in contemporary Russia* (Ислам в современной России), Moscow: Grand.
12. Ibid., p. 54.
13. Ibid.
14. Ibid., p. 59.
15. Gainutddin, R. (2004), *Islam in contemporary Russia* (Ислам в современной России), Moscow.
16. Interfax, 6th February 2006.
17. Malashenko, A. (2007), *Islam for Russia* (Ислам для России), Moscow: Rosspen.
18. Ibid.
19. Ibid.
20. Hunter, T.S. (1984), *Islam in Russia*, New York: ME Sharpe.
21. Iran its neighbours and the regional crisis: a Middle East Program Report// Chatham House, The Royal Institute of International Affairs- [S.I]. 2006, p. 40.
22. Malashenko, A. (2007), *Islam for Russia* (Ислам для России), Moscow: Rosspen.
23. Melkov S.A. (2001), *Islamic Factor and military policy of Russia* (Исламский фактор и военная политика России), p. 54, Moscow: Moscow Military University.
24. Tabdrabrifikovi (2004), Bashkiriya: Confessional Life of the Republic, p. 12.
25. Magomedov A.M. (2002), "Realisation of State Religious Policy in Russian Federation and Dagestan" in *State and Religion in Dagestan*, Makhaskala, 3: 12-13.

26. Hunter, T.S. (1984), *Islam in Russia*, New York: ME Sharpe.
27. Ibid., p. 95.
28. Ibid.
29. Ibid.
30. Hunter, T.S. (1984), *Islam in Russia*, page 96, New York: ME Sharpe.
31. Ibid., p. 96.
32. Ibid.
33. Ibid.
34. News agency Interfax 26th March 2004.
35. www.Islam.ru
36. Data given by the Ministry of Regional Development quoted in Silantev, R.A. (2008), *Encyclopedia Islam in Contemporary Russia (*Энциклопедия ислама в современной России), Moscow: Algoritm.
37. URL:http://www.newsru.com/religy/23oct2007/kadirov. html
38. Malashenko, A. (2007), *Islam for Russia* (Ислам для России), Moscow: Rosspen.
39. Ibid.
40. Albakov, D. (2004), "Application of Shariat in Inghushetia" in Islam and law in Russia, (2): 82.
41. Nizavismaya Gazyeta Religia, date 27 February 1997.
42. Shamiyev, M. (2005), I took responsibility for myself" in Russia and Islamic World,(9):59.
43. Hunter, T.S. (1984), *Islam in Russia*, New York: ME Sharpe.
44. Hunter, T.S. (1984), *Islam in Russia*, New York: ME Sharpe.
45. Iskhakov, G. (1999), "Islam in Tatarstan: History and Modernity" in *Islamic World*,(1): 24
46. Melkov, S.A. (2002), Islam's Key Factor and its Influence on the Military Policy of Russia (Ключевой фактор ислама и его влияние на военной политики России), Moscow: Military University Moscow.
47. Ibid.
48. Melkov, S.A. (2002), Islam's Key Factor and its Influence on the Military Policy of Russia, Moscow: Military University Moscow.
49. ARMS-TASS, http://www.armstass.su/?page=article$aid=20735$cid=43
50. Melkov, S.A. (2002), Islam's Key Factor and its Influence on the Military Policy of Russia, Moscow: Military University Moscow.
51. Vremyanovosti 5th December 2006.
52. Hunter, T.S. (1984), *Islam in Russia*, New York: ME Sharpe.
53. Gainutddin, R. (2004), *Islam in contemporary Russia* (Ислам в современной России), Moscow: Grand.
54. Ibid., p. 29.
55. Hunter, T.S. (1984), *Islam in Russia*, New York: ME Sharpe.
56. Ibid.
57. Ibid.
58. Ibid.
59. Ibid.
60. Ibid., p. 224.
61. Ibid., p. 136.
62. Hunter, T.S. (1984), *Islam in Russia*, New York: ME Sharpe.
63. Ibid.

5. Muslim Integration with Russian Society

State's Role in the Integration Process

The State is required to formulate policies for facilitating political participation of religious communities, their civil society activities and improvement of their socio-economic conditions. The secular state has to play a role in organising religious governance and institutionalisation of religion, while maintaining the secular character of the state. The State has to resolve the differences, not only between various confessions, but also within a particular religion. On the whole it is the State's responsibility to integrate people of particular faith with it for the sake of security, stability and harmony in society. Let us analyse the Russian state's role in integrating Russian Muslims into its society.

Russia's approach to Muslim integration is a product of its distinct historical and political developments. It has been strongly influenced by the dominant role of religion in its history and the need to protect the Muslim population's cultural originality, while integrating them into the State for the interest of national security. The integration process in Russia takes place under the State in conditions of multi-ethnicity, multi-confessionalism, multi-nationalism and cultural diversity. Russian approach to State –Islam interaction is complex and distinctive because of its prolonged historical association with the country. The Russian integration process involves integration of not only Muslim migrants but also own ethnic Muslims, living on its territory for centuries, even before advent of the dominant religion, which is Orthodox Christianity.

The Muslim communities of Russia with their distinct ethnic, political and religious characteristics, have strong regional differences, ranging from moderate Islam in the Volga region to its radical movements in the North Caucasus. The most striking difference can be witnessed between Muslims of the Volga region and North Caucasus in the context of integration. While the integration process has been more successful in the Volga region,the rebellious mood against the Russian state is seen in North Caucasus. That is why the state has to pursue different policies towards different regions for resolving the integration issue. The sense of belonging to the state is stronger and efforts to centralise regional administration are more acceptable in the Volga and Ural regions than in North Caucasus. While separatists movement is almost absent in the Volga – Ural region, North Caucasus has become hotbed of terrorism, extremism and separatism, and thus has become a major source of concern for state security. Aware of the separatist mood and rebellious character, the State does not try to enforce central authority in North Causus as much as it does in case of the Volga-Ural region. The State desists from the attempts to undermine traditional sources of local and religious authority. Rather it tries to establish its authority there with their help along with the judicious use of traditions.

Muslim integration in Russia has been the product of a top-down assimilation process, combined with preservation of cultural autonomy. Starting from Catherine the Great's era to Putin's presidency,the State has been engaged in a process of assimilation as well liberal accommodation while dealing with the Muslim issue, in order to defend its national security and internal stability. The repressive Soviet methods of dealing with religion for the sake of promoting atheism led to the weakening of Muslim institutions.

In the post-Soviet period,while Yeltsin's regime pursued a policy of religious revival and respect for individual identities, Putin stressed on a policy that focuses on Russia's 'unique and synthesised 'identity. The objective is to build a strong multi-ethnic, multi-confessional and multi-cultural state. This is reflected in the State's effort to build closer ties with 'traditional religions ' and make best use of religious and social institutions to protect multinational, multi-cultural and multi-confessional unity and spiritual revival. In 2007, President Putin in his address to the Muslim leaders emphasised the multi-religious coexistence as an ' absolutely new form of cultural cooperation between different peoples and religions that constitutes Russia's inner strength as a great and important world power.

What is significant here is the idea of spiritual revival reflecting a fusion of religious and secular values.

The idea of inter-faith dialogue and multi-ethnic and multi-cultural strength dominates the State approach to Muslim integration. State authorities miss no occasion to reiterate that Russia's success lies in the strength of its moral values and ideals based on tolerance, inter-faith and inter-ethnic cohesion. However, Orthodoxy's special status sometimes does not fall in line with state efforts to construct a multifaceted Russian identity. The discourse on a separate Muslim identity has been developed within the concept of unity in diversity. This concept provides the State additional motivation to promote a kind of Muslim education that would facilitate inter-faith dialogue and create interlocutors committed to such a dialogue. The State has a vested interest in training imams under a programme that would meet the requirements of its national security and social stability. Though some experts criticize large-scale state funding of Muslim education that promotes values of inter-faith dialogue and harmony, it is indeed a prudent and productive step towards secular regulation of Muslim integration with Russian society in the interest of national security and social stability. In Russia, where civil society has not been adequately developed, the State partnership with Muslim organisations and State intervention in Muslim civil society organisations and clergy find their reputation tarnished in the eyes of some sections of Muslims if their association with the State is too close. That is why, the State and Muslim civil society, as well as its religious boards seek to build a mutual relationship which is productive, mutually beneficial without risking reputations. There is an understanding between State officials and Muslim leaders that the social stability and spiritual revival of the nation requires a consolidation of Muslim structures of administration, which can be effective only in close cooperation with the State structures. Growing security concerns as well as issues of social stability, created as a result liberal reforms of the 1990s, have justified the State's greater role in handling Muslim affairs.

Unity in the religious community and existence of a single central authority makes it easy for the state to handle it. On the other hand,the State can use the contradictions and rivalry within the community to maintain its hold over it. A major source of division within Russian Muslim community is the rivalry between Russia's two most famous and important leaders- Ravil Gainutdin and Talgat Tadzuddin. A variety of factors that include ethnic differences– Gainutdin is a Tatar,whereas Tadzhudin is a Bashkir,there are doctrinal and political disagreements and also a bid to be the supreme Muslim leader, all which have contributed to the rivalry between the two prominent leaders of Russian Muslims. This rivalry came to the surface in September 1994 when Tadzuddin attempted to remove Gainuddin as leader of Moscow Cathedral Mosque as he was leading the prayer. Gainutdin, in response, resigned from the structure of the CSBM. Subsequently, during the 7th Extraordinary Congress of Muslims of Russia and European countries of CIS, organised at the initiative of Tadzhuddin in Ufa in January 1995, the delegates representing 2500 Muslim communities revoked the religious title of Mufti Ravil Gainutdin and prohibited him from performing his duties as a Muslim religious leader under the pretext that he was "supporting divisive actions of Arab organisations" and "violating traditional canons of Russian Islam." Since then, accusations of Wahhabism against Gainutdin and deviation against Tadzuddin have become a hallmark of their rivalry. Tadzuddin on a number of occasions has accused Gainutdin and his organisation of harbouring sympathy for Wahhabism. On one occasion, he called the All Russian Islamic University, established in Kazan with the support of RCM,the source of Wahhabi cadres for entire Russia.[1]

The Gainutdin-led RCM retaliated with the following statement:

In the television programme 'Itogi' of 14th November 1999, one of the leaders of Muslims, Talgat Tadzhudin accused practically all Muslims of Russia, and nearly all spiritual administrations of the country, of being the "enemies of the people" and "Wahhabites". We pray to the almighty Allah that He would forgive the unfortunate man, but resolutely oppose those forces that unleashed with his hands the Islamophobic campaign in the mass media.[2]

Doctrinal differences as well as varying interpretations of Islam constitute a major source of dispute between the two leaders. Tadzuddin's beliefs are considered as more eclectic and, even heretical, according to orthodox Muslims. His rather unorthodox views have disappointed many sections of Muslims and form a source of rivalry between the two leaders. In early the 1990s, statements made and events organised by Tadzuddin were viewed as by many sections of Muslims as heretical. He tried to create a fourth holy site for Muslims in Russia in the small town of Bulgar in Tatarstan. On many occasions, he participated in Muslim prayers wearing the mantle of an Orthodox Christian priest. In an interview to *Nezavisimaya Gazeta,* during a religious conference in Ufa, Gainutdin claimed that Tadzudin appeared at the Ufa Cathedral Mosque dressed as an Orthodox Christian cleric and proposed the idea of unifying all regions. He proceeded to place Orthodox

Christian icons in the mosque until the members of the local congregation disrupted his actions.[3]

The two leaders have divergent views on the question of Wahhabism in Russia. While Tadzhuddin has been consistently opposing the spread of Wahhabism in Russia, Gainutdin's views on the vexed issue are reflected in his subtle criticism of the Kremlin's anti-Wahhabi policies, rhetoric and reluctant approval. In June 2001 during President Putin's visit to the newly built Moscow Lya Lya Tyulpan in Ufa, Tadzhuddin expressed his opinion on the penetration of foreign Muslim missionaries in to Russia, stating, "We do not want to have Wahhabis in our country and also those who come from foreign lands and want to educate us... From ancient times Orthodox Christianity and Islam went hand in hand and for almost 300 years they were the foundation of our statehood."[4]

Tadzhuddin believes that the most serious challenges faced by Russia's Muslim establishment are the adverse impact of foreign-inspired doctrines and the necessity of revitalising traditional Russian Islam. In an interview to *NezavisimayaGazeta,* Tadzhuddin said, "The main problems of Russia's Muslims are to rebuild traditional Islam and to fight against religious extremism, terrorism, and one of its manifestations-Wahhabism."[5]

Tadzhuddin endorses government policies on other crucial issues touching Islam. Regarding Chechnya, he maintains, "The Chechen people should not be hostage of the so-called Islamist gang formations, Wahhabites, or similar pseudo religious figures, regardless of what they use to hide their criminal intentions. The actions of the authorities fully correspond to international and religious laws."[6]

By contrast, Gainutdin on these issues holds a somewhat different position. His views on Chechnya and Wahhabism appears more sympathetic to them and cautious. Gainutddin seems to have adjusted his views with passage of time, which is evident when you compare his statements on the first and second Chechen wars. Expressing his views on first Chechen war, in an interview he said, "The minority,Chechens are confronting the majority and the Russian army as a whole. We should have known their national character, their patriotic attitudes, responding to the call of the Holy Quran." However, adjusting his views on the second Chechen war, he adopted a less sympathetic position towards the separatist Chechen cause by saying, "Perhaps from a theological point of view Ahmad Kadyrov could have interpreted the invasion of Russian troops (in the first Chechen war) as an attempt to thwart the freedom of Chechen people. Then he had the right to do so. But now the situation is entirely different. The Chechen armed formations invaded the territory of Dagestan and drew fire upon them.[7]

On the problem of penetration of foreign radical Islam into Russia, and particularly spread of Wahhabism, Gainutddin's views have altered between tacit approvals to subtle condemnation. In an interview to Russian national daily *Nezavisimaya Gazeta*, he explained Wahhabism in the following way: "If we interpret Wahhabism as the media and politicians interpret it daily, then of course, I would view it negatively. The sad truth is that Wahhabism is understood only as the ideology of extremism and terrorism. However, Wahhabism is the official ideology of the Kingdom of Saudi Arabia, where there is no terrorism or extremism that would be rooted in Wahhabism". This view is not unconventional and corresponds to the views of Russian-baiter Western scholars.

Gainutddin does not buy the alarmist views about spread of Wahhabism in Russia. In this connection he stated, "I think all talks about some sort of targeted religious expansion against Russia by Muslim states are entirely unfounded." He issued warning against adoption of laws that would restrict religious activities of Muslim organisations, saying that "adoption of any legislation that would prohibit Wahhabism would be undoubtedly discriminatory to the rights and constitutional reforms of Muslims of Russia."[8]

Implications of Inter-Mufti Rivalry:

The rivalry between Tadzuddin and Gainutdin can have far-reaching implications for the organisations they represent as well as negative implications for Muslim community and various organisations at different levels across the country. The rivalry transcends the administrative boundaries and has serious potential to aggravate relations between Muslim organisations that are under the religious jurisdiction of competing centralised spiritual administrations. This potentially dangerous process can engulf regions, cities, towns, and villages across the country. For example, the Spiritual Board of Muslims of Omsk district under the leadership of Mufti Zulkarni Shakirziyanov is aligned with the CSBM and is bitterly opposed to the Spiritual Board of Muslims of the Asian Part of Russia, headed by Nafigulla Ashirov and associated with the RCM. Similar disagreements and conflicts exist in other places, particularly in Penza and Tyumen districts, the autonomous okrugs of Yamalo—Nenets and Khanty-Mansi, Krasnoyarski Krai and the Altai republic.[9]

There is a bitter struggle for establishing control over the mosque of the Volga region town of Bulgar in Tatarstan since 1997 between the Spiritual Board of Muslims of the Tatarstan, headed by Mufti Gusman Ishkakov, and the self-proclaimed Mufti of Tatastan, Farid Salaman, representing the interests of Mufti Talgat Tadzuddin in the republic. At the Unifying Congress of Muslims of Tatarstan held in February 1998, he was one of the six candidates for the post of chairman of the autonomous Spiritual Board of Muslims (SBM) of the Tatarstan republic. After losing the race to become the Mufti of Tatarstan, Farid Salaman worked in the newly constituted SBM of the republic as the chairman of the Commission on Compliance of Literature with the Shariat. Subsequently, after accusing the SBM of misappropriating funds and adhering to Wahhabism, he left the organisation and declared himself as mufti of Tatarstan under spiritual supervision of Tadzuddin. Salaman occupied the mosque in the city of Bulgar with the help of his supporters. All attempts to gain access to the mosque by a commission appointed by Tatarstan's SBM to investigate the dispute ended in failure.[10]

Finally in February 2002, the Tatar SBM, with the support of the local authorities, regained control over the mosque.[11]

There were similar incidents in other cities too.

Competition for Government Sympathy

Differences and rivalry between Gainutdin and Tadzudin lead to unhealthy competition by the two leaders for getting more support and sympathy from Kremlin. They regularly issue public statements endorsing the Kremlin position on important issues in order to be in its good books. Gainutddin, who had differences with Kremlin on critical issues, has adjusted his views over time to demonstrate loyalty to the federal centre. To illustrate, on 16th March, 2000, supreme mufti Talgat Tadzhudin supported the counter-terrorist campaign in Chechnya and said that the war in Chechnya is not against Islam, but for the restoration of law and order. In his speech, commemorating the end of the holy month of Ramadan at the Moscow Cathedral Mosque in January 2001, Mufti Ravil Gainutdin echoed the same sentiment. Commenting on President Putin's speech on the same occasion, he said, by speaking in defense of our religion against groundless accusations, he stressed that Russia does not fight with Islam, nor does it wage war against people practicing Islam. This shows how both Muslim leaders strive to demonstrate their loyalty to the regime.

Gainutdin devoted a lot of time and effort to develop contacts within both executive and legislative branches of the Russian government. According to Farid Asaddulin, Ravil Gainutdin established regular consultations and meetings with the members of the cabinet of ministers of the Russian Federation as well as with influential political figures on a nall-Russia scale, such as president Vladimir Putin, Ramazan Abdulatipov, Gennady Zuganov, Valei Kokov,Yuri Luzhkov, Mintimir Shamiyev, Boris Gromov and others".[12]

As a result, the spiritual structures controlled by Gainutdin enjoyed the support of officials from the presidential administration and the Moscow mayor's office. The distribution of federal funds to Muslim religious organisations is a good indicator of the quality of the relationship between the government and various spiritual administrations. In 1995, the Supreme Coordinating Council of Spiritual Boards of Muslims of Russia received 1.2 million rubles in government subsidies, Gainutdin's Spiritual Board of Muslims of the central European region of Russia received 3.5 million rubles, and the CSBM of Tadzhuddin received 2.2 million rubles. Until the late 1990s the Kremlin administration under Vladimir Putin supported Gainutdin and his organisation because they succeeded in guiding Muslims in favour of Putin in the presidential elections of March 2000.

Gainutdin on his part has stressed his loyalty to President Putin whenever he has had a chance to do so. In the fundamental principles of the social programme of Russian Muslims, he compared Putin's statement to the sayings of the Prophet Muhammad.

The Russian government has made attempts to bridge the gap between rival groups of Muslim clerics. The first step in this direction was taken by the participants in the aforesaid roundtable discussion on 'The Islamic Factor in Russian Politics' on the occasion of the inauguration of the Tauba mosque in Nizhny Novgorod. The participants did not come to a comprehensive agreement on all issues of concern. Nonetheless, they signed a joint resolution that outlined their common aspirations. In particular, the declaration expressed the signatories' willingness to work together on unifying standards in all Muslim educational institutions of the Volga federal district, irrespective of their official religious affiliations. The participants unanimously pledged to oppose the spiritual and moral decay of society, not to allow inter-ethnic and inter-confessional animosity, to counter religious deviation and sectarianism that are potentially dangerous for the society, and to implement multilateral programmes aimed at lowering the level of crime, alcoholism, and drug addiction. The fact that Talgat Tadzhudin and Nafigulla Ashirov, who represented the interests of the RCM and its leader Ravil Gainutdin, sat at the same table was in itself remarkable.

The Nizhny Novgorod meeting could potentially be a promising development, and under favourable conditions, could promote the normalisation and stabilisation of Muslim spiritual life in Russia. Yet despite Ashirov's participation in the conference, Moscow still plays the two leaders against on another, depending on the situation. For example, in 2000, Moscow began shifting its favours from Gainutdin to Tadzudin. Several factors accounted for this deterioration of relations between Gainutdin and Russian government. First of all, the relative deterioration in relations between the federal government and the republic of Tatarstan, where Gainutdin enjoys lot of support, gave rise to disagreements between Gainutdin and the Kremlin, particularly regarding the cultural and religious rights of Tatar Muslims. These disagreements are partly related to Moscow's recentralisation strategy and partly owing to Tatar leadership's decision to change the alphabet in the republic from Cyrillic to Latin, there by raising Russian fears of Turkification in Tatarstan. Secondly, as relations between the Russian council of muftis and government have strengthened, Gainutdin has displayed more assertiveness and independence. On a number of controversial issues, Gainutdin's opinions, though always not very consistent, have frequently demonstrated ambivalence towards and occasionally divergence from the official position. This assertiveness has led to certain degree of disillusionment among government officials who previously favoured Moscow's mufti. Thirdly, the Orthodox Church to some extent has promoted Tadzhudin. The proposal to invite Tadzhudin to participate at the meeting of the inter-religious council of Russia came from the representatives of the Russian Orthodox Church, which has the leading role in the council. This position of the Church is not surprising, given Tadzhidin's more relaxed and less orthodox beliefs, which appear less challenging to the Church.

According to some Russian scholars, the Kremlin's recent support of Tadzhudin reflects the view in some circles of the Russian government. It is more expedient to have strong relations with Tadzhudin and his centre in Ufa rather than with Gainuddin and his headquarters in Moscow. Some scholars maintain that this change in government's attitude is also related to Kremlin's decision to employ various Islamic authorities to popularize pro-Moscow policies. Under these circumstances, Gainutdin's more and more independent stand and his relations with foreign Muslim organisations make him a less desirable partner for the Russian government, which is keen on exercising more and more control over Muslim religious leadership.

Islamic opposition in the country consists of Muslims opposed to the state authority,spiritual leaders refusing to cooperate with the authorities and contemplating Islamic alternative for which a jihad should be launched. This opposition is supported by religious fanatics, terrorists,Muslim fundamentalists, extremists etc. According to Malashenko, Islamic extremists take resort to banditry while criminals use Islamic rhetorics, trying to project them as fighters for faith.

However, there is democratic Muslim opposition in the country, that fights against state's sometimes undesirable intervention and put forth demands to improve socio-economic conditions of Russian muslims.

Terrorism in Russia is associated with radical Islamic opposition in the country. The State has waged a relentless war against Islamic extremists and terrorists and their actions often evokes anger among the Muslim masses, loyal to the state as a whole.

Inter-Faith Dialogue and Islam

Russia is a multi-ethnic and poly-confessional state. Many experts, however, fail to understand that multi-ethnic and multi-confessional character of Russia is different from that of countries like US, Britain or France which practice multi-culturalism. One has to take note of the difference between the multi-ethnic character of Russia or India on the one hand and US, France, Britain on the other. Contrary to the US or France, Russian believers practicing traditional religions, live in predominantly compact territory. For example, Russian Muslims have been living in the Volga-Ural region and North Caucasus for centuries. Nearly 18 % of population,not belonging to Russian ethnicity, live in their historical territory, accounting for half the territory of the Russian state.

While speaking about interaction of ethnic and civilisational factors, it is important to note the special feature of Russian civilisation, reflected in mutual interaction between Russian ethnos and other Russian people.

In contrast to the North American 'melting pot', Russian people played the integrating role in Russian civilisation, being the centre of cultural attraction, not only for Slavic but also for Turkic, Finno-ugric and other people. It must be said that in the civilisational aspect, Russian people act as Russiski people rather than just ethnic Russians. Without the integrating role of the Russian people, and particularly the Russian language, Russian society cannot survive; at the same time there can be no Russia without the voluntary union of other ethno-confessional people living on its territory.

Long collective living within the framework of a single state, centuries-old spiritual, social and human links, a joint creation of cultural values and state structure, its joint defense, common fortunes and misfortunes—all these form common feelings by multi-ethnic and poly-confessional people for the destiny of Russia. There are centuries old traditions of tolerant co-existence while preserving original ethno-confessional culture. Russian Muslims have inherited this from the Tatar-Mongol Golden Horde, during whose rule Orthodox Church did not pay tax, possessed judicial rights over its subjects and used the freedom to elect spiritual leaders. The Russian Orthodox Church also had similar traditions of not only tolerant co-existence but also support to people of other faiths.

It goes without saying that as a result of centuries-old co-existence, interaction and inter-penetration between Orthodox Christian Culture and Islamic culture, Russian Muslims deeply integrated with Russian society and became integral part of its historical development. It is dangerous to ignore this fact or belittle its importance. That is why opposition to Islam or a fight against Islam in Russia would tantamount to fighting against its own people.

It is a paradox but true that co-existence of Orthodox Christianity and Islam continues in Russia from the period of Golden Horde led by Tatar-Mongols. It should be mentioned that there was a strong influence of the Orthodox Christianity in Russia during the rule of Golden Horde. Orthodox Christianity lost its status officially when Khan Uzbek tried to convert all his subjects to Islam and hanged all those who protested against his policy.[13]

It is possible that Islam was embraced by the entire ruling class while different religions were practiced by various sections of common people. In this context, leading Russian expert on Islam, Professor R. Landa says that it is surprising that during this period the strengthening of Islam in the Golden Horde was accompanied by the strengthening of Orthodox Christianity in Rus.[14]

The Tatar –Mongols inherited wonderful tolerance, in any case to some degree till the rule of Khan Uzbek, which largely determined the formation of the Russian super-ethnos. Subsequently, Russians continued to show a tolerant attitude towards the sovereignty of the Khan for centuries. This helped Russians to preserve their religion and culture. Even during the dominance of the Golden Horde, Orthodox Christianity played a leading role in the spiritual life of Russia and the Russian East. From this period, Orthodox Church became the owner of vast swathes of property. The metropolitans were functioning independent of the local kings. Many Russian kings receiving the permission from the Golden Horde to rule over their territory voluntarily sent their children for education in the ambit of the Golden Horde. While all this is very well, it must be also emphasised that the Golden Horde played a devastating role in the history of Russians and Russian state by slowing down its socio-economic progress. There is a viewpoint that the Tatar-Mongol impact facilitated the formation of a unified, centralised Russian state from out of the warring and bankrupt kingdoms— and that the Golden Horde is the source of centralised Russian statehood. The Golden Horde played its role in spreading Islam in Russia, in the formation of Russian super-ethnos and centralised Russian state.

While speaking about the Golden Horde, White Horde and Blue Horde, it should be said that they were states in which an important role was played by very different people and cultures, not just the Tatar-Mongols. Eminent Russian scholar Lev Gumilev assesses highly the Golden Horde's contribution to the formation of the Russian state, though this view is believed to be highly exaggerated by other scholars.

The Destiny of Russia was always strongly associated with the Islamic world, which is why the Russian state incorporated the khanates of Kazan, Astrakhan, Siberia, Crimea, Caucasus and Central Asia into its territory. This is also part of Tatar-Mongol heritage.

In the history of the Russian people and Russian state, relations between Orthodox Christians and Muslims were complicated but tolerant. Their inter-relations intensified after incorporation of the khanets of Kazan, Crimea, Siberia and then Caucasus into Russian territory. The Islamic influence was reflected in Russian architecture. This is particularly seen in the St. Vasily Blozheni Church, located in the Red Square in Moscow, and the monasteries of the Kremlin Palace.

Lev Gumolev in his writings shows how intensive were the interactions between the Russians and Tatars. Russian historians Kantemir and Karamzin, poets and writers Derzhabin, Ogarev, Turgenev, Dostoyevski, Kuprin, Bulgakov,great scientists like Mendeleyev, Mechnikov, Pavlov, Timiryazev, famous artists like Anna Pavlova, Galina Ulanova, Skryabin, Taneyev, Shishkin etc had Tatar-Muslim roots. According to Lev Gumilev, Czar Boris and Fyodor Godunov, the wife of Vasily 111 and wife of Czar Fydor Ivanovich also had Tatar roots.[15]

From the time of penetration of Islam into Russia there is an ongoing process of not only its expansion but also 'postizheniye'.This process takes place in the dialogue with orthodox Christianity and other traditional faiths of Russia. This complex process took place over centuries and continues currently. This process was discontinued during Soviet period but still had its own special feature. During the Soviet era, the authorities fought against religions but at the same time fought as fiercely against interfaith conflict. The relevance of co-existence of Orthodox Christianity and Islam has grown in the post-Soviet Russia,because there is an attempt to use the new-found freedom to establish the supremacy of truth and faith, even by those who are far from truth and faith. That is why there is a need for tolerance, culture and respect for other faiths because everybody is convinced about the genuineness of his choice. Russia covered the path from the declaration of Islam as a false religion— to being the enemy of the Orthodox Christianity — to the recognition of the necessity for equal dialogue with it. In principle they shared the common destiny of one and the same country.

Cooperation between various religions is a complicated and contradictory process not only in Russia but in many other multi-confessional countries. Though, on the surface one finds tolerance in the country, existing religions have questions and pretensions against each other. There are serious differences within Orthodox Christianity and Islam. There is a search for religious identity by the people. But here it is important to preserve civil identity. It is not always possible to talk about tolerance towards Islam in Russia, but it is a fact that Islam was always tolerated and respected. This is a significant achievement in comparison to many countries of Europe. It must be recognised that the former head of the Orthodox Church, Aleksei-11, current head of Russian Orthodox Church Metropolit Kiril, mufti Ravil Gainutdin, Talgat Tazudin, Nafigula

Ashirov,Saigid Abubakarov, Akhmad Kadyrev,Mahammed Albogachiyev, chief Rabin of Russia A, Shaevich, head of the Armenian Church Tiran Kyurekian, archbishop episcope (bishop) of theCatholic Church Tadeush Kandrusevich and the Buddhist community of Russia have all contributed greatly to promote inter faith dialogue in Russia.

It is believed that there was a policy of 'Russiafication and Christianisation 'in pre-revolutionary Russia and the former Soviet Union. This is only partly true. However it is not at all prudent to look at the events of the past retrospectively as a special policy against any particular people or religion. Those processes touched all religions of Russia-Orthodox Christianity, Islam, Buddhism, Eudaism etc. However, it must be acknowledged that there was a process of co-existence between Orthodox Christianity and Islam in a country with a predominantly Orthodox Christian population. This process was very difficult and did not always pass through peaceful stages.

Certain developments in the post-Soviet Russia evoke misunderstandings when in a secular and multi-confessional country you find authorities giving priority to one particular religion for political purpose. Interestingly, the nearer Russia becomes to the West,the stronger is the threat to Russians by Islam.

The explosion of religious consciousness in the absence of necessary intellectual training and spiritual maturity of the people leads to the rise of mutual intolerance, not only between followers of different religions, but even within one faith. The real state policy should be built taking multi-ethnicity and multi-confessionalism into account. Ethnic and religious factors are part and parcel of social-spiritual structure of Russian reality and statehood.

There are various forces which try to discredit Islam as they do it with other religions too. Quite often everything is done to discredit Islam with a political objective and to project Orthodox Christianity as the official religion of the Russian state. In certain Muslim dominated regions of Russia Islam is also projected in a similar manner. Such actions bring back the memory of how the Czarist autocracy deliberately planted Orthodox Christianity in Muslim dominated regions.

The interfaith situation in Russia largely depends on relations between Orthodox Christian Church and Muslim spiritual boards, Orthodox Christians and Muslims. Today these relations are quite positive. The State has to create conditions for equal dialogue between confessions and should not permit discrimination of citizens on the basis of religion.

Islam and Muslims are not looked down upon as alien to Russian reality. It has to be understood that Russian spirituality would be incomplete without Islam and Islamic culture. At the same it is necessary to understand the important role played by Orthodox Christianity in uniting Russian people and formation of the Russian state.[16]

However, hyping the exclusive role of Orthodox Church in the formation of Russian state is lopsided and undesirable. This kind of thought process can be harmful for the unity of Russia's society and state.

There has always existed a philosophical and ideological basis for dialogue between Orthodox Christians and Muslims in the Sate, and it exists even today, because it is believed that these two religions are close to each other in terms of content and major principles. In this context Islam and Orthodox Christianity are basic elements of Russian spirituality. All the Russians are united by the common historical destiny of Russian confessions and common historical responsibility for Russia and for its spiritual situation.

An Inter-confessional council was set up in December 1998 for the first time after the All Russia Islamic Conference and this organisation united representatives of all major confessions of the country. However, its activities have been limited without adequate state support.

The complex of Church, Mosque, Synagogue etc built at Poklonoya Gora, Moscow is destined to play important role in the interfaith dialogue. The dialogue between Orthodox Christianity and Islam is important for maintaining stability in Russian society. This can be based on the accumulated experience over centuries. People of both faiths have shown their inclination for this through their actions.

The desire of traditional confessions for strengthening indigenous foundation of Russian statehood, their support for national traditions and the original culture of people play an important role in this, particularly during the critical periods of history. Similar positive contributions of traditional religions (Orthodox Church, Islam, Buddism, and Zorastrianism) can be found in the prevailing complex political and spiritual situation of Russia.

The peace-loving activities of leaders of traditional Russian religions are quite commendable in contemporary Russia. The spiritual leaders of Orthodox Church and Islam have contributed significantly in resolving conflicts in regions like Chechnya and Tatarstan. The majority (almost

70%) of the people believe in the peace-building potential of religious organisations. The majority of the population dismiss the possibility of inter-confessional conflicts in Russia. Around 75% of Orthodox Christians and 68% Muslims do not accept the exclusive character of any religion. Many people believe that inter-ethnic and inter-confessional conflict may lead to the collapse of the state. The call to build a religion- based state can hardly strengthen the society. Supporters of such an idea forget that the equal and free development of the ethno-confessional originality of the people, which links their historical destiny with Russia, constitutes the basis for preservation of unique Russian civilisation.

Dialogue between Orthodoxy and Islam in Russia

There has been a mutual dialogue between Orthodox Christianity and Islam in Russia for centuries. This dialogue is one of the popular themes in the press and is often addressed by spiritual leaders of both confessions. In conditions created by a multi-confessional country, this dialogue is no doubt very essential, but has never been easy. One of the aspects of this dialogue is mutual understanding and mutual tolerance between Orthodox Christians and Muslims.

During the Soviet era, there was no problem since inter-confessional differences were being ignored. However, the post-Soviet period has witnessed the revival of religious identity, which at times brings inter-faith differences to the fore. Inter-faith differences do create problems in national consolidation. For example, during Russo-Turkey war in the beginning of 19th century, Russian Muslims refused to fight against their co-believers, and their desire not to fight against their religious brothers was taken into consideration by the government. If we look at more recent period, starting from the Afghan war– to conflict in Yugoslavia, Moscow has been involved in a situation that has a strong Islamic dimension. During the Balkan crisis, while the Russian government and Russian Orthodox Christians were expressing solidarity with their Orthodox Christian brothers in Yugoslavia, many Russian Muslims were showing sympathy for their Muslim brethren there. Despite the inter-faith harmony that dominates in Russian society,the rise of Islam-phobia, for whatever reason, can not be ignored. Tension between the two communities in different regions has been also reported in the press. However, leaders of both faiths, despite certain suspicions of each other, are engaged in efforts to maintain inter-faith harmony. Regular interaction between the leaders of both religions no doubt plays an important role in maintaining this harmony and constitutes part of inter-faith dialogue.

Proximity between Russian political leadership and the Orthodox Christian leadership and repeated statements of members of ruling elite about their loyalty towards Orthodoxy, have caused some dissatisfaction among Russian Muslims. The statement of Ravil Gainutdin, chairman of Russian Mufti Council, that Islam also has the right to enjoy similar favours that Orthodox Christianity enjoys from the authorities, is a pointer in this direction. The Russian Muslim spiritual leadership does not have a common stand on how to develop a dialogue with Orthodox Christianity. A major part of the Muslim spiritual leadership, consisting of leaders like Ravil Gainutdin, head of the spiritual board of Asian part of Russia Nafigulla Ashirov, Nizhegorod mufti Omar Idrisov etc, insisting on equal status for both the religions, argues against dominance of any particular religion in the multi-confessional democratic state. The other part of the leadership led by Talgat Tazuddin, head of the Central Muslim Spiritual Board, is inclined to accept the special status of Orthodox Christianity. He misses no occasion to emphasize his close relations with Moscow Patriarchy and enjoys its goodwill.

It is interesting to compare the social concept advances by both the religions in this context..The basic social concept of the Russian Orthodox Church approved in August, 2000 and the basic tenets of the social programme of Russian Muslims prepared by Russian mufti council in 2001 reflect the perpetual relevance of issues of interaction between the two main confessions of Russia. Geopolitical sustain ability and societal harmony of Russia to a great extent are determined by the accord and understanding between the two cultural-historical entities- Orthodox Christian and Muslim communities. In this regard Christian–Islamic dialogue is one of the central elements for civic accord in Russia.

Doctrinal interactions between the two religions require consideration of their differences. The famous Russian religious philosopher and historian L. Krasavin in this regard had said, "Religious tolerance cannot lead to recognition of similar values of all, even of conflicting religious teachings. Then it would become non-religious indifference from religious tolerance. It can be said about spiritual- practical tolerance, which means principled refrain from violence towards people other faith".

Orthodox Christianity historically witnessed the experience of a close co-existence with Islam. As a result, it is not doctrinal but a practical element in which cultural- civilisational interaction is more important than theological dispute that becomes the determining factor in Christian- Islam dialogue. This is true for Russia where Orthodox Christians and Muslims, starting from 13th century, lived in one state, first in the Golden Horde era and subsequently in the Russian state. Moreover, people of Muslim culture constitute part of the state–forming Russian people.

Under such conditions, in Orthodoxy–Islam dialogue, practical requirements took precedence over doctrinal differences, which reinforced mutual tolerance in their consciousness. Close interaction with the Muslim world facilitated formation of such feature in Russian character like religious tolerance.

All this created favourable conditions for close cultural interaction. It is believed that in the early historical period,the Muslim culture of the Turkic people was a donor for the Slavic-Christian culture. Orthodox Christians accepted the achievements of the Islamic world in the sphere of military organisation, state building etc with pleasure. The two faiths exchanged their roles in the subsequent period. Muslim culture became the recipient from Russian Orthodox Christian culture, particularly in the sphere of art, natural sciences, and technical knowledge etc. Towards the beginning of 20th century the Muslim population of Russia identified itself as the 'Russian Muslim community.' The great Russian religious thinker Ivan Ilin noting the influence of orthodox Christianity on the faiths of other Russian people wrote that, "Orthodox Christianity preserved and carefully developed all that other branches of Christianity, Islam, Eudism and Paganism left on it".

As a result of Catherine The Great's religious reforms, the Orenburg Spiritual Assembly, with a mufti as its head, was created. And the Muslim community in Russia got an hierarchical organisation similar to Church, though the institute of the Church is absent in Islam. The Islamic influence can be seen in the church architecture of the 16th-17th centuries.

Contrary to the Catholic Church which pays significant attention to issues related to status of other religions, the Orthodox Christian world does not have a holistic doctrinal approach towards Islam. Eminent Church leaders of Russia emphasise their respectful attitude towards Islam. Famous Archbishop Vladimir in his interview to Russian national daily *Nezavisimaya Gazetta* described Islam as a friendly religion of Orthodox Christianity, whose main characteristics are enlightenment, religious tolerance and openness.

The emergence of an official social doctrine of the Russian Orthodox Church and the Muslim organisations of Russia heralds a new stage in the dialogue between Orthodox Christianity and Islam. Although the document, drafted by Russian Council of Muftis,lags behind in the concept developed by Orthodox Church in terms of details, it lays down the basic principles of religion-state relations and position of Muslim organisations on social issues.

A comparative analysis of both documents shows that none of them claims the status of state religion and both of them recognise the secular character of the Russian state and maintain patriotic positions. Both the religions advocate social partnership with the state and stand for constructive interaction acknowledging mutual obligations. The Muslim social doctrine favours cooperation with the secular state, pleading for the concept of accord that suggests mutual obligations accepted by state and Muslim organisations.[17]

The document stands for participation in resolution of social problems including preservation of spirituality in the society, high moral standards, religious tolerance, and fraternal relations between people of different nationalities. There are similarities in both the documents on issues of inter-ethnic relations, issues of war and peace, science, culture and education, preservation of cultural heritage etc.

The chapter on Church and Nation in the Orthodox Church's document and the chapter on 'Islam and Nation' in the Muslim document emphasises the supra-national character of both religions, without supremacy of any religion over others. Both the documents stress that different countries and people possess full rights for their national and cultural originality.

On the chapter on 'War and Peace', both documents permit the possibility of war for defending their motherland. In this connection, the Islamic social programme provides a special explanation of 'jihad', which according to it does not have anything in common with war with religious objectives.

Both the documents give importance to the preservation and multiplication of the cultural heritage and traditions of people of Russia. While the Orthodox Christian concept says cultural traditions help in preserving and multiplying spiritual heritage in the dynamically changing world, the Islamic document notes that they are sources of national-religious self-consciousness.

The chapter on 'Relations of Muslims towards Representatives of Other Religions' has a lot of significance for inter-faith dialogue in Russia. The chapter notes that a tolerant attitude towards representatives of other religious traditions is determined by not subjective human desires but by the will of Allah and canonic foundation of religious tolerance comes from Quran and Sunna. Mutually respectful dialogue and cooperation in the social sphere with the believers of other traditional faiths of Russia is recognised as a very important task.[18]

Similar approaches and positions of both the social doctrines on a wide range of issues create an objective basis for constructive inter-faith interaction and dialogue.

The Cooperation between Orthodox Church and Islam could be most effective in the following areas -peace-keeping and patriotic activities, prevention of interfaith and international conflicts between both Orthodox Christian and Muslim communities.

While talking about interfaith dialogue between Orthodox Christianity and Islam, we must pay attention to the media discourse about the possibility of geopolitical turmoil in Russia as a result of large scale conflict between the two against the backdrop of the Huntington's concept of Clash of Civilisations. The proponents of the concept maintain that wherever Islamic world comes in touch with non-Islamic world, there emerge 'bloody borders', which is confirmed by Palestine-Israeli conflict, developments in Kosovo and Chechnya. There is also a viewpoint that such confirmation does not stand on firm foundation, and is a reaction of western political science with the aim by Muslim countries to form independent strategic policy towards us and their allies.

According to Russian expert Professor Mchedlov, world experience shows that most prolonged and acute conflicts with religious colour occur not in those regions where there is no multi- religious composition of population but rather in those regions where confessional groups live compactly in their historical territories. Russia has two such zones – the Volga–Ural region and the North Caucasus. The geopolitical sustainability of Russia, as well as perspective of further development of Russian society and state, depends on the level of constructive interaction between Orthodox Christians and Muslims. In this connection it is pertinent to look at the contemporary relations between Orthodox Christians and Muslims in those regions, including the historical status of Russian Orthodox Church there.

Orthodox Christianity penetrated into the Volga-Ural region long before they were incorporated into the Russian state. Structures of Orthodox Church emerged here during the rule of the Golden Horde. After Tatarstan and Astrakhan Khanet were incorporated into Russian territory, one of the largest centres of Russian orthodox Christians emerged in the Volga-Ural region. With the opening of Kazan Spiritual Academy in 1797, Kazan emerged as one of the most important centres of Orthodox Christian thoughts and spiritual education.

Christianisation and Islamisation of the people of the region led to both faiths acquiring an ethnic niche. Largely people of Slavic origin (Russians and Ukranians), Fino-Ugor and some Turkic people formed the foundation of Orthodox Christian historical community,whereas Islam was rooted among the Tatars and Bashkirs.

Towards the beginning of the 20th century, Orthodox Christianity as well as Islam became an integral part of the spiritual life of the people of this region. Both the faiths obtained their firm niche, which formed the foundation for good neighbourly relations between them. During the Soviet era the state-sponsored atheism facilitated the removal of inter-faith contradiction and formation of relations of certain solidarity between the believers and spiritual leaders of Orthodox Christianity and Islam.

In the post-Soviet period, the natural parity of Orthodox Christianity in the region could be preserved, thanks to the efforts of representatives of spiritual leadership and local administration, which outlined its policy taking into account the bi-ethnic and bi-confessional nature of related regions of Russian federation and considering confessional factor as a phenomenon of culture.

The people practicing Orthodox Christianity and Islam enjoy close neighbourhoods in all the regions of the Volga–Ural territory. The cases of Tatarstan and Bashkortstan are interesting as the proportion between Orthodox Christians and Muslims is almost equal. Similar situation prevails in Astrakhan and Orenburg districts where the Muslim population is between 20% to 30 %. That is why it is interesting to analyse the relations between Orthodox Christians and Muslims in these regions.

Regarding the peaceful co-existence of Orthodox Christians and Muslims in each of the above mentioned regions, it should be noted that religious leaders of both confessions perceive division of population on the basis of religion as natural phenomena but confirm the thesis that 'one people–one faith' and people historically practicing Islam come under local mufti council,and people linked to Orthodox Christianity come under one roof. In this context both the confessions refused to have mutual prozelitism, which facilitated their mutually respectful co-existence.

Nevertheless, there is a problem with those who convert themselves to the alternative confession. Conversion of ethnic Orthodox Christians into Islam and ethnic Muslims into Orthodox Christianity does happen as a result of interfaith marriages and individual spiritual search. However, unusual ethnic and faith-based combination does not evoke negative reactions.

The conversion of Russians to Islam has been noticed in Kazan, Ufa, and Naberezhny Celna. Kazan has a mosque where prayer is conducted in the Russian language. On the other hand,one can see representatives of Tatar and Bashkir people in majority of orthodox Churches of Kazan and Ufa. Interestingly, there are more than ten bishops of Tatar and Bashkir origin serving in Kazan Churches. According to Orthodox Church leaders there is no problem with mutual conversion as such. However, some experts believe that this kind of situation may have negative consequences, which is why spiritual leaders and believers from both the faith should be careful.

A major indicator of inter-faith consensus in the Volga-Ural region is equal parity to revival of religious life and development of confessional infrastructure linked to it like the opening of churches, mosques, monastries and spiritual schools. Revival of religious life flows here with full force and spirit. If towards the end of 1980s, Tatarstan had 18 Muslim and 15 Orthodox Christian associations, by the year 2000 number of Muslim religious organisations reached 700 and Orthodox Christian organisations reached more than 150. In Bashkortstan, during the same period,a number of Muslim associations jumped from 30 to 500 and Orthodox Christian organisations rose from 32 to 140.

If you take into account the fact that number of ethnic Muslims and Orthodox Christians in Tatarstan and Bashkortstan was almost equal in the early 1990s, you get the impression that Muslim revival is taking place more actively than Orthodox Christian revival. However, significantly the rise in number of Muslim religious organisations is explained first of all by the special nature of distribution of different confessional groups. More Tatar and Bashkir people live in rural areas, as a result of which a large part of Muslim religious associations are represented by communes of small village mosques.

Russian population is concentrated usually in cities where Orthodox Christian churches are much larger and more crowded. Interestingly,the proportion between Orthodox Christian churches and mosques was almost the same in the pre-revoltionary Russia. In 1917, there were 2,507 mosques and 489 Orthodox Christian churches in Ufa province. More Orthodox Christian religious associations are to be found in other provinces of the Volga-Ural region. However, if we take into account that the percentage of Muslim population in those places is much less, then we can talk about the same tendency. For example, there are 120 Orthodox Christian churches and more than 80 mosques in Orenburg district, and there are more than 80 Orthodox Christian churches and 30 mosques in Astrakhan district.[19]

Starting from 1988, the process of returning to churches and mosques, which were used as monuments, Orthodox Christians and Muslims has been highly active. Equal respect to both the faiths is evident from the fact that the restoration of the Orthodox Christian and Muslim monuments like Kazan Kremlin and Great Bulgar began at the same time. The reconstruction of the Kazan Kremlin began as a result of the decision taken by Tatarstan government in 1994. According to the director of Kazan Kremlin Museum the main objective of this reconstruction is restoration of Kremlin complex by giving it Tatar-Muslim as well as Russian–Orthodox look. The Kazan Kremlin is considered a symbol of inter-faith peace and religious tolerance in the republic.

The reconstruction programme in the region includes research and restoration of historical monuments belonging to both confessions. According to the director of Bulgar Historical Muscum, R. Mahmudov, paying equal attention to the monuments of different faiths is a necessary condition for preservation of historical reality. Great Bulgar was always a multi-national and multi-confessional city which had Russian, Armenian and Jews segments, and mosques peacefully co-existing with churches and synagogues.[20]

Similar examples can be found in other parts of the Volga-Ural region.

The practice of mutual assistance for construction of mosques and churches from representatives of both confessions was also prevalent in the region. For example, in Bashkortstan more than 50 churches and mosques were built with the assistance from collective farms, enterprises and commercial structures, where both Orthodox Christians and Muslims work together during the last several years.

In Tatarstan a famous church was built with the participation of and donations from Muslims. A number of churches and mosques have been constructed in the republic from donations received from the people of both religions. Churches have been built by Tatar Muslim architects and mosques have been constructed by Russian Orthodox Christian architects.

Cooperation between traditional confessions in the republic develops within the framework of the international charity fund of the UNO 'Peace Temple',with the objective of construction and restoration of cultural buildings in Bashkortstan. The Bashkir republican branch of this organisation was founded by the Ufa Orthodox Church,the Spiritual Boards of Muslims, the Jewish community of Bashkortstan and religious association of Buddhists s. A spiritual- enlightenment centre for traditional religions of the republic is under construction in Ufa as a joint initiative of Orthodox Christian, Muslim and Jewish spiritual leadership, supported by the political leadership of Bashkortstan. The complex would comprise an Orthodox Christian church, mosque and a synagogue.

The joint fight against destructive sects and pseudo-religious organisations is one more area of cooperation between believers and spiritual leaders of Orthodox Christianity and Islam. The so-called 'new religious movement' carrying on under the name of 'religion of new age' evokes serious concern in Russian society. Unfortunately, the issue has not caught the attention at the level of inter-faith dialogue in a serious manner. The emergence of 'new religious movements' has a varied nature. Religious quests and the emergence of a new religious stream linked with it is a historically objective process. However, new religious movements include anti-social sects and movements that bear destructive consequences for the spiritual, psychological and physical health of the individual and the society. Often these organisations act as a cover for political and commercial objectives. Seontology Church, Aum Sinrike, Satanic sects, neo-pagan movements bordering on political extremism (such as fascism)are examples of such destructive organisations.[21]

According to some experts, the proliferation of such anti-social and pseudo-religious organisations is the result of a forcible break up of a significant number of people from traditional Russian faiths during the Soviet era through its militant atheism. People representing all traditional faiths had fallen victim to such movements. All this suggests that there is reason for joint action by Orthodox Christianity and Muslim against such sects and movements. Kazan has experience of such inter-faith cooperation against harmful religious movements and sects. The Orthodox Church and the Muslim spiritual board in Tatarstan jointly created a centre for rehabilitation of victims of totalitarian sects. The participation of Muslims in the centre is very significant. The deputy mufti of Tatarstan Valiualla-Khazryat is in charge of running the centre.

Thus, relations between Orthodox Christians and Muslims in regions of the Volga-Ural territory are very positive and productive. Attempts to destabilise the situation emanate not from believers but radical nationalists. Such conflicts were provoked in 1998-2000 in Naberezhniye Chelny in connection with the construction of the Orthodox Christian spiritual centre with churches around it. According to the former mufti of Tatarstan, G. Galiullin,Orthodox Christians are closer to him than the radical nationalists.

The other Russian region where Orthodox Christians and Muslims live in close peaceful neighbourhood is North Caucasus. It should be noted that in the 40s of the first century, apostle Andrey Pervozv any propagated the teachings of Christ among the Adygeas whereas Islam came there in the year 642 when Arab troops invaded Dervent (Dagestan). Thus, both the religions started setting roots here soon after their From the 4th to 12th centuries North Caucasus was part of the orbit of political and religious influence of Christian states like the Byzantine empire, Georgia and Ancient Rus as a result of which the Adygeas, Ossetins and Voinakhs adopted Christianity.

From the middle of 13th century, North Caucasus was in the zone of interests of Muslim states like the Golden Horde,the Ottoman Empire and Iran. As a result of this Islam received a strong boost in the region, whereas Christianity witnessed a decline.. Till the 19th century North Caucasus had a multi-confessional landscape as it was inhabitated by not only Muslims and Christians but also believers from Eudism, Zorastrianism, and traditional pagan cults.[22]

Orthodox Christianity received a new impetus in North Caucasus in connection with the emergence of first Russian Cossac settlements in the second half of 16th century. Orthodox Christianity in North Caucasus received a further boost as a result of Cossac community in Kuban with its original Church.

The Orthodox Church from the very beginning never made any attempts to convert the local mountain people to Christianity, as a result of which

Islamization of the local population was completed during the 18th -19th century. Ossetins were the only exception,who while formally remaining Orthodox Christians practiced a faith demonstrating the combination of Christian as well as Muslim rituals as well as traditional pagan cults. Parts of the Assetins living in the Kabardino kingdom were subjected to forced conversion to Islam. The Ossetin Spiritual Commission was set up to function from Kizlyar and Vladikavkaz in order to counter the spread of Islam. However, here missionary activities were conducted cautiously for the fear of evoking dissatisfaction among Assetins, and preserving loyalty to Russia in the Caucasus war.

After incorporation of North Caucasus into Russian empire, many incidents of harmonious relations between the local mountain Muslims and representatives of Orthodox Christianity could be seen. Archbishop Agafodor, heading the Stavropol Church between 1893- 1919 and famous for building schools for children of mountain people, enjoyed much popularity among the mountain people. There are incidents of Muslims protecting Orthodox Churches from the onslaught of bandits.

Thus, in the beginning of the 20th century a complicated and multi-level system, based on the balance between Orthodox Christianity and Islam, emerged in North Caucasus on the basis of a combination of ethnic and confessional groups. Subsequently national-confessional relations in the region became seriously deformed. At present they are in a situation of unsustainable balance, when any ill-concieved action of the authorities could lead to unpredictable consequences, which is specially reflected in the Chechen war.

Currently, North Caucasus,which includes ten federal subjects — Adgea, Dagestan, Ingushetia, Kabardino-Balkaria, Karachaevo-Cherkesia, Norh Ossetia –Alania, Chechnya, Krasnodarski and Stavropoliski Krai- as in the past, presents a combined ethnic and religious composition with the predominance of Russia's two largest ethno-confessional communities – Orthodox Christianity and Islam.

Russians and Ukrainians constitute the basis of the Orthodox Christian community that includes representatives of sub-ethnic groups such as different forms of Cossacks and representatives of non-Slavic ethnic groups like Ossetins, Georgians and Greeks. The Islamic community includes North Caucasian ethnos related to Abkhaz-adygea (Agygeas, Shapcugi, Abazani, Cherkesi and Kabardins), Nakhso-Dagestanis (Chechens, Ingush and, people of Dagestan), and Turkic (Karachaev, Balkar, Kumyk, Nogaits, Turkmeni and Ajerbaijani) language groups etc.

The population, historically identifying itself with Orthodox Christianity, dominates in Rostov district, Krasnodar and Stavropol krais, accounting for 85-90% of the inhabitants there. The Orthodox Christians constitute a significant portion of the population in the ethnic subjects of the Russian Federation, ranging from 10% in Dagestan to 70% in Adygea. On the other hand, a significant Muslim population lives in Stavropol and Krasnodar krais and Rostov district.

Thanks to the efforts of Orthodox Christian and Muslim spiritual leadership, it was possible to maintain inter-faith harmony and peace in the North Caucasus region during the 1990s. Significant credit for this should go to the late metropolit of Stravropol and Vladikabkaz Dokukin, who during the course of first and second Chechen wars launched peace initiatives in the region. Though the result of his initiatives was not very significant, Muslim spiritual leaders of the region highly appreciated his sincere efforts to bring peace. Good relations and mutual understanding between the spiritual leaders of both the faiths made significant contribution towards Chechen events, avoiding snowballing into a religious war, though Chechen militants captured and killed Orthodox Christian spiritual leaders. On the other hand, Muslim spiritual leaders were also killed by Chechen terrorists.

The level of understanding between leaders of both faiths permits development of various directions of interfaith cooperation between Orthodox Christians and Muslims such as humanitarian help to victims of military conflicts, mutual assistance in the construction and restoration of church's and mosques, joint fight against destructive movements and sects. In October 2000 priest Dokunin gave part of the humanitarian assistance brought from Germany to the Chechen mufti, Ahmed -khaji Shamayev. The humanitarian assistance was meant for the Chechen people suffering from military action. Mufti Shamayev in response promised to help in restoring the Orthodox Church on Chechen territory.

Funds collected from both Orthodox Christians and Muslims were used for construction and repair of churches and mosques in Adygea. Similar activities were carried out in other republics of North Caucasus.

One can often see the joint fight of traditional religions against destructive religious movements and totalitarian sects. There were several meetings organised by the local authorities of Kabardino-Balkaria and Dagestan in participation with representatives from Orthodox Christianity and Islam for fighting the totalitarian sects. As a result of this, local law on the regulation of religious activities came into force in these republics.

There are only two major traditional confessions existing within the system of relations between the state and religion in most of the Republic of North Caucasus. This system is most developed in Kabardino-Balkaria, where the council on religious organisations, under the president of the republic, includes representatives of three confessions, considered as traditional such as Islam, Orthodox Christianity and Eudaism. This kind of approach facilitated religious tolerance towards Protestants, though from the end of 19th century North Caucasushas been one of the centres of Russian Protestantism.

Thus,relations between Orthodox Christians and Muslims in the Volga-Ural region, as well as North Caucasus, are characterised by sufficient stability and mutual respect and does not have conflicting nature. However, it needs to be mentioned that the number of factors concerning domestic politics, as well as that which has external dimension such as the Chechen war, influx of migrants from near and abroad, expansion of 'trading minority' of non-Slavic origin, coupled with the aggravation of socio-economic crisis, facilitate a kind of 'Islamophobia' in Russian society. Social tension aggravates as certain political forces use Islamophobia as an instrument in their political game. This has become the reason for the emergence of a conflicting situation, linked to the transfer of mosques to the Muslim community or the construction of new mosques etc.

The return of conservative Islamic rituals such as wearing of the burkha or hizab in schools etc also create unpleasant situations in certain regions of North Caucasus. For example, the use of hijab the in certain schools Stavropol Kraihas provoked a lot of controversy and tension in the region, leading to the registration of legal cases. Another serious incident took place in Stavropol. The cafedral mosque built in 1915 was a real attraction of the city. In 1930 it was closed and was subsequently used to house the archives. In 1992 after the Soviet break up, it was given to the United Museum of the Krai. The Muslim community of the region demanded its return to them in mid-1990s, which was approved by the local authorities. However, local Cossack organisations joined by many Russian refugees from Chechnya protested against this decision. There were even demands to blast the mosque in response to terrorist acts in Buinask, Moscow and Volgodonsk. As a result, the decision to return the mosque to the Muslim community could not be executed and the fate of the historical monument still remains undecided. A similar incident had happened in the city of Taganrok in Rostov district where the Orthodox Christian spiritual leadership, Communists and Cossacks protested against the construction of a mosque. As a result, the mosque could not be built though the City Hall had given its consent for its construction.

Local and federal authorities and the spiritual leadership have to strictly abide by the law on freedom of conscience, in order to prevent such negative developments. Experts believe that only in conditions of political and economic stability such conflicts can be avoided.

It is widely believed that cooperation between Orthodox Christians and Muslim organisations can be effective in the following areas.

- Peace-keeping and patriotic activities, prevention of interfaith and inter-ethnic conflicts between the two communities,formation of good neighbourly relations and solidarity between the believers of the two faiths at regional, federal and international levels.
- Joint activities for preservation of cultural heritage of Orthodox Christians and Muslims, mutual assistance in restoration and preservation of religious monuments of history and culture of both the confessions.
- Fight against pseudo-religious movements and destructive cults and neutralisation of negative consequences of their activities.

Historical experience shows that there is hardly any country with a significant Christian and Muslim population that has escaped inter-faith contradiction and tension. Russia can not really be called an exception in this context though its inter-faith harmony, it has to be admitted, has been far stronger than in any other country. It is, of course, not possible to overcome these contradictions completely. Without a successful inter-faith dialogue, it would be difficult to achieve national consolidation in a multi-confessional and multi-ethnic state

Notes

1. Hunter, T.S. (1984), *Islam in Russia*, New York: ME Sharpe.
2. Ibid.
3. Ibid.
4. Ibid., p. 105.
5. Hunter, T.S. (1984), *Islam in Russia*, New York: ME Sharpe.
6. Hunter, T.S. (1984), *Islam in Russia*, New York: ME Sharpe.
7. Ibid.
8. Ibid.
9. Ibid.
10. Ibid.
11. Ibid.
12. Ibid.
13. Landa R.G. (1996), Islam in the history of Russia, p. 55, Moscow.
14. Landa R.G. (1996), Islam in the history of Russia, p. 53, Moscow.
15. Abdulatipov, R.G. (2002), Faith of Islam in Russia, Moscow: Mysl.
16. Ibid., p. 176.
17. Op. Cit., Hunter (1984).
18. Ibid.
19. Ibid.
20. Ibid.
21. Ibid.
22. Ibid.

6. Islam and Russian Foreign Policy

History

While one group of Russian specialists believe that the history of Islam in Russia began in the year 642 when the first groups of Muslims reached Derbent, the other school argues that the year 922, when Islam was adopted in Bulgaria on the Volga, should be considered as the year when history of Islam began in Russia. However, the real interaction of Russia with Islamic civilisation started not earlier than 15th century. In the year 922, the embassy of the Baghdad Khalifa al- Muktadir, one of the leaders of which was the famous chronicler Ibn Fadlan, reached the country of the Volga Bulgars, which expressed its desire to voluntarily adopt Islam. In the year 932,the son of Bulgar Tsar went on Hajj, which ultimately established links between the Volga Bulgars and the Islamic world. This country was perceived as the northern most outpost of Islam.[1]

In the year 987, King Vladimir received the delegation of Volga Bulgars while deciding about Russia's new religion. This is considered the first diplomatic move for spreading Islam on the territory of Russia. Subsequently, the history of interactions between Rus and Volga Bulgaria was full of wars with rare periods of peace. Nevertheless, the interaction between the Russian principalities with the Muslim world was very intimate. Arabs, Persians, Khoresans sold silk, gold, silver, spices, glass utensils, jewellery, specious metals in Rus. The merchants of Vladimir-Suzdal principality, the main trading partner of the Muslim world, supplied it with nylon cloth, leather, honey, wood etc.

At that point of time, the Muslim merchants familiar with the local language, acquainted with the traditions of the host countries and enjoying the most freedom of movement, played an important role in diplomacy. The acquaintance with Islam within Russian territory took place primarily them. As a result, the first mosques in Moscow were built in its port cities like Yaroslavle, Kostroma, Tver and Arkhangelsk to cater to the spiritual needs of these Muslim merchants. Special palaces were built in large Russian cities for providing shelter to diplomats and traders. In the middle of 18th century, Tatarskaya Kargala or Seyotov Pasad near Orenburg became the main Russian centre for Muslim merchants/diplomats; it was famous for its madrassa and in time became a major trading and spiritual centre for the Tatars Muslims.

The Tatar- Mongol invasion in the 13th century brought to end the history of the Volga Bulgars and opened a new stage in the history of interaction of Rus with the Muslims. In the year 1257, the first Khan-Muslman-Berke headed the Golden Horde of the Mongols, and in the year 1313, Khan Sultan Mohamed Uzbek declared Islam as its state religion. This move resulted in the spread of Islam amongst the multitude of Turkic tribes — from Crimea to Siberia. At the same time, Uzbek had a tremendous respect for orthodox spiritual leaders and instructed his subjects not to insult orthodoxy. His son Zanibek continued his father's tradition and cultivated a very warm relationship with the Moscow metropolit, Aleksei. According to some experts, this was the time when inter-faith dialogue took its roots in Russia.[2]

The acquaintance of Moscow state with Islam took place mainly through contacts of members of Tatar nobility who came to serve Russian kings. For example, in the year 1445 the great king of Moscow, Vasily-11 Tyomny, gave the town of Gorodets-Meschersky to Kazan Prince Kasim for his military assistance, which heralded the beginning of Kasimov rule on the banks of the Ok River. Muslims coming to live there organised their life as they liked, built mosques and enjoyed full religious freedom. Other towns like Serpukhov, Zvenigorod, Kashira, and Yuriyev were given to the Tatar khans for establishing their rule over these territories. However, their authorities could be reinforced only in Kasimov.

In the 16th century, the conquest of Kazan and Astrakhan, Nagai kingdom and Siberia khanet led to the incorporation of a significant Muslim community into the Russian state. Russian czars had a policy of tolerance towards for Muslims and did not make any special effort to convert them to Christianityand encouraged their conversion exclusively through economic measures. However, there were serious obstacles before the Muslim missionaries.

According to the Sobornoye Ulozheniye, a special decree issued in 1649, Islam received legal status here. During the Smuta or dark times of the early 17th century, Muslim Tatars extended support to the patriotic troops led by Minin and Pozharsky and subsequently participated in the Zemsky Sobor (Assembly) called in 1613. The Tatars took active part in the establishment of the Romanov dynasty. It was after this that the process of integration of

Muslims with the orthodox Russian state gradually started characterising the features of an orthodox multi-confessional state. Even Soviet experts on Islam recognised the contribution of the Muslims in the formation of Russian state.

It can be assumed that State repression was launched not so much against Islam as against Muslim communities whose loyalty was at times questionable. It should be mentioned that Kasimov Muslims had full religious freedom and could occupy the highest posts in the state apparatus. Representatives of their elite were involved in diplomatic missions in Central and South Asia, direct contacts with whom could be possible after the fall of the influential eastern neighbours of Russian state.[3]

In the beginning,Moscow exchanged embassies with Bukhara and Khiva, and subsequently, attempts were made to replicate the route travelled by Afanasi Nikitin and to revive contacts with India.

In the year 1675, Tsar Aleksei Mikhailovich sent a mission to India with Mahamed Yusuf, a Kasimov Tatar at its head, tasking him to establish trade relations.. Yusuf's diplomatic mission, meant for finding the shortest route to India, buy Russian prisoners and establish trade ties with Moghul India was unsuccessful However, starting from middle of the 17th century, the Muslim subjects of Russia were involved in highly responsible diplomatic activities.[4]

In the 18th century, there was no principled change in the conditions of Muslims in Russia. However, the pro-western Tsar Peterthe Great took some steps, leading to discrimination against them, though it is he who had ordered the first translation of the Quran into Russian.. Kulu-Muhamed Teblekov, a talented diplomat, who became a close confidant of Peter the Great significantly strengthened Russian position in Kirgizia and signed the agreement with khan Abulakhair,which set the stage for a merger of Kazakhstan with Russia. For his significant achievements, Tebkelev was decorated with the title of Major -General.

The attitude of the authorities to Muslims took a sharp turn for the better under the rule of Ekaterina (Catharine) the Great. The expansion of the Russian empire, as a result of the conquered territory with a Muslim population, particularly Crimea, set the agenda for reglamentation of the life of Russian Muslims. In the year 1773, a decree was issued under the order of Catherine the Great, which formed the foundation of a secular state in Russia. Catherine subsequently issued several decrees that eased the life of Muslims in Russia.

Mufti Mohamedzan Gusseinov was appointed as the head of the newly established Ufa spiritual assembly by Catharine the Great,and his selection was not accidental. Subsequently, he was sent by the Russian ministry of foreign affairs with a secret mission to Bukhara and Kabul, where he presented himself as a student wishing to receive higher spiritual education.

Husseinov was given the task of establishing relations with representatives of Kazakhs belonging to small and middle Zhuzov, and headed the Russian mission to Kazakhstan several times. The main objective of this mission was to bring the Kazakhs into the orbit of the Russian empire, and encourage the spread of moderate Islam, free of any anti-Russian and pro-Turkic attitude. Other Muslim spiritual leaders helped Husseinov in his diplomatic task. As a result of a well- conceived work, Husseinov managed to win the sympathy of the Kazakh elite. In the year 1797, the Khan Council was set up at the initiative of Husseinov for ruling Mali Zhuz. On the recommendation of the Mufti, Aichubak, who was loyal to Russia was elected as the khan, and daughter of Husseinov married Zhangir, the last khan of Bukeivskoi Horde.

Other regions were also brought under Husseinov's sphere of interests. In 1805,the mufti took part in the 'Secret Commission on Affairs of Turkmen' and organised a family judicial system in North Caucasus.

Gabdessalam Gabdrahimov, the Imam of Orenburg mosque, headed the spiritual board after the death of Husseinov in 1824. Like his predecessor, Gabdrahimov was also assigned diplomatic as well as secret missions in Kazakhstan and Central Asia by the Rus government. In 1823 and 1824, Gaddrahimov was a member of the commission set up to resolve Kazakh affairs under the chairmanship of Khan Aichubak. In order to establish close contacts with the Kazakhs he gave their children education in his madrassa.

As the Russian empire expanded and its relations with Turkey and Iran started deteriorating, the priority for the authorities was to establish good relations with Muslims of Caucasus and Crimea, which required a special approach and special structure. The objective was to win their sympathy for Russia and reduce foreign influence over them.[5]

After the October Revolution in 1917, the Bolshevik government required not only internal but also external recognition. The continuing First World War compelled the warring nations to look for sympathisers in the East. First of all, it was the Russian provisional government that thought of using the Islamic factor in its foreign policy. It wanted to use the fact that part of Russian Muslims were sympathetic to Turkey, which could be used to conclude a separate peace treaty.

On the other hand, the group of Muslims led by the Cadet leader Sadri Maksudi protested against the plan of a decisive defeat of Turkey and establishment of Russian control over Constantinopole, Bosfor and Dardanell. Speaking in the 7th Congress of Cadets Party, Maksudi said that Muslims with sympathy for Turkey would support the Cadet party only if they delete the clause about dismemberment of Turkey and destruction of Constantinopole from their programme. He made similar statements after two years while addressing the Paris Peace Conference in 1919 -1920 on behalf of all Russian Muslims. He warned the participants of the conference that if Istanbul, along with the channels, are taken away from Turkey, then the allied countries would lose the support of Russian Muslims and subsequently this would leaded to the spreading of Bolshevik ideology.[6]

The Tatar democratic intelligentsia organised a strong agitation against Russia's provisional government which decided in favour of continuing the war, particularly against the Cadet leader Milyukov, a strong supporter of the conquest of Constantinopole. As a result foreign minister Milyukov prepared a special statement of the provisional government about the objectives of the war, which declared the refusal of making slaves out of each others people.[7]

In this connection S.M. Iskhakov writes that in the autumn of 1917, Muslim countries had their own views about international situation. In this context he looks at the appointment of Daut Aitov, the leader of "Peoples Will", as Consul General in Paris in September 1917.[8]

In July 1917, members of Higher Muslim Council – the Milli Shura, took a decision to send a delegation of Russian Muslims to the international Socialist Conference in Stockholm, and in November, the head of the council, Akhmed Tsalikov, expressed concern about the statement made by British foreign minister Artur Balfur, which sowed the seeds for the creation of a Jewish state in Palestine.

"Muslims of Russia support the sovereign rights of Muslim population of Palestine with all the forces at its command and would do everything to oppose the efforts of violence over this wishes," said Head of the Milli Shura.[9] It can be said that the fight of Muslims of former Russian Empire for the rights of Palestinians began particularly from this statement.

It is true that many Russian Muslims had sympathies for Turkey and were concerned about its destiny. Bolsheviks taking note of these circumstances indicated in the address of the peoples commissars for 'The Working People of the East' that the secret agreements of the ousted tsar about the occupation of Constantinopole, which has been confirmed by ousted Kerensky, stands annulled and destroyed. The republic of Russia and its government and council of peoples commissars are against occupation of foreign land: Constantinopol must remain in the hands of Muslims, and the agreement on dismemberment of Turkey stands annulled.[10]

The Bolsheviks pursued a similar policy regarding Iran, declaring that the agreement on the division of Persia stands annulled and destroyed. Because of this, Iran recognised the Bolshevik government in 1917, and in June 1918, the Soviet government sent a message to the government and people of Iran, which promised to cancel the entire amount of Iranian debts due to Russia, to stop all control over Iran's state revenues and handed over all roads and telegraph lines under Russian control to Iran.

Russia's benevolent policy towards the East brought immediate result. After the declaration of independence in 1919, the Afghan leader Amannula-Khan sent a letter to the Russian President Mikhail Kalinin, expressing the desire to establish friendly relations with Soviet Russia. Diplomatic relations between the two countries were established in the summer of 1919 and Yakov Surits became the Soviet ambassador to Kabul.[11]

In the beginning of 1918, the delegation of Young Turks arrived in Moscow in order to hold talks about the fate of Turkic prisoners of war and to establish diplomatic relations between Turkey and the Soviet Union. The delegation included Yusuf Akchurin, a Muslim leader of Russian origin, leading the activities of Red Cross and fulfilling the delicate task assigned by government of Turkey.

Akchurin became the successor to the founder of the Russian pan-Turkism, Ismail Gaspirinsky. Akchurin, a native of Simbirsk, shifted to Istanbul at the age of 7 along with his family and was educated in the military college. He came in close contact with young Turks during his college career, and took active part in their activities, for which he was even imprisoned for sometime. Subsequently he studied at Sorbonne in Paris and returned to Russia on the eve of 1905 revolution. He took part in the struggle against Czarist rule and actively participated in the propaganda of Zadidism and the setting up of the "Ittifak –al- Muslimin' party. Akchurin launched a newspaper called *Kazan Mokhbir* and taught history and geography at a Kazan madrassa.[12]

After his arrest, because of anti-government activities, he moved to Turkey where the Young Turks came to power in 1908. In 1915 he formed a 'Committee for Defense of Rights of Muslim Turkic-Tatar People of Russia', which was engaged in political propaganda against the Russian government in the name of human rights activities. The members of the committee often travelled to Europe where they narrated the precarious conditions in which Turkic-Muslims live in Russia and demanded the revival of the Kazan and Crimean Khanates.[13]

Being a well-recognised human rights activist, Akchurin was involved in diplomatic activities, visiting European countries as a member of Turkic delegation. He met Lenin in Zurich in 1916, during which he came to learn about Bolsheviks nationality policy. He appreciated the nationality policy of the Bolsheviks, who regarded Russia as a 'Prison House of Peoples".[14]

As a result of the revolution in April 1920, Mustafa Kamal Atatyurk came to power in Turkey. His government immediately expressed a desire to establish diplomatic relations and form a military alliance with Soviet Russia. Soviet foreign minister Chicherin sent a positive response to the proposal, and the Soviet-Turkey treaty of friendship and brotherhood was signed in March, 1921. This treaty was in the interests of Turkey as the Bolsheviks supplied it with weapons to defend its territorial integrity. By then Akchurin had also risen to became advisor to Kamal Atatyrk on cultural and political affairs he fulfilled his mission in Russia very successfully.

In the year 1921, a delegation of the Indian National Congress visiting the Volga region and Siberia, was accompanied by mufti Galimzhan Barudi and Musa Biriyev, a Mukhtasib from Petrograd. This delegation was received by Lenin.[15]

The eastern division of the secret organisation GPU was formed in 1922 on the orders of the Central Committee of the ruling Bolshevik party, whose objective was to coordinate the activities of the local bodies of state security in fighting against espionage and counter –revolution,keeping in mind the specific situation in Caucasus, Central Asia, Tatarstan, Baskiria and Crimea. The members of this committee largely shaped the state policy towards Muslims and were in charge of using the Muslim leaders to achieve their foreign policy goals.[16]

During the mass hunger in the Volga region in 1921-22, a commission was set up with Kazi Kashafudin Tarzimani at its head for distributing relief amongst starving people. The commission established contacts with the ambassadors of Turkey, Persia and Afghanistan, and through them addressed the Muslims of those countries for providing assistance to the starving people. The commission established contacts with charitable organisations of some countries, and sent its representatives to Siberia, Chinese Turkestan, Turkey, Estonia, Finland, Latvia and Lithunia. Appeals were issued to the Christian spiritual leadership of the West in French, English, and Germany languages. Mufti Galimzan Baridi worked very hard in the commission. He came to Moscow to meet with Stalin for discussing the relief issue.[17]

Kashafudin Tardzhimani conducted talks with K. Karabeker, commander of Turkic Caucasus front, who offered to send 2000 starving children of Tatar, Bashkir and Kirgyz nationalities to Turkey. As a result of vigorous diplomatic activities of the Muslim leaders, it was possible to mobilise a substantial amount of assistance for the starvation-hit people.

In 1923, Soviet Peoples Commissariat for Foreign Affairs launched a campaign under the slogan that shariat and socialism do not contradict each other. About 150 loyal Muslims helped the ministry in the campaign. The Third All Russia Congress of Muslim Spiritual Leadership, held in 1926, sent a telegram to the Soviet foreign minister Chicherin which said, "Muslim people understand that their freedom and cultural-economic development depend on close cooperation of Muslim world with the proletariat world with Soviet power at its head".[18]

After formation of the Union of Soviet Socialist Republic in December 1922, the Soviet government once again paid attention to the Muslim countries, in which the maximum attention was given to the newly independent state, the royal Kingdom of Saudi Arabia.[19]

In 1907 speaking in the Islamic conference in Cairo,the father of Zadidism, Ismail Gasprinsky, advanced the idea of convening a global Muslim congress as the general spiritual and political centre of the Muslims of the entire world, and proposed to have annual an Muslim congress at Cairo or Istanbul. One of the objectives of such a congress, according to him was to mobilise Russian Muslims towards Turkey, pan-Turkism.[20]

In 1926, mufti Rizaedin Fakhredin sent a telegram to Soviet leader Stalin, in which he shared his views about the venue and specifics of such a congress. He argued that such congress should be convened in a country situated outside the sphere of influence of imperialist powers, and in this context opposed holding the congress in pro-British Egypt.

The second All Russia Congress of Muslim spiritual leaders showed special interest in the destiny of the Khalifat and discussed the information about the revival of the independence of Khalifatin Turkey. This reform was supported by Russian Muslim spiritual leadership, which even sent a congratulatory message to the great national assembly of Turkey. This proved the open pro-Turkey orientation of Russian Muslim leadership and its recognition of Abdulmazid, the newly elected khalifa, as the spiritual leader of all Russian Muslims. Thus the efforts of the Tsar's regime to free Russian Muslims from Turkic influence went in vain.

Mufti Rizaedin Fkhredin's proposal about the venue of the World Muslim Congress was not accidental. In 1920 after the annexation of Khidzaz by the British Mufti Galimzan Barudi and Rashid Ibrahim appealed to Soviet power to defend Muslim rights and oust the British colonisers from Mecca and Medina. Russia's official contacts with the Arab states began in 1922 when in the course of the Lozzan conference the Russian Federation People's Commissar on Foreign Affairs,Chicherin, met with the representatives of the King of Khidzaz, K. Lotfalla; during this meeting an agreement was reached for establishing diplomatic relations between the USSR and Khidzaz. In 1924 Kerim Hakimov was appointed as the Soviet Consul General in Khidzaz. Chicherin wrote to him that to visit Mecca is of utmost importance for us. That is why we are appointing a Muslim as a consul general so that he can stay in Mecca. Though we have searched for the right person among Muslims for long, we did not find anyone better than Hakimov.[21]

Hakimov continued in this position for not too long. The war between Wahhabis of Nedzhda and Hashemits of Khidzazwas coming to an end with the former winning it. Chicherin wrote to Hakimov that Soviet interests on the Arab issue are to unite Arab lands into a single state.[22]

Soon after Ibn Sauda occupied Mecca, and Hakimov started negotiations with Wahhabis which were successful. Following this,the Soviet government sent a letter to the king of Nedzhda recognisingthe future Kingdom of Saudi Arabia. There was a positive response from the Saudi king on the Soviet position and Ibn Saud became the most trusted ally of Communists in the Middle East. At that point of time the Soviet diplomats were not concerned about the religious teachings of Saudis, who were regarded as natural allies in the struggle against imperialism.[23]

The young state of Nedzhd, Khidzaz and adjacent districts tried to project themselves as serious players in the world affairs and also as an alternative centre to Turkey and Egypt in the Muslim world. As opposed to the Khalifat congress planned to be held in Egypt supported by Britain, Ibn Saud proposed to convene the World Muslim Congress at Mecca, the most sacred city for Muslims. Russian Muslim leaders extended strong support to this proposal.

The first congress on Khalifat issue, supported by Britain and the Ullemas of Cairo University, opened in Cairo on 13th May 1926. However, no significant decision could be taken in the congress which was quite low profile. Against this backdrop, the world Muslim congress held in June 1926, with delegates from 57 major Muslim countries which included India, Indonesia, Palestine, Nedzhda, Khidzhaza, Asir, Turkey, Afghanistan, Sudan, Yemen and USSR looked like a very significant event. Delegates from states of Arab peninsula, controlled by Ibn Sauda dominated the congress.[24]

A Representative of Hidzhaza was elected as the chairman of the congress while the leader of the Indian delegation and mufti Rizaedin Fakhredi from USSR were elected as vice-chairman. The two major issues in the congress were to be—Independence of the Muslim world and the unity of Muslims in the framework of World Muslim Congress—which was chosen to be a permanent body with an annual congress in Mecca or in any Muslim country without foreign influence, were. The discussion of such important issues pushed the Khalifat question to the bottom of the agenda making it a non-issue. Britain was very disturbed by this development. The participation of Soviet Muslims in the Congress facilitated its success to a large extent, noted Soviet diplomats with some satisfaction.[25]

The World Muslim Congress had discussions on mutual relations between the major streams of Islam and access for all Muslims to the sacred places of Khidzaz. The head of Indian Association of Ullemas, Mohhamed Kafayatulla, proposed to permit Muslims to offer prayer according to their traditions. While the host country opposed this proposal, delegates from Afghanistan and Soviet Union supported this. Ultimately it was decided to limit non-tolerance of bad behaviour towards other Muslims when they visit Mecca and Medina.

The discussion on equal rights for Shiaites and Sunnis, and tolerance inside Islam, became new direction in Muslim diplomacy, promoting dialogue between different streams of Islam. As evident from the materials of the above Muslim congress, Russian Muslims with their experience in Shia-Sunni dialogue in Caucasus, made a significant contribution to the healthy process beginning in the Muslim world.

With direct participation of Muslim leaders from the USSR and Soviet diplomats, the state headed by Ibn Sauda projected itself as a leading Muslim power.Soviet diplomacy and Muslim spiritual leaders of USSR made serious contributions in changing the history of the entire Islamic civilisation.[26] Saudi Arabia reaped the benefits of success in 1969 when it became the founder of Organisation of Islamic Conference and proved its leadership in the Muslim world. Soviet Muslims did not get any positive result for themselves from the World Muslim Congress. Subsequently, the southern borders of the USSR were closed,creating obstructions for conducting the hajj. After the murder of Kerim Hakimov by the Stalinist regime in 1938, the Soviet diplomatic mission in Saudi Arabia was closed.[27]

Subsequently, Saudi Arabia came under British and then US control. Soviet diplomacy was a complete failure on the issue, which became evident during Afghan war. Many Soviet experts on Islam did not have any illusion about bringing Saudi Arabia into Moscow's orbit and rightly concluded that Britain by inciting Bedouins against Turkey succeeded in preserving serious levers of influence on King Ibn Sauda.

Mecca is the Centre for international relations of the Muslim world and primary source of religious forces of Islamic teachings. It is the source of pan-Islamism, and besides that was under British influence. Because of this the Soviet government did not permit citizens to go abroad for conducting hajj. This is how Soviet secret service argued in favour of the ban on pilgrimage to Mecca just like their colleagues did in the 19th century.[28]

It is interesting how mufti Rezauddin Fakhredin in his report at the Mecca congress expressed his sincere happiness that the October Revolution made the fear about pan-Islamism baseless. However, his happiness was short-lived as the idea of reducing foreign influence on Russian Muslims was relevant under any government by any means and it is still required till today by bureaucrats and secret service.[29]

When it was known that a huge number of Muslims in the British colony recognise only the 'right', pro-British khalifa, it became clear that the issue of the future of khalifa started emerging as a significant factor of international politics. Secret documents of the eastern sector of the Commintern in 1921 bear testimony to the fact that its members considered it necessary to compete with Britain for control over khalifat institute and facilitate the appearance of a pro-Soviet khalifa rather than pro-British khalifa.[30]

Keeping this in view, the Soviet leadership invited Anwar Pasha, son-in-law of the last khalifa of Turkey to Moscow to use him in igniting a mass Muslim protest against British colonialism. Anwar-pasha was a famous political and military leader. He was closely associated with Young Turk movement and took active part in the revolution of 1908. Anwar Pasha dreamt of creating a great Turkic state, with Samarkand as its capital. After Turkey's defeat in the First World War, he was forced to leave the country and using his wide contacts proposed his service to the victorious nations, and also to Soviet Russia. Anwar Pasha succeeded in convincing Bolshevik leader Karl Radek about his usefulness. Radek organised his visit to Baku in 1921 to participate in the conference of representatives of eastern people. This conference attended by Zinovyov, Radek and the Hungarian Communist Bela Kun gave a call for a sacred war against imperialism. Anwar Pasha, supporting this call proposed to wage a war against imperialism from the territory of Central Asia through which they could attack key British colonies.[31]

In October, 1921 Anwar-pasha was sent by the Bolsheviks to Turkestan for organising a war against Britain and Basmachi. Anwar Pasha after reaching Bukhara along with a group of Turkic military officers opened his cards by joining hands with the basmachis of Ibrahim-Bek, who shortly made him chief commander of his forces. Anwar Pasha declaring himself as the Emir of Turkestan gave an ultimatum to Moscow for recognising the independence of Central Asia and to withdraw the red army from its territory. Anwar Pasha dreamt of reviving the empire of Timurlane by conquering Afghanistan, East Turkestan and Kazakhstan and then sent his troops to India. Anwar Pasha along with his close colleagues was eliminated near Tajik village Chagan in August 1922.

Second World War and the Muslim Factor

Soviet Muslims were living in a bad situation when Hitler attacked the Soviet Union. All the muftis who defended state interests were annihilated or had gone through Stalin's repression. Bolshevik leaders could hardly imagine that Muslim leaders would be once again be as useful as they were during dark times. However, Hitler's invasion compelled the government to mobilise all resources, including the Muslims to defend the motherland from the fascist onslaught. Moreover, the fascists did everything possible to draw the

Muslim minority to their side promising them full religious rights and an opportunity for self-determination in case of their support.

The other unpleasant surprise for the Soviet government was the position of Turkey. According to Soviet historians, after the beginning of Second World War in 1939-40, Britain and France, through their diplomatic channels, tried to make Turkey their ally by supporting pan-Turkism, so that Turkey could launch attacks on Soviet Union.. Western countries advised Turkey to pay attention to the precarious situation in which Soviet-Turkic people lived and were waiting for their freedom from the "Soviet yoke". However, Turkey scared of the USSR, maintained neutrality, without falling victim to western provocation.

After the war began, Turkey restrained itself from taking part in military activities, and thus managed to avoid German occupation. After the defeat of France and Britain at the hands of Germany, Turkey changed its foreign policy seeking alliance with the winning side. Subsequently, Hitler in a secret meeting in Berlin in March 1941 stated that Caucasus would be given to Turkey.

Hitler in 1941 began to set up spy schools in order to train agents for working for its interests in North Caucasus and Trans-Caucasus, seeking support among the Muslim political immigrants and Muslim prisoners of war. The late Anwar Pasha's relative, the Turkic general Nuri Pasha Killigil advised the Germans to separate Muslim prisoners of war from the rest and conduct a propaganda among them in order to form military units that would constitute the backbone of the Turkic national movement. The idea was immediately implemented by separating war prisoners on the basis of religion.[32]

This practice was witnessed during Russo-Japanese war and the First World War Through this practice, Muslim volunteers were mobilised for Turkey's army that was to help them in gaining freedom from 'Russian yoke'. Muslim war prisoners were kept in special camps where living conditions were better. Mullas from Turkey with Tatar origin used to visit these camps to launch anti-Russian propaganda, acting as agents of German imperialism.[33] Russian pan-Turkists like Gamilzhan Idrisov and Berdi Kemal also took part in those camps in anti-Russian campaign.

In 1941, a division was set up in the ministry of foreign affairs of Germany to look after pan-Turkey movement and Muslim factor. Pan-Turkism was designed to be used as an important instrument against Soviet interests.

Towards the end of 1941 and beginning of 1942, Muslims loyal to fascists started forming Muslim legions like Turkestan legion, Caucasus legion, Tatar legion "Idel-Ural' etc. Hitler openly declared that he considered Muslims as a reliable ally and did not perceive any threat from the formation of Muslim military units. Mullas and propaganda- experts were mobilised to work among Muslims and the famous Bashkir nationalist –immigrant Ahmedzaki Balidi was one of them.

Muslim units in the German army took active part in military actions. Some of the Muslims living in Caucasus were really collaborating with fascists and were engaged in subversive activities. The newspaper "*Gazabat*", launched with the help of Germany, conducted active propaganda among Muslim legions under the slogan "Allah is over us and Hitler is near us".The fascists set up special schools in the occupied territory for training mulla-collaborationists, which were given special tasks in the ideological war.

A special wing was set up in the Ministry of Eastern Affairs of Germany to deal with the Volga-Tatars. Tatars loyal to Hitler were mobilised in the "Union of struggle of Turk-Ttatars Idel- Ural" with its help and organised a large kurultai (parliament) in Graifsvald.

By 1942, it was clear that fascists were effectively using the religious factor against the USSR and were actively involved in building mosques and shrines in huge numbers in the occupied territory. The fascists also reopened the muftiat in Crimea. This action soon brought dividends for them. The Crimean Muslim committee 'Azat Creamia' in its newspaper published an appeal to Hitler as the "man who brought freedom to oppressed people."

The Soviet government understood that Hitler was using opening of shrines in its propaganda activities and launched a host of counter measures. Realising that in spite of years of atheist propaganda, the religious factor was still very strong and could play a decisive role in victory, the Soviet government decided to reduce pressure on religion. Orthodox Christians and Muslims were permitted to open their places of worship the Russian Orthodox Church was permitted to re-establish its patriarchy and Muslims were permitted to run their system of spiritual administration. Its results were immediately felt.

In the beginning of the war, the Muslims of Tashkent issued a Fatwa for launching a Zihad against fascist Germany, addressed to all the Muslims of USSR. In May 1942 the Muslim spiritual board, under the leadership of Mufti Gabdrakhman Rasulev, issued an appeal to Muslims about fascist aggression against USSR, which was full of patriotic feelings. This appeal was translated in all languages of Muslims of Soviet Union as well as in the Arabic, Turkic and Persian languages. Izvestia published a telegram by Mufti Rasulev for the collection of funds from Muslims for formation of tank unit and he contributed 50,000 rubles for the fund. Stalin himself had expressed his gratitude to the mufti for this initiative and gesture.[34]

As the war drew nearer, a tragic incident took place in the history of Soviet Union, particularly in the history of Soviet Muslims. Nationalities such as Tatars, Chechens, Ingushits, Balkar and Cherkes, who had embraced Hitler's pan-Islamic idea, were deported from their motherland to different parts of Soviet Union by Stalin. The history of deportation clearly demonstrated what kind of fate the foreign provocators had planned for Soviet Muslims.

The centuries-old bid to bring about a clash of Muslims with Russian authorities was close to its goal during years of war. The tragic consequences of deportation of Muslims is still felt in the country. Its adverse impact on inter-ethnic as well as inter-faith relations is till felt. Whole nationalities lost their trust in the Russian state.

Muslim Diplomacy during the Cold War

The Soviet Union emerged as one of the great powers in the post-war period owing to its decisive contribution in the victory over fascism. The western world scared of this rising great power contemplated plans to contain and check the Soviet Union, which was subsequently known as the Cold War. British Prime Minister Wilson Churchill's speech at Fulton is regarded as the beginning of the Cold War which was to continue over the next 40 years.. The Cold War required special efforts in the propaganda and counter-propaganda war between the capitalist and socialist systems, to prove the supremacy of one system over the other. One of the directions of the war was the struggle for world peace and countering the anti-Soviet propaganda. The Soviet Union was projected as an atheist country, which does not have religious freedom, and suppresses religions.

Being one of the two superpowers,the Soviet Union was to work for its image abroad, which was tarnished by the alleged militant atheism practised in the country. On the other hand, Stalin had positively assessed the contribution of Orthodox Christians and Muslims to the war efforts, and subsequently started relaxing militant atheism in the country. Khrushchev's de-Stanilisation campaign also improved the situation in religious freedom.

Relations between the state and religion significantly improved during the Cold War years.

One of the important dimensions of Soviet foreign policy was towards the Middle East, Russia's traditional friend. However, relations with the Muslim world, particularly with the Middle East was strained after Soviet Union played a positive role in the creation of Jewish state of Israel. The Arab countries obviously did not appreciate the Soviet role in the creation of Israel. The Soviet Union had to address the issue and improve the situation by several means, including using the Soviet Muslim factor.

At the outset, it was decided to involve the Soviet Muslims in the world peace movement and disarmament process. In March 1950, Soviet National daily *Izvestia* published a statement by DUMES, signed by Mufti Gabdrahaman Rasulev, which on behalf of all Soviet Muslims expressed full support to the Stockholm resolution of the World Peace Congress. In September 1951, *Izvestia* in an article noted the active struggle of the Soviet Muslims for world peace, quoting from Mufti Eshon Babakhanov's speech launched in one of Tashkent's mosques, in which he strongly condemned the anti-human policies of US-British imperialists, trying to ignite the war fire, by appealing to all Muslims to put their signatures on the World Peace Council Resolution.[35]

In 1945 Tashkent hosted a conference of Muslim theologists of Central Asia and Caucasus which took a decision to establish close contacts with foreign Muslims, the first being all Arab Muslims. After two years the future SADUM Mufti Ziauddin Babakhanov went on a long trip to Muslim countries for raising his qualification at Al-azhar University and the maddrassas of Mecca and Medina. He was elected as the vice-chairman of SADUM upon his return to Moscow.

Visiting Muslim objects in some regions became part of the programme of the visiting foreign delegations to which it was required to demonstrate full religious rights in USSR. Muslim delegates representing DUMES participated in the third National Congress of Supporters of Peace held at Moscow in 1953, and DUMES Mufti Shakir Khiyalatdinov had gone to Helisinki to attend the World Peace Council meeting in 1955.[36]

In 1953,Mufti Babakhanov led a group of pilgrims to Mecca, and this group was warmly received by Saudi king Abdulaziz ibn Saud during this tour. Babakhanov during his visit to Egypt signed an agreement with the vice-chancellor of Al-Azhar for educating Soviet Muslim students.[37]

In 1955,the SADUM mufti as a member of the World Peace Council participated in the Delhi International Conference of Public Figures Fighting for Relaxation of International Tension, where he established contacts with Indian Muslim representatives. In 1958, he took part in the World Conference of Religions, and 1961 participated in the International Conference of Religious Leaders held in Japan;in 1962 he was a delegate to the World Islamic Conference held in Baghdad.[38] In 1961 a major event took place with the opening of the international department that looked after issues of pilgrimage, sending and receiving of delegations etc. The intensity of international activities of Soviet Muslims required a permanent body for coordination of activities at the national level. The International Relations Department (IRD)of Muslim organisation's of the USSR was set up in July 1962 under the Council of Religious Affairs of Soviet Union, which became an independent body. The decision to set up this organ was taken at the level of CPSU Central Committee, which wanted this body to analyse materials about relations of Soviet Muslims and prepare recommendations. Muslim spiritual leaders in the framework of their international diplomacy were expected to fight for world peace and counter anti-Soviet propaganda in international media and explain real situation with Soviet Muslims to the outside world.[39] IRD was in charge of certain publications and making of films about life of Soviet Muslims. However, important delegations were handled directly by CPSU Central Committee.

The international diplomacy of Soviet Muslims yielded a lot of positive results for the Soviet state. A warm reception was accorded to foreign delegations in Muslim centres like Tashkent, Kazan, Ufa, and Moscow also improved the image of USSR in their eyes. Mufti Shamsuddin Babakhanov recalled how Lebanese mufti Hassan Haled visiting Tashkent in 1967 admitted that his perception that USSR was a country of militant athesism that does not have religious freedom was completely changed as a result of his visit to Soviet Union. According to him Islam had not only been preserved but also developed in the Soviet Union.[40]

In 1967, Soviet Muslims reacted strongly to the Arab-Israeli 6-Day War, and after which the USSR broke diplomatic relations with Israel. Mufti Ziauddin Babakhanov speaking on Tashkent Radio expressed a strong protest against Israel aggression. While Mufti Babakhanov travelled to Cairo to participate in the meeting of Afro-Asian Solidarity Committee, convened to condemn Israel aggression, Soviet Muslims took part in demonstrations protesting against Israel aggression against Middle East countries.

In the 3rd conference of Representatives of All Religions of Soviet Union, held at Zagorsk in 1969, Babakhanov releasing a report on the situation around Palestine, announced that SADUM has collected 250 thousand rubles for the Muslims suffering from Israel aggression.[41]

SADUM hosted the International Conference on Muslim Unity and Cooperation for World Peace, which was dedicated to the issues of Middle East. The conference was attended by delegates from 25 countries representing Asia, Africa and Latin America. In 1973 mufti Babakhanov organised an international conference in support of the people's struggle for freedom, national independence and social progress at Tashkent, which was attended by theologists from Egypt, Iraq, Libya, Yemen, Kuwait and other Muslim countries. The conference passed a resolution in support of brothers of Arab countries fighting for unity, independence and national sovereignty.

The international conference organised by SADUM in 1974 at Samarkand on "Imam al-Bukhari and Modern Times" in its resolution demanded immediate withdrawal of all troops from the occupied Arab territory, the creation of conditions for return of refugees and granting of self-determination rights to the Palestine people.[42] In 1978 at the Asian Islamic Conference held at Karachi,in response to a question on equal rights of Muslims with Christians in USSR,Mufti Babakhanov said Muslims in USSR enjoy absolutely equal rights with Christians. The other strong argument was equal rights enjoyed by men and women in USSR.

The first ever visit in the post–war period by a Muslim delegation from Turkey, led by one of the ministers in 1978, facilitated establishment of contacts between Muslims of two countries and exchange of regular delegations.

The Islamic revolution in Iran taking place under the anti-imperialist and anti-Communist slogans created a dilemma for Soviet foreign policy towards the East. CPSU General Secretary Leonid Breznev speaking at the 26th party congress said that freedom struggle, as well as counter revolutions, can take place under the banner of Islam.

In 1984, there was an attempt to assess the activities of IRD during its two-decade existence. Around 123 Soviet Muslim delegations undertook visits to 51 countries when 103 foreign delegations from 46 countries visited USSR during this period. Soviet Muslims established close contacts with Organisation of Islamic Conference, Arab league etc.[43]

After the election of young and energetic muftis like Shiekh–Ul–Islam Allakhshukura Pasha-zade and Talgat Tazuddin as head of DUMZAK and DUMES, along with the death of Mufti Babazanov, the dominance of Tashkent in the life of Soviet Muslim community came to an end. The next international Islamic conference 'Muslims for World Peace' was organised at Baku in 1986, which was attended by 600 delegates from 60 countries, making it the largest ever international conference of this kind in the history of USSR. This made Pasha-zade, the new head of Muslims of Caucasus, the real leader of Soviet Muslims.[44]

The US State Department which was expecting the Baku conference to criticize Soviet intervention in Afghanistan was concerned about its outcome. As a result of the Baku conference in 1986, OIC general secretary S.Pirzada paid a visit to USSR and held talks with Soviet foreign minister Edward Shaverdnadze. Consequently, Ajerbaijan became the first Republic of erstwhile USSR to get OIC membership even before the collapse of Soviet Union.[45]

The Soviet people have always been veery sympathetic to the people of the East fighting for their freedom. They were also sympathetic to the warring people of Morocco, and so they launched a movement to show their solidarity with the people of Egypt, and supported the freedom struggle in Algeria, Lebanon, Syria, and Palestine. The USSR had warm relations with Turkey and its leader Ataturk. It was the first country to recognise the sovereignty of Saudi Arabia in 1926 and concluded an agreement with Yemen in 1928. After the Second World War, the majority of Arab states received their political independence with direct support from Russia.

A new chapter in the history of relations between the USSR and Arab countries began from the middle of 1950s when mutually beneficial multifaceted ties developed in political, economic and cultural spheres. The USSR stood by the Arab countries during the Suez crisis when Egypt was subjected to attack from three colonial countries. The Soviet Union supported the cause of the Palestine people fighting for their homeland and has contributed hugely in resolving Middle East problem. More than 400 industrial and other enterprises have been built in Arab countries with Soviet technical assistance. Tens of thousands of Arab specialists in various areas have received their training in the former Soviet Union.

According to some Russian experts, Soviet diplomacy towards Muslim world was not very successful as a whole. Turkey,which had received significant Soviet assistance during years of its formation as a nation-state, was seriously considering an alliance with fascist Germany, and subsequently joined NATO. Iran after the Islamic revolution considered the USSR as a 'Junior Saitan'. Military intervention in Afghanistan, with which Moscow always enjoyed friendly relations, turned out to be disaster. Saudi Arabia which had managed to have a meaningful role in the Muslim world, thanks to Soviet effort, turned its back against Moscow, and financed anti-Soviet Muzahiddins in Afghanistan and Pakistan. The information war with US for Muslim sympathy in the world was largely lost, and Russia's prestige and influence in the Muslim world touched rock bottom.[46]

However, it must be remembered that there were also strong allies of the USSR in the Middle East such as Syria, Iraq, and Libya etc. The USSR lost its influence in those countries because of its own wrong policy starting from the late Perestroika years.

As a result of the lop-sided foreign policy pursued in the final years of Perestroika, more so after the Soviet break up, Russia lost its influence in the region. The vacuum created as result of Russia's voluntary withdrawal from the region was immediately filled by West, particularly the US. Russia lost tens of billions of dollars as a result of the loss of the Middle East weapons market, which was subsequently captured by the West. Around 20 billion dollars used to come to Moscow's coffers from arms supplies only to Iraq and Libya.[47]

There is a section of Russian elite and media who lost no occasion in arguing that 'Moscow was feeding these countries' in order to maintain Russian presence in the region. As a result of their activities, Russian lost its geo-political, geo-economic and geo-strategic advantage in the region.

However, the failure of Soviet foreign policy towards the Muslim world can not be attributed to the Muslim-diplomats but to the mistakes and lack of vision of the foreign policy makers of the country.

It must be said that the idea of using the Muslim factor in Soviet foreign policy was useful, first of all for Soviet Muslims themselves. Thanks to the activities of IRD Muslim organisations of Soviet Union, they could maintain ties with Muslim world; build friendly relations with foreign political and spiritual leaders; gain rich experience in diplomacy which came in handy after Soviet break up.

During Gorbachev's perestroika period the Soviet foreign policy went through a drastic change under the 'New thinking' concept. Though the new thinking concept did not touch Islam directly, the Islamic factor did play a role in shaping Gorbachev's foreign policy, first and foremost, because of the Soviet defeat in Afghanistan. After all, the resistance to Soviet military presence was organised under the banner of Islam. The West's policy towards the Soviet military presence in Afghanistan was drafted in close cooperation with a host of Muslim countries. There was concern among Soviet leadership that radical Islamic thoughts might spread to parts of Soviet space inhabited by Muslims, and might encourage a pro-independence movement.[48]

Muslim Diplomacy in the Post-Soviet Period

The establishment of the Russian foreign policy after the Soviet disintegration was dominated by Euro-Atlantists who pursued a predominantly Euro-centric foreign policy. The Muslim world was largely neglected by them, a situation which was not popular with Russian Muslims. The Eurasian school strongly opposed the Euro-Centric foreign policy pursued by Euro-Atlantists, that made Russia a junior partner of the West. The Eurasianists criticised Russia's foreign policy in the 1990s as it did not pay adequate attention to the former Soviet republics, their Muslim neighbours.

The Eurasianists stressing the significance of geopolitical factors argue that Russia's geopolitical realities require a multi-vector policy that dos not over emphasize relations with the West at the cost of other important regions. There are differences within the Eurasian school on the role and importance of Islam. However, they are unanimous in emphasizing Russia's geopolitical imperative to pay adequate attention to the Muslim world. Citing the long history of Russia's relations with Muslim world, they argue that this asset should not be squandered. They plead in favour of a more nuanced, balanced and prudent policy towards the Muslim world. Russian scholars argue that the Russian approach to the Muslim world should be qualitatively different from that of US policy. They advocate that Russia should not join the West in forming the anti-Muslim front. Eurasianists believe that Russia should exploit the tensions between the West and the Islamic world to its advantage.

One of the major objectives of Russian foreign policy is to build a multi-polar world, and the Muslim world is generally perceived to be a partner in striving to build such a global order. Even as Russia considers the Muslim world as a partner in the struggle to build a multipolar world, it does perceive a serious threat from Islamic radicalism and terrorism to its security and stability. This dualism is reflected in Russian foreign policy. While fighting

Muslim terrorism within its territory, it tries to pursue a balanced policy towards Muslim countries. Aware of the fact that Muslim population would evince keen interest in Muslim countries, the state seeks to maintain good relations with them.

After Soviet disintegration, significant changes took place in Russian foreign policy. Moscow established diplomatic relations, on the one hand with Saudi Arabia in 1990 and with Israel, on the other. The ideological element in Moscow's policy towards Middle East was removed. However,Yeltsin's regime became junior partner to US in the domain of foreign policy matters. Moscow did not support Iraq, its staunch ally from the Soviet period during the latter's military conflict with the US. Yeltsin's policy towards the Middle East was completely diluted as a result of which Russia's influence in the region touched rock-bottom. The situation improved for Russia in the Middle East only during President Putin's period.

Moscow's Iran policy went through significant change starting from the Iranian Revolution. Soviet leadership initially saw progressive elements in the Iranian Revolution that occurred in 1979. However, it turned out that Moscow had unrealistic expectations about the Iranian Revolution. Nevertheless, Soviet-Iranian relations did improve significantly compared to the pre-revolutionary period inspite of the fact that "US was the larger Satan and USSR was smaller Satan for" Tehran. The revolutionary Islam turned out to be a potentially destabilising factor in the Muslim dominated regions of Russia. Iran's policy of ' export of Islamic revolution' also contained challenges for Russia's integrity. However, relations between the two countries gradually developed significantly encompassing cooperation in peaceful nuclear, defence and energy spheres. Iran became one of the few Muslim countries which supported Russia on the Chechen issue while the entire West was vociferous in criticizing Moscow's Chechen policy. Iran was perhaps the only Muslim country that took a public stand on the Chechen issue showing solidarity with Russia. According to some experts,.though Iran is a Shiite country whereas a vast majority of Russian Muslims are Sunnis, Islam did play a positive role in shaping Russian-Iranian relations. Iran perhaps is the only Islamic nation with which Russia enjoys a strategic partnership.

Turkey is another big Muslim country with which Russia's relations have been uneven historically. The Russian Empire had fought the largest number of battles with Ottoman Empire. However, Moscow's relations with Ankara improved dramatically in the post-revolutionary period. Notwithstanding the fact that Turkey was a NATO member and USSR supported left forces in that country, Moscow and Ankara enjoyed fairly productive and mutually beneficial relations in trade and economic spheres. Turkey tried to strengthen its influence in the former Soviet space following Russian withdrawal from that territory. This did irritate Moscow, but it could do little to curb Turkey's growing influence, particularly in Central Asia and Caucasus. One can witness a great competition between Moscow and Ankara for influence in this space.

Relations between Moscow and Ankara have been shaped by competing interests of Russia's economic, political and security elites. The security establishment views Russia's big business favours and growing ties with Turkey as a rival because of Turkey's NATO membership The fact that Russia has a huge population of Turkic origin within its national borders and in its 'Near Abroad' has no doubt influenced dynamics of bilateral relationship over the years. Though Moscow has been peeved by Turkey's support to the Pan-Turkic movement within its territory and historic zone of interest, it has not stood in the way of the dynamic development of trade and economic relations between the two countries. Bilateral cooperation particularly in the sphere of energy is noteworthy and promises huge dividends to both countries in the future, apart from the geopolitical implications of this cooperation. The latest summit between the two countries at Baku in June, 2015 has drawn lot of attention in this context.

The Islamic factor had a determining effect on Russia's relations with Afghanistan. Moscow's policy towards Afghanistan, went through many ups and downs over the decades. After Soviet military withdrawal from Afghanistan, the Nazibulla regime in Kabul could have survived if Moscow would not have cut off critical supplies to that country. The Taliban takeover in Afghanistan posed a very serious challenge to Russian security. The Taliban-led Afghanistan became the breeding ground for international terrorism and turned it into a safe haven for Islamic terrorists, including Chechen terrorists who were fighting against Russian troops. Chechen terrorists received military training and mobilised funds on Afghan territory. Afghanistan turned into a huge centre for norco production that found market in Russia. Terrorism and drugs emanating from Afghanistan have become a huge problem for Russia. Russia's relations with post-Taliban Afghanistan has been normalised. Russia extends support to war-torn Afghanistan's economic re-construction and supplies transport helicopters to that country but refrains from military involvement. Russia expects deterioration of security situation in Afghanistan after the withdrawal of NATO troops from that country and perceives a security threat to Central Asian countries, from where it can have a spillover effect on Russia's Muslim dominated territories. Russia tries to tackle terrorism and find a solution to Afghan problem through CSTO, but more importantly through SCO.

Pakistan was another Muslim country where Islam had a definite impact on its relations with Moscow. Pakistan's membership in the pro-US military blocks during Cold War, its proximity to Washington had its negative impact on development of its ties with the USSR. Nevertheless, the USSR made efforts to get back Pakistan from US orbit in 1960s. Unequivocal Soviet support to India during the Bangladesh liberation war alienated Pakistan further from Moscow. Pakistan's support to Afghan Muzahiddins— Islamic fundamentalists fighting the Soviets in Afghanistan, strained its relations with Moscow further. There was an attempt to normalise ties between the two countries in the early 1990s in the immediate aftermath of Soviet disintegration. However, the Taliban takeover of Kabul and Pakistan's full support to the Taliban regime there dashed Moscow's hopes for improving ties between the two countries. The Pakistan-backed Taliban attempt to export militant and fundamentalist Islam to Central Asia caused serious concern in Russia. Tajik extremists fighting a civil war were reported to be receiving military training and other assistance in the camps located in Afghanistan and Pakistan, which became a cause of worry for Moscow. Gradually, Pakistani Islamic missionaries were found to be quite active in the Muslim-dominated regions of Russia.

Official relations between the Pakistan-backed Taliban regime in Kabul and Russia's rebellious Muslim region, Chechnya, grew stronger after the Hosyurt Agreement, leading to a ceasefire in Chachnya and its de-facto independence. The Pakistan-backed Taliban regime in Kabul, which did not receive international recognition, was the only country to extend official recognition to Chechnya's illegitimate government led by rebel leader Aslan Maskhadov. According to some experts, the Taliban regime's establishment of diplomatic relations with extremist Chechen government was largely based on Islamic solidarity.

Chechen –Taliban bonhomie could not have been built without active support from Pakistan's military-political establishment. Extremist Chechen leaders like Zelimkhan Yanderbiyev and Salman Raduyev, visiting Pakistan, had meetings with members of Pakistani leadership and mobilised funds for their extremist and terrorist activities back at home. There were reports of Pakistani generals being stationed in a camp called 'Caucasus' imparting military training to Chechen terrorists. According Russian sources, Pakistani nationals were involved in hostage-taking operations by Chechen rebels led by Raduyev.

The fall of the Taliban regime in Kabul opened a new window of opportunity for normalisation and improvement of relations between Moscow and Islamabad. Pakistan President General Musharaf's visit to Moscow in 2003, during which he declared that Chechnya is an integral part of Russia and Pakistan territory will never be used for terrorist activities against other countries, including Russia, became a landmark event in the history of Russia-Pakistan relations. Russia's growing engagements with Pakistan during the past decade,particularly the possible supply of certain military equipments to that country, have caused concerns in India.

Russia's relations with other Muslim countries of South and South East Asia like Bangladesh. Malaysia and Indonesia have also seen improvements over the years.

Central Asia is another important region where Islam plays a role in determining Moscow's policy towards it. Central Asian countries were pushed to the bottom of Russian foreign policy agenda in the aftermath of the Soviet disintegration. However, Russian authorities very quickly understood the wrong premises of this policy and developed the concept of 'Near Abroad'. Soon one of the top priorities of Russian foreign policy became the development of relations with its Near Abroad consisting of Central Asian Muslim countries. The importance of the Muslim factor in Moscow's policy towards Central Asian countries can be judged primarily by two factors—first, the apprehension of the spread of radical Islam from this territory to Russia's Muslim-dominated regions, and second, the growing influence of major Muslim countries like Turkey and Iran in Russia's own strategic yard, to the geopolitical disadvantage of Moscow. Russia's renewed policy regarding the countries of the Central Asian region can be explained largely by these two factors, apart from geopolitical competition from other major players. This explains Russia's military assistance to the Tajik government which was fighting against militant Muslim fundamentalists in the fierce civil war that has engulfed the whole country. Russia enjoys close relations with Kazakhstan, which is its strategic partner number one and member of

Eurasian Economic Union and CSTO, the two Moscow- led economic and security organisations. Russia's relations have been uneven with Uzbekistan, which sometimes comes closer to Moscow and sometimes distances itself from Moscow. Uzbekistan has suspended its membership in the above-mentioned Moscow-led economic and security organisations, though it tries to maintain friendly ties with Moscow on a bilateral basis. Russia's relations are equally uneven with Turkmenistan which proclaims neutrality as the core of its foreign policy. Moscow has been able to build productive relations with Kyrgyzstan and Tajikistan over the years. While Kyrgystan has joined both the Eurasian Economic Union and CSTO, Tajikistan is a member of CSTO but is yet to join Eurasian Economic Union, though it has declared its intention to be part of this burgeoning union.

The Euro-Atlantists dominating the Russian foreign policy establishment perceived major threats to country's security from radical Islam spreading to Russia and other parts of former Soviet space. Finally when radical Islam did begin to play havoc in Central Asia and Caucasus, the Western countries displayed no sympathy for Russia; rather, they supported the armed separatists and terrorists. The West's policy towards Chechnya created deep anguish among Russians and reinforced their impression that West was trying to further disintegrate Russia using the Islamic card and supporting the Islamic brand of terrorists and separatists. Russia resented the double standards of the West on the issue of fighting terrorism. While the West was pleading to build an international coalition to combat terrorism, it showed absolutely no sympathy to Russia in its fight against terrorism on its own territory. The Western double standards of combating terrorism were exposed by its stand on Russia's fight against terrorism in Chechnya.

Freedom and democracy in the post-Soviet period opened a new chapter for Islam in Russia. The first Muslim summit in post-Soviet Russia was organised in Kazan and Naberezhni Chelni in July 1992; it was attended by business representatives and Muslim leaders. Among Russian muftis, Ravil Gainutddin, the head of DUM of European part and the Russian mufti council, received the maximum opportunity for establishing international contacts. High level delegations from Muslim countries were taken first to Moscow,which was under his control. Gainutddin's base in Moscow helped him maintain contacts with embassies and other missions of OIC member-countries. This also helped him to be part of activities organised by Russian foreign ministry.

DUMER became the first organisation to create a department to look after international activities. In 2007, this was converted into the international department of Mufti Council of Russia.

In the aftermath of Soviet disintegration, when the Russian Muslim community went through a phase of sharp domestic conflict,splitting the old as well as new Muslim structures,it rarely expressed views on international issues and maintained relations with foreign Muslim organisations mainly for receiving funds. Participation of Russian Muslims in international Islamic conferences virtually came to an end as organisers of those events did not know who truly represented the Russian Muslims and whom to invite from Russia, since the IRD of Muslim organisations of Russia—the permanent partner of foreign Muslim organisations for decades, had practically ceased to function. Till 1997, new Muslim organisations of the post-Soviet Russia were so busy in their internal squabbling that they had hardly any time to react on international developments, and all public statements were reactions to domestic developments and revolved around the internal tussle amongst the muftis. Rarely did their newspapers write about role of Russian Umma in the new uni-polar world.

Russia's important Muslim organisations started publicly reacting to global developments relevant to the Muslim community starting only from the middle of 1990s. Russian Muslim organisations first reacted to the developments around Palestine very sharply. They were very concerned about Islam-phobia. Muslim diplomats of the new generation succeeded in achieving some success, by establishing contacts with most influential Muslim international organisations and putting their representatives in those organisations. Muslim leaders of North Caucasus, in course of their foreign visits, could convince the Muslims of foreign countries that Russia is not an enemy of the Muslim world, and the Chechen war does not have a religious character.

The International Islamic Mission was set up in 1997, and was to become the successor to the International Relations Department of Muslim organisations of the USSR. Its leaders like Tahir Khalilov, Sabir Mamedov and Safig Pshikhachev, with the help of Ajerbaijan's Board of Muslims of Caucasus, could launch the process of integration of CIS Muslims, which resulted in the creation of a Consultative Council of CIS Muslims, with Sheikh -ul-Islam Allakhshukur Pasha-zade as its head.

The experience of Muslim diplomats was of great help for the work of Russian foreign ministry which paid special attention to the Islamic issue from 2003, particularly after the US aggression against Iraq. In 2010, the Muslim community of Russia was integrated with the Muslim world, optimizing its international activities with the help of the government and gaining certain immunity from destructive foreign influence.

Mufti Ravil Gainutdin was part of the Russian foreign ministry delegation that visited Egypt, Syria, Israel, and Lebanon in March 1995. From this time onwards,Russian muftis were regularly taken as members of government delegations visiting Muslim countries. Among the foreign countries Saudi Arabia, Turkey and Kuwait the showed most interest in Russian Islam. It is their governments as well as non-government organisations that set up shop in Russia and established control over local Muslim centres.

It is not only the Sunnis but also the Shiites who showed heightened interest to Russian Islam. Iran under its embassy here opened a cultural wing and foundation for research on Islamic culture. Russian muftis started showing interest in the life of Muslims living in the countries of Russia's Near Abroad. The priority partners for TSDUM there became the DUM of Ukraineled by mufti Ahmed Tamim, DUM of Belorus led by Mufti Ismail Voronovich, DUM of Moldavia headed by mufti Albir Babayev etc. On the initiative of the mufti of Kazan,Kiev mufti office was set up with Kanafei Khusnutdinov at its head.

The Russian mufti council chose to establish contacts with the alternative muftis of Ukraine and Belorus, and also with DUM of Kazakhstan and Muslims of Tajikistan. Mufti Ravil Gainuddin signed an agreement for cooperation with Islamic Centre of Tajikistan in 1999. The other direction of the international activities of mufti council was to establish contacts with Muslims of Finland, who were earlier attached to Orenburg Mohmedian Spiritual Assembly.

In July 1996, the Union of Muslims of Russia conducted a press conference on Muslim community against rising Islamophobia in Russia, which became the starting point for the fight of Russian Muslims against internal as well as external Islamophobia. In December 2005 Russian President Vladimir Putin, speaking in Chechen parliament said, Russia was always the most loyal and sincere defender of Islam, thus giving new dimension to international relations. That is why it was not surprising that Russia was the only Christian country that so strongly condemned the Dutch caricature scandal.

Starting from 1998, Russian Muslims started taking an active public position on international issues. In December 1998 the Mufti Council of Russia issued a special statement condemning the new barbaric acts of intervention and military pressure against the fraternal people of Iraq and demanding immediate cease of bombardment on Iraq.

Parts of Russian Muslim community reacted strongly to developments around Yugoslavia. Some circles close to the Russian mufti council expressed their doubts about that Russia unconditionally supporting Yugoslavia in this conflict. In 2008 some Russian Muslims expressed support to the declaration of independence by Kosovo.

The US military intervention against Afghanistan in November 2001 triggered a lot of dissatisfaction and anger amongst Russian Muslims whose several organisations condemned US aggression against Afghanistan. However, some Russian Muslims went so far in their anti-US tirade that they solicited the wrath of the Russian government as well as from some religious organisations. Indeed, some Muslim leaders like Hafigulla Ashirov, Ismail Shangarev and leader of the Eurasian Party of Russia Abdul Wahed Niyazov gave a call to support the Taliban. The statements, by supreme mufti of Asian part of Russia on the US aggression, against Afghanistan were regarded as an appeal to Russian Muslims to join the Taliban movement in order to fight against the US troops.

In November 2001, Ashirov and Shangariyev along with Geidar Zamal, the leader of the Islamic Committee of Russia, participated in the anti-US meeting along with National Bolsheviks as a result of which a kind of 'red-green international' was declared. Around 20 Muslims from North Caucasus and Tatarstan expressed their desire to go to Afghanistan as volunteers to fight against US troops. Some of them were arrested by the US troops and were sent to the Guantamo camp. The episode of Russian Taliban came to an end when seven of them were returned to Russia in 2004.

Ashirov's radical call on behalf of Mufti Council of Russia put the organisation in a precarious situation, which forced Mufti Ravil Gainutddin to publicly denounce the statement of his co-chairman.

In 2002, Ashirov, along with Chairman of Islamic Committee, Geidar Zamal, took part in an international conference organised to extend support to the struggle of Palestine people against Israel and US. The resolution passed in the conference approved use of suicide-killers against Israel, which was regarded as provocative by the Washington administration.

In the beginning of 2003 the most important topic for Russian Muslims was the US aggression against Iraq, which was condemned by all Muslim centres. On 15th February 2003, a huge anti –war demonstration took place in Makhachkala which was attended by thousands of Muslims expressing their desire to fight for Iraq's freedom. Russian officials did not criticize the anti-US attack by Muslims, but silently did everything so that Muslim volunteers coulds not go to Iraq to fight against NATO troops there.

Against the backdrop of this anti-Western mood, TSDUM proposed to send a multi-religious delegation to Iraq with a peace mission. This idea was welcomed by the Orthodox Church. Subsequently, a delegation of Muslim and Orthodox representatives paid a visit to Iraq to demonstrate their solidarity with the people of Iraq. Supreme mufti Talgat Tazuddin, Perm district Mufti Muhhamadgali Khuzin, Rostov district Mufti Zagofar Bikmayev, Moscow and Moscow district Mufti Muhmad Belitov, Maldova Mufti Alber Babayev and Belarus Mufti Ismael Voronovich all represented Russian Muslims, while episcope of Magadan and Sinegorski Feofan represented Orthodox Christians in the delegation. During their two-day visit, the Russian delegation met Muslim and Christian spiritual leaders and held talks with foreign ministry representatives.

The NATO bombardment triggered unprecedented anger among Russian Muslims. Supreme mufti Talgat Tazuddin, speaking at a meeting in Ufa on 3rd April, 2003, made an emotional speech, calling Russian Muslims to extend all kinds of assistance to people of Iraq. The central element of his speech was the declaration of a sacred war against the main proponents of anti-Iraq coalition- of the US and Britain.

While writing about Muslim diplomacy in post-Soviet Russia, it is not possible to not to mention Chechnya's young President Romazan Kadyrev's activities in this sphere. Kadyrev was the first Russian to be invited to Saudi Arabia in 2007 for participation in Kaaba ceremony, which is held twice in a year by the elite of the Muslim world. He visited Jordan and met with king Abdullah-11 in the same year. This enhanced his prestige and elevated him to one of top twenty leaders of Russia.

Interaction with International Islamic Organisations

Islam gradually started becoming an important factor in international politics. The reasons for it were the failure of national, socialist and related models of development, politicisation of Islam,the mushrooming of Islamic parties advocating Islamic alternative, the unending conflict in the Middle East etc. Attention to Islam from the major actors of international politics while taking strategic decisions, is becoming inevitable.

Towards the end of 1970s, the influence of Islamic revolution in Iran and resistance to Soviet military intervention in Afghanistan made Islam a formidable factor in Soviet foreign policy. While the Communist state had a negative attitude towards religion,and Islam being no exception, the CPSU Central Committee report to the 24th Party Congress, said 'freedom movement can take place under the banner of Islam'. Historical experience including the experience of the recent past bears testimony to that.[49]

The following reasons explain the growing Islamic factor in the foreign policy of major international players,

- The political inclination of Islam
- The mandatory membership of the country in international Muslim institutions.
- Observation of Muslim solidarity at the state and society level.
- Presence of radical religious- political movement in the society
- Existence of transnational Islamic organisations
- Intolerance towards other confession
- Existence of multi-million Muslim migration.

Source: Malashenko, A. (2007), Islam for Russia (Ислам для России), Moscow: Rosspen

For Russia, the additional factor in this regard is its vacillation about its geopolitical choices. Russia's attempt to be part of Western civilisation in the post-Soviet period hit a serious roadblock, which made it look towards the East, including the Muslim world. In many ways it is easier for Moscow to find a common language with Muslim world than with the West, in spite of its cultural and civilisation closeness with the latter. Russia, of course, does not strive to be a full-fledged member of the Muslim world. Its civilisational standards may have some similarity with Islam; nevertheless it strongly differs from Islam. Islam, contrary to Western requirements, does not demand Russia's full ideological and value –system assimilation.

Leaders of Muslim countries do not raise the issue of human rights or democracy in Russia, nor do they strongly criticise Russia on the Chechen issue. Russian experts take note of the fact that Russia and the Muslim countries, particularly Saudi Arabia, were on the same side in the human rights commission meeting in Geneva. Russia on its part does not call Muslim countries to adopt democracy; does not interfere in their domestic affairs, expressing understanding of the prevailing authoritarianism in the Muslim world.

The existence of the multi-million Muslim community in Russia makes it a factor in its foreign policy making. Moscow cannot afford not to listen to their voices.

The Islamic factor is important for Russia on account of religious extremism. Almost all terrorist acts were conducted by mujahidins, which compels Russia to make a common front with the West for combating terrorism.

Although Russia became the successor-state to the USSR, after its disintergration, there was absolutely no continuity in the foreign policy of post-Soviet Russia.

Russia positioned itself as an altogether different country. The de-ideolisation of its foreign policy brought radical shifts in its foreign policy, making the friends of Soviet Union, enemies of Russia overnight. Anti-imperialism disappeared from Moscow's lexicon. Russia gave up its independent stand on the Middle East, fully toeing the US policy on the issue. This is how relations with Iraq, Libya, Syria, and all friends of former Soviet Union, cooled so quickly and without any good reason. This can be called part of President Yeltsin's appeasement policy towards the West, particularly the US. Russia gave up strategic autonomy in its foreign policy making. Russian defense minister Pavel Grachev's flight over Golan Heights in an Israel aircraft symbolised the end of Russia's independent policy towards the Middle East. The countries of the Middle East expressed indignation over Russian foreign policy. This did not change the course of Russia foreign policy towards Middle East under Yeltsin. Moreover, Russia got entangled with myriad domestic issues, including military conflicts across its former territory, which left no scope and time for Moscow to pay sufficient attention to foreign policy. After all, Russia had hoped to resolve its domestic problems with Western assistance.

However, degradation in relations with the Muslim world and indifference towards it did not lead to total disappearance of Islamic factor from Moscow's foreign policy agenda. Soviet disintegration accompanied by end of bi-polar world saw Islam emerging as a strong factor in international politics.

This was no doubt important for Russia. We can say there was some continuity in Moscow's foreign policy in the context of Islamic factor. One of the factors that contributed to Soviet disintegration was Moscow's decade long war in Muslim-Afghanistan. However, soon after the Soviet disintegration, Moscow discovered its new Islamic front in Chechnya. Just like Soviet Union's Afghan war, Russia's Chechen war had its international ramifications.

Russia saw serious threats to its security stemming from the rise of radical Islam within its territory. Since the West was also facing major threats from radical Islam, this became an additional argument for Russia-West partnership. President Boris Yeltsin had called for joint Russia-US defense system against Islamic militancy. However, Russia soon discovered Western double standards on the issue of combating Islamic brand of terrorism. There was a growing feeling in Russia that the West was trying to use Islamic terrorism and separatism to weaken Russia. Despite the fact that Russian President Vladimir Putin was the first world leader to call US president immediately after 9/11 promising Russian support and solidarity and despite the fact that Russia joined the US-led anti-terrorist coalition, the West supported militant Chechen separatists to disintegrate Russian Federation. This was bound to have its impact on Russian foreign policy.

The growing Islamic factor started impacting on Moscow's policy towards its Muslim 'Near Abroad' countries, where the Islamic 'renaissance' played a significant role in shaping post-Soviet identity. Islam was incorporated in the official ideology, influencing the local elite, particularly in Tajikistan and Uzbekistan. Their bid to demonstrate that they belonged to the Muslim world distanced the Muslim republics of the former Soviet Union from Moscow. The ruling elites in those newly created states did not want to be fully part of the Muslim community. However,the appeal to Islam created additional space for manoeuvring in the foreign policy. Muslim countries of the former Soviet Union used the Islamic factor for receiving more assistance from the Muslim world.

Re-Islamization of the former Soviet Muslim republics made them a happy -hunting ground for countries like Turkey, Iran, Pakistan, countries of Middle East etc. Russia in the aftermath of Soviet disintegration voluntarily withdrew from this space which had earlier been inaccessible for Muslim countries. The first half of 1990s saw the unrestricted expansion of Muslim countries, each in its own way, to this new territory. Muslim countries wanted firstly to control the markets of these newly created states against the backdrop of Moscow's absence there. Turkey was most active among these new players, using pan-Turkism idea and cultural and linguistic affinity with Turkic people of these countries. Education became most important area for cooperation. Hundreds of young people were brought to Turkey for giving them education. Turkey used its soft power image by demonstrating its confidence that it would be soon admitted into the European Union. This was to enhance its prestige among Muslims of former Soviet Union. Turkey also used the religious factor by harping on the fact that they and the people of Central Asia practice the same kind of Hanifa stream of Sunni Islam, which is the most tolerant form of Islam that facilitates and promotes reform and harmony.

It is the Arab Muslims who used Islam most intensively and actively in the Muslim republics of former Soviet Union, particularly with the help of international Muslim organisations that funded the building of mosques, institutions, Muslim publications and financed the education of thousands of young people from Central Asia in Arab countries.

Iran's activities, limited only in Tajikistan and Azerbaijan, were attributed to lack of sufficient finances and differences in culture. Iranians are Shiite, and local Muslims are scared of radical Islam associations with Iran.

However, the honeymoon in the relations between the former Soviet Muslim republics and the Muslim world was short-lived, inspite of some progress in trade and economic relations. By the mid-1990s, the expectations for receiving huge economic assistance by former Muslim republics from the above-mentioned countries were denied. The above-countries had their own objectives in making the Muslim republics of the former USSR their client states, but this did not happen. The local elites did not like the prospect of being dependant on them— and being raised in Soviet secularism they did not wish to be very active, enthusiastic Muslims. It is interesting to note that the Muslim world occupied the third place after the US and Russia in terms of foreign policy priority.[50]

However, Russia could not but take into account the formation of Muslim enclave on its southern borders while shaping its foreign policy.

In 1994, Evgeny Primakov, the then head of Russia's foreign intelligence agency, in one of the scenarios, forecast the rise of the Islamic threat to Russia. The threat perception came from expansion of Islam from Tajikistan which was going through a civil war, and from Afghanistan, which had turned into the epicentre of international terrorism. The first Chechen war in 1994 and

Taliban's advent of power in Kabul in 1996 destabilised the situation in the entire region. Extremists from Central Asia and Chechnya received training in Afghanistan.

The attack on the twin towers in New York, on 11th September, only demonstrated the acuteness of the problem. Russia joined the international anti-terrorist coalition after 9/11. It joined efforts with the West to combat terrorism– their common enemy. The threat of Islamic extremism forced Russia to bring corrections in its foreign policy. In order to combat the terrorist menace, Russia promoted the formation of CSTO under its leadership. A CIS anti-terrorist centre was set up, and a similar structure was organised in the framework of CSTO. Russia had to strengthen its military presence in Central Asia for facing any eventuality. Combating terrorism, extremism and separatism was incorporated into the SCO agenda. Russia had proposed that Uzbekistan and Tajikistan set up an alliance for combating radical Islam. However it did not materialise.

Russia can ill-afford to intervene in any Central Asian state if it faces a mass movement under Islamic slogans, or if the country faces instability as a result of radical Islam. Against the backdrop of experiments like Afghanistan and Iraq, Russia can barely think of sending troops to foreign country. Russia does not seem to be ready to play the role of mediator in Central Asian conflicts. President Putin's statement in this connection is interesting. He has on record said, "We are not ready; we do not want and will not take responsibility for complete resolution of conflicts. We do not want that any of the conflicting sides put the responsibility of resolving the crisis on us".[51] Moscow is very clear in its policy that it would deal with those who accept the rules of the game, irrespective of the fact what place religion has in their world view or official ideology. But the question here is whether Russia will hold talks with Islamists in case they come to power in Central Asia. According to Aleksei Malashenko, the answer is 'yes'. Moscow has the experience of holding talks with Islamists during Tajik civil war. Moscow facilitated to signing of peace treaty between secular forces and united Tajik opposition led by local Islamic Party of Revival in 1997.

Russia respects the semi-traditional character of post-Soviet Muslim regimes. It is used to the Islamic challenge and adopts it to its policy. Moscow also recognises the independence and original character of the Central Asian states and has no intention of interfering in their internal affairs. All this makes it easy to maintain a dialogue with the local ruling classes and helps strengthen its presence there.

Russian elites' hatred for Islamists does not stand in its way for developing understanding with it in the domain of foreign policy. Moscow has started positioning itself as a mediator between the Islamists and the West. This is clear in the case of the Iranian nuclear crisis.

In 2006, Russia got a chance to play the mediator's role after the victory of HAMAS in the Palestinian elections. Victory of this radical political group became a milestone in Middle East politics. The victory changed the co-relation of forces inside the establishment in Palestine. This provided a chance to Moscow to return to Middle East politics as an independent player. Russia invited a HAMAS delegation to Moscow for holding talks in March 2006. In the same year Moscow took another important step by dropping HAMAS and Hezbollah from its list of terrorist organisations, prepared by the Federal Security Service. This was a challenge to the US who had kept these two organisations in its list of terrorist outfits.

The HAMAS delegation to Moscow, led by its top leader Haled Mashal, had unofficial meetings with parliament members and diplomats. The delegation was received by the Chairman of the International Affairs Committee of the Federal Council, the upper house of the Russian parliament. The delegation took part in a the common prayer held in Moscow cafedral mosque, chaired by the head of mufti council Ravil Gainutdin. Russian contacts with HAMAS continue. In 2007 the foreign minister in HAMAS government, Mahmud Zakhar, undertook a visit to Moscow during which he met with Russian diplomats for discussing the Middle East crisis. Russia's Muslim community strongly approves a dialogue with Islamists of the Middle East.

Russia tries to maintain special relations with the Muslim world as has been discussed in earlier chapters. Such relations are built on the fact that Russia is a multi-confessional country and is regarded as a Christian-Muslim country, which gives it the right to be in two civilisations simultaneously. Moscow strives to be a link, or bridge between the West and the Muslim world.[52]

In 2004, a parliament group 'Russia and Muslim World: Strategic Dialogue' was set up in the State Duma with the objective of providing legislative support to the development of Russia's relations with the Islamic world and international Muslim organisations, firstly with the Organisation of Islamic Conference and to create conditions for a constructive dialogue between the political and economic elites of Russia and Muslim world.

The special ambassador of Russia, Venyamin Popov, regularly maintains that Russia must stand for Christian–Muslim dialogue. According to Ambassador Popov, Islam is the only religion which has created its own inter-state structure—the Organisation of Islamic Conference (OIC). Russia's special relations with the Muslim world has facilitated its admission into OIC in the capacity of an observer. The Soviet Union had sporadic contacts with OIC, which had played an important role in the return of Russian prisoners of war from Afghanistan. After Soviet disintegration OIC general secretary had paid visits to Russia twice in 1994 and 1997.

As mentioned above, Azerbaijan became the first republic of former Soviet Union to be a member of OIC, which was followed by new-born states of Central Asia and Kazakhstan. Admission into OIC promised certain dividends to its member-states. However, OIC membership for Orthodox Christian Russia was problematic for many reasons. This did not prevent Russia to cultivate a close relationship with OIC. Head of DUMES, Mufti Talgat Tazuddin in the year 1992, in his speech in the first world congress of Tatars, made a statement that Tatars should return to the great Islamic world and this should be done through OIC membership. Tazuddi further said that when he met OIC general secretary in Istanbul, he asked him to convey to the presidents of Tatarstan and Bashkortstan, that if they make an official request, these two republics would be granted OIC membership.[53]

Following the example of Azerbaijan, perspective of Russia's Muslim regions joining OIC at that time did not seem a big deal. However, the growing division in DUMES created obstacles in this direction. Nevertheless, in April 1993 the deputy chairman of Russian Supreme Soviet Committee on religious affairs, Murad Zargishev, raised the issue of Russia's membership in OIC, which was rebuffed by Russian expert on Islam Aleksei Malashenko.[54]

In the meantime, Russia's contacts with OIC continued to grow. In 1997 the leader of the Union of Muslims of Russia NadirShah Khachilayev raised the issue of Russia's membership in OIC. Khachilayev took the initiative of organising a Round Table on the issue in the State Duma.

In December 1999, the OIC delegation, led by Iranian minister of foreign affairs K, Kharazi, paid a working visit to Russia, which was received by Russian leader Vladimir Putin. The Iranian foreign minister visited Moscow for the second time next year during which he had talks with Russian foreign minister Igor Ivanov. Taking advantage of Russia's growing contacts with

OIC, Mufti Ravil Gainutdin sent a letter to Iranian president Muhamed Khatami to provide observer status to Russia in OIC.[55]

In January 2003, the OIC general secretary A. Belkaziz met with Sergey Mironov, speaker of Federal Council, foreign minister Igor Ivanov, deputy foreign minister Alexander Saltanov and Mufti Talgat Tazuddin and Ravil Gaunutdin at Moscow. In April 2003, President Putin during his meeting with Tajik mufti Amonulla Nematzade talked about the possibility of Russia joining OIC as an observer, noting that Russia to large extend belongs to Muslim world. Russian Orthodox Church head patriarch Aleksei and head of Russian the mufti council Ravil Gainutdin welcomed this.

The Russian foreign ministry was given the task of creating conditions for Russia's admission into OIC. Russian President Vladimir Putin missed no opportunity to remind about Russia's special ties with Muslim world. The Russian foreign ministry created a post of special ambassador for looking after relations with OIC and other Muslim organisations, and Venyamin Popov, earlier working in Yemen, Libiya and Tunisia as senior diplomat,was appointed to that post.

President Putin during his official visit to Malaysia in August 2003 made a statement that said that Russia is likely to get an observer's status in OIC. Ultimately it was decided that Russia would apply for OIC observer status and organise one of its future summits at Moscow. In October 2003, President Putin attended the 10th OIC summit held in Kuala Lumpur as a guest where he made a speech. President Putin said, "We know that vast majority of member states of the organisation supported our initiative for development of relations with OIC. I am confident that Russia's participation would not only enrich the bright landscape of the organisation but would also bring new possibilities for its work and would reflect weight and voice of huge Muslim community of Russia, which does not look at it as separate entity from world Muslim community and is ready for fruitful cooperation in its spiritual, cultural and political life." The presence of leaders of certain Muslim regions of Russia and Chairman of Coordination Centre of Muslims of North Caucasus Mufti Ismail Berdiyev in the summit spoke of Russian government's warm relations towards Muslim community of the country. Russian delegation at Kuala Lumpur included property minister Farid Gaziulin, Deputy Chief of Kremlin administration Zakhan Poliyeva and Chechen president Ahmed Kadyrev.

The political gains of Russia's closeness to OIC were evident very quickly. The Muslim world's understanding of Russian policy in Chechnya started growing and it is noteworthy that OIC sent its observers for the presidential election in Chechnya scheduled for October, 2003,noted special ambassador Venyamin Popov.

Obviously it is not only Chechen issue that demanded Russia's association with OIC. More than anything else it is the issue of Russia's place in the world and strives to compensate the loss in the relations with the West that prompted Moscow to get admission into OIC. There is no doubt that the role of Islamic factor in foreign policy got reinforced under President Putin.

In May 2004, Russian foreign minister Sergey Lavrov sent a letter to OIC General Secretary with the request to provide Russia with an observer status in the organisation. The 32nd session of the council of ministers of foreign affairs of OIC member countries held in Sana, June 2005, granted observer status to Russia. Moscow received similar status of observer in the Islamic Organisation on education, science and culture.[56]

OIC's loyalty to Russia is evident from the fact that its representatives, along with Arab League delegation, were present as observers in the Chechen presidential election held in 2003, in which Kremlin–supported candidate Ahmed Kadyrev was declared elected.

In 2006 a group called 'Russia and Islamic world' was set up under the patronage of former Prime Minster Evgeny Primakov, which launched some important projects with the participation of famous public figures, state and spiritual leaders. This group organised four important events at Moscow, Kazan, Istanbul and Zhida, with the participation of representatives of Orthodox Church.

Russia's integration with OIC led to the creation of the post of special ambassador in the foreign ministry to look after relations with OIC member countries. Russia's association with OIC became possible as a result of the Government's own serious efforts, and not through lobbying by Muslim spiritual leaders. None of the Russian muftis was involved as a negotiator with OIC, though it is they who reaped maximum of benefit out of Russia's observer status in OIC. Apart from OIC, Russian Muslim centres established contacts with number of international Muslim organisations, including the World Islam League and international assembly 'Islamic Appeal'.

Not all Muslim countries welcomed Russia's entry into OIC. For example, Pakistan was very vocal among those who opposed Russia's admission into OIC, arguing that Russia is a Christian country and in terms of political orientation, its history is replete with wars and conflicts with Muslim countries. Lastly, Russia's entry into the organisation would change the configuration in the organisation. However, the main reason why Islamabad was opposed to the idea of Russia's admission into OIC was that it might open the door for India's entry, a country with similar ethnic and religious composition like Russia and Pakistan's adversary for decades. Pakistan's opposition paled in front of support for Russia's admission into the organisation from such countries like Malaysia, Iran, Syria, and to an extend Saudi Arabia. Finally, Russia received an observer status in OIC in June 2005.

The soft attitude of Muslim countries towards Russia can be explained by the fact that the Muslim world needs additional allies against the backdrop of the US expansion and hegemony in global affairs. In the face of imminent democratisation of the greater Middle East demanded by the US, the ruling Arab elite,concerned about instability looks for an alternative support base. Russia provides this support base, however weak it might be, in many conflicts starting from Iranian nuclear programme to the conflict in the Middle East. Though the countries of the Middle East do not want to exaggerate Russia's significance, they are not inclined to refuse additional support for them.

Russia's entry into OIC did not bring about dramatic improvement in Moscow's relations with the Muslim world. Moscow also never expected exclusive preferences from OIC entry. Russia's entry into OIC just fixed its 'special place' in the global space and served as reminder that being largely a Christian country, there are no stereotype perceptions about it in the Muslim world as it exists about the West. The conscious strengthening of Muslim direction in Russian foreign policy is accompanied by statements that the West is trying to block the promotion of Russia's relations with the Muslim world by pitting it against the later. This is explained in the Western concept of clash of civilisations. Particularly the neo-Eurasianists and Muslim spiritual leaders make this kind of argument.

In contrast to the West, Russia demonstrates a great deal of understanding of the Muslim world. Whenever there is any scandal in the West in connection with Islam, Russia always appeals for calm..

For example, during the scandal linked to publication of Prophet Mohammed's caricature in Dutch newspaper *Yulands Posten,* which rocked the entire Muslim world, President Putin expressed understanding with the position of Muslims, comparing the prophet's caricature with child pornography.

During the scandal, linked to Pope's statement in 2006 at Regensburg that had created great upheaval in the Muslim world, president Putin appealed to everybody to be responsible and maintain restraint, emphasising that Russia would do every thing possible to establish a dialogue of civilisations.

Notwithstanding the official statement about love and sympathy towards Muslim world, Russian policy towards it is described as 'ambivalent' or at best 'tactical' by some experts.[57]

Conclusion

Approximately 15-20 million Muslims constitute roughly 14% of Russia's total population, and that makes Islam multi-confessional Russia's second most professed religion. Russia's interaction with Islam began in the 7th century much before Orthodox Christianity was adopted as country's official religion by King Vladimir of Kievan Rus. The reign of the Tatar-Mongolian Golden Horde during 13-th and 14th centuries provided a strong impetus to expansion of Islam in Rus. In the year 1313, Golden Horde ruler Sultan Muhhamed Uzbek declared Islam as his country's official religion. As a result of this,a multitude of Turkic tribes from Crimea to Siberia adopted Islam as their religion. His son Zanikek continuing his father's tradition established warm and harmonious relations with Moscow metropolitan, Aleksei, who had helped in healing his wife.

In the 16th century, the conquest of Kazan, Astrakhan and Siberian khanates led to incorporation of this huge territory with its Muslim population into the Russian Moscovite state. Russian kings more or less had a tolerant attitude to their Muslim subjects and seldom took coercive measures to convert them into Orthodox Christians, rather encouraging conversion through economic measures. However, strict measures were taken against conversion of Christians into Islam.

Beginning from the second half of the 15th century, Tatar settlements appeared in Russian towns like Kashir, Serpukhov, Kolomna, Zvenigorod, Podolsk etc. Islamic norms were reflected in the family as well as in public life of these settlements. It must be noted that Christians and Muslims had peaceful co-existence in those places, largely thanks to Golden Horde's wise policy in this regard.

However, Russian Czar, Ivan the Terrible had issued an order to convert the people in the conquered territories to Christianity. Russian authorities had thought that Islam could be uprooted in the Volga region and Siberia. Steps were taken to motivate Muslims materially in order to convert them into Christianity. There were discriminatory practices against Muslims. Czarist authorities took away the land from Muslims and gave it to those who got converted into Christianity.

Russian rulers gradually changed their policies towards their Muslim subjects in the 18th century. While Peter the Great facilitated translation of the Quran from French to Russian in 1704, his successors Elizabeth Petrovna, Catherine the Great issued decrees in order to regulate Muslim religious and public life and permitted the building of mosques for their Muslim subjects. These decrees ensured official legal status to Islam in Russia. As a result of prudent policies pursued by the Russian rulers, Muslims joining Russian empire did not regret it. Muslim spiritual leadership in return did not support the uprisings against the Czarist Government, rather they extended assistance in establishing order and stability on their territory.

Catherine the Great allowed the peaceful propagation of Islam in some parts of her empire and permitted building mosques and religious schools in Bashkortstan and the Kazakh steppes. This enlightened policy brought rich dividends for Russia in terms of economic prosperity, social harmony and stability.

The turn of 20th century witnessed growing political activities by Muslim representatives. The factors that promoted this were Russia's defeat in Russo-Japanese war of 1904-05, developments in Muslim countries and uprisings by workers and peasants. The first Russian Revolution of 1905-07 compelled Czar Nikolas -11 to initiate certain political reforms that created space for political movement of Muslims. In 1905 the Muslim movement succeeded in building a unified political platform that demanded religious self-determination, fair land reform etc. The building of common platform was followed by a major initiative to convene the first ever Congress of Muslims of Russia (CMR) that appreciated the step for creating the Russian Duma and called for inclusion of Muslims in the reform process. The second congress held in 1906 took the decision to create a political Party, Union of Muslims (UM), which was liberal and pro-reform. The third congress held in Nizhni

Novgorod, adopted a programme that was close to that of Constitutional Democrats.

While Russia's Muslim political leadership developed a Muslim agenda through All Russia Muslim Congress, the Ittifak party tried to establish itself in Russia's newly constituted State Duma. Muslims had 25 members in the first Duma and 39 members in the second Duma. The Second Duma, despite the rise in the number of Muslim members, witnessed decline of the Ittifak party's influence as a result of infighting and factionalism. The dissolution of the second Duma by the Czar in 1907 coincided with virtual break up of Ittifak as an effective party.

The fourth congress held in 1914 was almost a non-event with just 30 delegates and failed in its attempt to revive Ittifak as a viable political party. Although Ittifak and the All Russia Muslim Congress lost much of its influence, nevertheless it remained as an united platform championing Muslim cause.

The fall of the Czarist regime and victory of the October Revolution offered plenty of opportunities to Muslims to obtain greater autonomy in the sphere of culture, religion and politics. Some Muslims even aspired to gain full independence, and some even achieved it for a brief period.

After the fall of Czarist regime, Muslims emerged as a strong political force between the period of the February Revolution and the October Revolution. The All Russia Muslim Congress got a new lease of life to influence the political developments in the country and its congress held in May 1917 gathered more than 800 delegates from host of Muslim organisations across the country. The congress despite differences on host of issues, took decisions in favour of an unified Russian state and formation of separate Muslim regiments in the army to serve in Muslim dominated territories. Delegates of the next congress recommended that the Muslims of inner Russia and Siberia should resolve issues concerning their territorial autonomy, religion, culture, education and language etc. The Congress took a decision in favour of setting up a Council, consisting of 12 members, headquartered in Ufa, to take steps for creating Muslim national-cultural autonomy. There was a strong move to create the Volga-Ural Republic with adequate autonomy.

After the October Revolution the Bolsheviks offered an opportunity to Russian Muslims to organise themselves politically and promised to provide national self-determination, particularly in religious and cultural spheres. The Bolshevik government issued a "Decree on the Rights of Peoples of

Russia "that stipulated equality and sovereignty of the peoples of Russia and the right of non-Russian peoples to self-determination, including the right of secession. The Bolshevik leadership in its famous "Appeal to All Toiling Muslims of Russia and the East "promised religious as well as host of other freedoms to Muslims. The Muslims supported the Bolsheviks because they met their aspirations contrary to the White Guards. During the civil war Muslims on the whole fought on the side of the Bolsheviks. Reformist Muslims were convinced that Muslim revival would be much easier under the Communists than under reactionary While Guards. The nascent communist government declared to permit Muslims certain degree of cultural, religious and national autonomy.

Historically, Muslims had aspired for greater political and cultural freedom and autonomy. The idea to form separate units with majority Muslim population under the federal political system was always strong. There were proposals to form three major political–territorial units with dominant Muslim population, namely, one in Volga region incorporating Tatars and Bashkirs, the second in Central Asia, and third in North Caucasus.

However, there was a radical shift in the policy of the Bolsheviks about religion as a whole from 1928, and Islam was no exception on the issue. While the 1918 constitution had permitted both religious and anti-religious propaganda, Stalin launched a full-fledged onslaught against religion from 1928 from an ideological point of view in order to achieve the objective to create a "Soviet Man", forgetting all religious and ethnic differences. The attack against Islam was not exception. As a result, the country saw massive closures of hundreds of churches and mosques. This attack on religion affected the clergies from both Orthodox Christianity and Islam. The Law on Religious Associations, promulgated in 1929, stipulated state authority to supervise and regulate religious life in the country. All regions including Islam suffered as a result of this law which placed severe restrictions on religious practices.

During World war II, there was a serious change in the attitude of the government towards religions as it needed to mobilise the entire population using all means, including religious feelings. That is why there was a relaxation of restrictions on religious practices during the war years, and Islam of course benefited from this. The more or less relaxed atmosphere in case of religion continued after Stalin's death, during Khruschev's period too. The Breznev period did not see excesses in the sphere of religion though the atheism remained the state religion. The situation in it started improving only during Gorbachev's perestroika years.

In the post-Soviet period, there was an interesting change in the Islamic discourse in the context of Russia. The conventional view that the USSR was engaged in a coercive exercise to destroy and annihilate nations and religions has now been challenged seriously by the argument that Soviet authorities engaged in a systematic attempt at ethno-national construction and were significantly successful in this exercise. With the disintegration of USSR the salience of these Soviet constructed ethno-national identities has only grown. One way in which ethnicity continues to assert primacy over religious identity can be seen in the conflation of religious and ethnic identity.

An analysis of Russia's almost 1500 years of interaction with Islam brings out a number of conclusions and is significantly different and distinct from Europe's interaction with Islam. Islam is one of the traditional religions of Russia, and it is considered more as a native religion than an alien one. Islam has contributed immensely to the evolution and enrichment of Russian culture and civilisation. Though Russia is primarily a Christian country with 80% population belonging to Orthodox Christianity, its civilisation is closer to European civilisation,and at the same time it is different and distinct from it because of number of factors —one of them being Islam. Russian history, culture, psychology, art and civilisation as a whole have been strongly influenced by Islam.

The discourse on Russia's evolution as a nation and formation of its civilisation is usually dominated by Russia's interaction with Europe and Christianity. The role of Islam in the evolution of Russian civilisation, formation of its world view, mindset, culture has not received adequate attention and is often seems to be ignored by scholars, with the exception of Eurasian school and particularly, one of its tallest proponents, noted scholar Lev Gumilev.

The Tatar–Mongol period and its influence on Russia is largely viewed negatively and is held responsible for Russia's alienation from Europe resulting in its backwardness. Some scholars believe that Russia's authoritarian political culture is a product of Tatar-Mongol rule.

While Islam became the official religion of Tatar–Mongol empire, under which Orthodox Christian Russia had to survive for almost one and half century,Tatar –Mongols did not try to destroy Christianity, or push it to the corner in Russia. When the Russian Moscovite state emerged as a strong state, following the defeat of the Tatar-Mongols, initially there was some kind of harassment unleashed against Muslims in Russia. However, subsequent Russian rulers, first and foremost, Catherine the Great took a number of steps to organise Muslim public and religious life in the country in order to integrate them with Russian state and promote co-existence of country's two main religions.

Muslim self-consciousness and political activities witnessed significant rise in the period between the two Russian revolutions. Muslim representatives took active part in the activities of State Duma that existed between the two revolutions. Muslims by and large supported the October Revolution and the Bolsheviks as their slogans for self-determination and greater autonomy appealed to them. Till 1928 Muslims supported the Bolshevik government. Muslims were alienated and antagonised from 1928 when Stalin unleashed his anti-religion campaign by destroying hundreds of churches and mosques and killing religious leaders. It should be noted here that Stalin's campaign was launched against all religions, and Muslims were never singled out or a special target as some scholars try to stress.

The state attitude towards religion took a positive turn after Hitler invaded USSR. The Soviet state wanted to mobilise all means (and believed that religion can be a strong instrument to mobilise people) in its war effort against Nazi Germany. That is why there were relaxations in the restrictions over religions and Muslims did reap benefits from this policy.

The post-Soviet period saw the mushrooming of Muslim political parties and movements which took active part in the political and social life of the country. These parties and movements took part in the national as well as local elections. A number of Muslim leaders became State Duma members; Muslim organisations also became active in the civil society movement of the country. However, a number of significant Muslim Political Parties and Muslim leaders have declined over the years.

Muslim revival took shape in the sphere of education also as a result of expansion of Muslim education. The establishment of a viable educational system that could help revive indigenous Islam of Russia and provide adequate number of qualified leaders for Muslim communities and institutions has been proven more problematic than building any physical infrastructure. But this was absolutely necessary from the political point of view to preventing infiltration of extremist elements among poorly educated Muslims. The major hurdles in creating an adequate number of Islamic educational institutions have been lack of sufficient funds, inadequate human resources (particularly the lack of qualified teachers) and political factors. When local funds are inadequate, foreign funding's should be welcome. However, foreign funds for creating educational institutions have diluted the educational agenda and helped promote extremism and fundamentalism. This has created a serious problem for the country. As per political considerations, both federal as well as regional authorities have some scepticism about building of Islamic educational institutions. This scepticism has grown in the back drop of some Islamic educational institutions serving as breeding grounds for religious extremism, fundamentalism and terrorism

The Muslim revival in post –Soviet Russia could be seen in the media sector. DUMES revived publication of its newspaper in 1990 which was closed after some time because of financial difficulties. Its publication started again in 1997 with the help of Mahmedgalli Khuzin, mufti of Perm district. Iman, the Muslim literature publishing house was inaugurated in Kazan in 1991; it also published a newspaper by the same name. Journal "*Islam Nuri*" started getting published in Kazan from 1993. Islamic Newspapers "*Vera* 'and "*Yakin*" got published from 1994. After the split in DUMES, the break away group of muftis started publishing their own newspaper. The Muslim Spiritual board of Bashkortstan founded the Russian language paper "Islam and Society" in 1992, and DUMER started publishing monthly paper "*Islam minber*" from 1994. Dagestan Muslims too started publishing their own periodicals from the beginning of 1990s.

By the end of 1990s, the majority of centralised Muslim organisations had their own newspapers. The most regular among them was "*Islam Minber*" which became the mouthpiece of council of muftis of Russia. Different Muslim communities too tried to publish their own newspapers, which did not last long.

Islamic revival could be seen in Muslim book publishing and Halal industry which saw its boom in the post-Soviet period.

Russia's state approach to Muslim integration with the society is a product of its distinct historical, cultural and political developments over centuries. It has been strongly influenced by the dominant role of religion in the history of Russia and the need to protect the Muslim population's cultural originality while integrating it in the interest of national security. The integration process in Russia takes place under state control in conditions of multi-ethnicity, multi-confessionalism, multi-nationalism and cultural diversity. The Russian approach to State –Islam interaction is complex, distinct because of Muslim's prolonged historical association with the country. The Russian integration process involves integration of not only Muslim migrants but also own ethnic Muslims, living on its territory for centuries, even before the advent of the dominant religion, which is Orthodox Christianity.

Muslim communities of Russia with their distinct ethnic, political, religious characters, have strong regional differences, ranging from moderate Islam in the Volga region to radical movements in the North Caucasus. The most striking difference can be witnessed between Muslims of the Volga region and North Caucasus in the context of integration. While the integration process has been more successful in the Volga region, the rebellious mood against the Russian state is evident in North Caucasus. That is why the state has to pursue different policies towards different regions for resolving the integration issue. The sense of belonging to the state is stronger and efforts to centralise regional administration are more acceptable in the Volga and Ural regions than in North Caucasus. While the separatists movement is almost absent in the Volga – Ural region, North Caucasus has become a hotbed of terrorism, extremism, separatism and thus is a major source of state security. Aware of the separatist mood and rebellious character, state does not try to enforce central authority in North Caucasus as much as it does in the case of the Volga-Ural region. The State desists from the attempts to undermine traditional sources of local and religious authority. Rather it tries to establish its authority there with the help of the local religious authority and judicious use of traditions.

Muslim integration in Russia has been the product of top-down assimilation process, combined with preservation of cultural autonomy. Starting from Catherine's period to Putin's presidency, the State has been engaged in a process of assimilation as well as of liberal accommodation while dealing with Muslim issue, in order to defend national security and internal stability. The repressive Soviet methods of dealing with religion for the sake of promoting atheism led to weakening of Muslim institutions

Radical Islam

Though Islam played a consolidating role in the fight of radical Chechen separatists against Russia, the slogan to build an Islamic State did not find support amongst the majority of Muslims. The propaganda of radical

Muslim fundamentalists could not have much impact on most Muslims. Nevertheless, various interpretation of Islam and fight for its realisation have triggered differences among the Muslims of Caucasus. Differences of this nature can be found among Muslims of other regions of Russia as well. However, these differences are not so sharp among Muslims of Tatarstan, Siberia or Moscow. The issue debated among Muslims of these regions are how to practice shariat in a secular country, where Muslims constitute the minority.

The rise of radical Islam in Tatarstan, Bashkortstan, Ural region is attributed to functioning imams and madrasa teachers, who have received their education in Saudi Arabia, Tunisia, Egypt, Morocco etc. There have been reports in Russian press that militant muzahidins were trained in mosques and madrassas, which were under the control of radical imams, for taking part in military actions against official Russian troops.

One of the sources of expansion of radical Islam in Russia are the activities of dubious international Muslim organisations functioning in Russia. They spread Muslim fundamentalism and teach a non-traditional form of Islam to Russian Muslims. Muslim missionaries from foreign countries try to spread ' clean Islam', which hugely differs from traditional Islam practiced by Russian Muslims. [58]

Tatarstan became the worst affected region by increasing presence of proponents of 'clean Islam'. The full-scale penetration of Wahhabism into the republic began in 1993 when the Saudi charity organisation 'Taiba' signed an agreement with the newly formed Naverezhno-Chelno madrassa 'Ioldyz' for implementing education programme, which led to transformation of the madrassa into a training centre for militants.[59]

In the autumn of 1999, Denis Saitakov, a product of this madrassa became one of those suspected in the terrorist act that took place in Moscow. Subsequently, the involvement of some other students of this madrassa in terrorist acts was also proved. It has been also established that Chechen terrorist leaders Basayev and Hattab were imparting military training in this madrassa. Subsequently, this madrassa was closed by the special commission of the council of muftis of Russia and was converted into a female madrassa. However, this did not resolve the issue of spread of Wahhabism in Naberezhni Chelny.[60]

After Naberezhny Chelny, there were reports about active Wahhabism centres in other regions like Nizhnekamsk, Kukmor, and Almetyevsk etc.

There were reports about the successful penetration of Wahhabis in the power structures of different regions— even into the leadership of Kazan muftyat.

The Muslim community's unity was disturbed in many regions by the penetration of Wahhabism. There were reports about clashes between traditionalists and Wahhabis in many places including Moscow, Ulyanovsk, Volgograd, Perm, Izhevsk, Petrozavodsk, Ekatirinburg, Tyumen, Omsk and many other cities.[61] While discussing the radical organisations functioning in Russia, special attention should be given to organisations with Turkic origin that propagates ideas of Saed Nursi. Their interests were represented by organisations like 'Tolerance' in the western part of the country, Toros foundation and Eflyak company in North Caucasus, Sehat company in Volga region, Ufuk foundation in Ural and Siberia. These organisations were actively engaged in recruiting people for the Nurdzhular sect banned in Turkey for their extremist activities.[62]

The emissaries of Nurdzhular set up tens of thousands of schools and colleges in different parts of the country. These schools, colleges and other educational institutions, run by this sect, drew the attention of law and order department in 2003 for their propaganda of pan-Turkism in these institutions. In spite of the fact that this sect is banned in Turkey, its representatives could take their students from Russian regions without any problem homeland, where values of Nursism were being openly taught. The Neo-Sufi organisation of Turkic- origin Suleman Zhidar and some other organisations like Grey Fox of Bashkiria were engaged in propagating values close to Nursism.[63]

Starting from 2004, most of the arrested Wahhabis were found to be members of Khizbut –Tahrir which was dominated in the beginning by Uzbek dissidents coming to Russia.[64]

By then the party had its branches in most of the major cities of Russia. However, their presence was particularly strong in Tatarstan, Bashkortstan and Tyumen district. The relative weakness of Hizbut Tahrir in North Caucasus led to the belief that there was some kind of division of sphere of influence between various Wahhabist groups.[65]

Russian authorities rose to combat radical Islam since 1999, particularly after President Putin came to power. The Russian Government banned representative offices of Al-Harmein foundation, Al Igasa foundation andTaiba foundation; closed educational institutions run by Turkic sect

Suleimanzhar 'and 'Nurdzhular; it prohibited activities of odious publishing houses and media. Members of Hizbut Tahrir were also arrested on a mass scale. Certain legal steps were taken to ban Wahhabism.

In February 2003, the Supreme Court of Russia in an open session looked into the case for declaring certain organisations as terrorist organisations and banned their activities on Russian territory. According to the verdict of the SupremeCourt the above-mentioned organisations were declared as terrorist outfits with all its consequences.

Contrary to Catholic Church which pays significant attention to issues related to status other religions, the Orthodox Church does not have holistic doctrinal approach towards Islam. Eminent Church leaders of Russia emphasize their respectful attitude towards Islam. The Famous Archbishop Vladimir described Islam as a friendly religion of Orthodox Christianity, whose main features are enlightenment, religious tolerance and openness. Official social doctrines of the Orthodox Church and Russian Islam herald a new stage in the dialogue between Christianity and Islam. They maintain similar views on state-religion relations and social issues. None of them claim status of state religion and both of them recognise secular character of the state. Both religions advocate social partnership with the state and plead for constructive interaction between the two faiths.

Orthodox Christianity historically gained some experience of co-existence with Islam. Historical experience shows that there is hardly any country with significant Christian and Muslim population that has escaped inter-faith contradiction and tension. Russia can not really be called an exception in this context though its inter-faith harmony, it has to be admitted, has been far more stronger than in any other country.

A process of co-existence between Orthodox Christianity and Islam has been going on in a country with predominantly Orthodox Christian population. This process was complicated and not always a smooth one. The Inter-faith situation in Russia largely depends on relations between Orthodox Christian Church and Muslim Spiritual Boards; Orthodox Christians and Muslims. Today, these relations are quite healthy, sound, forward- looking and positive.

Islam and Muslims are not looked down upon as alien to Russian civilisation and society. It is widely believed that Russian spirituality and civilisation can hardly be complete without Islam and Muslim culture. Russian Islam emphasises mutually respectful dialogue and cooperation in the social sphere with members of other traditional faiths of the country.

Russian Muslims' efforts to gain adequate recognition and at the same time become an integral part of the Russian society have been hampered by number of factors. Firstly, because the intra-Muslim conflict and contradictions have weakened their bargaining capacity with the secular state and consequently damaged their position in the society;secondly, strengthening of radical Islam, rise of terrorism and extremism in the Muslim-dominated regions have dealt a serious blow to the status and privilege of Islam as a whole across Russia.

There has always existed a philosophical and ideological basis for dialogue between Orthodox Christians and Muslims, and it does exist today, because it is believed that these two religions are close to each other in terms of content and major principles. In this context, Orthodox Christianity and Islam constitute basic elements of Russian spirituality and civilisation.

Historical experience shows that there is hardly any country with significant Christian and Muslim population that has escaped inter-faith contradiction and tension. Russia can not really be called an exception in this context though its inter-faith harmony, it has to be admitted, has been far more stronger than in any other country. Here what is significant is the idea of spiritual revival reflecting fusion of religious and secular values.

The idea of inter-faith dialogue and multi-ethnic and multi-cultural strength dominates the state approach to Muslim integration. State authorities miss no occasion to reiterate that Russia's success lies in the strength of its moral values and ideals based on tolerance, inter-faith and inter-ethnic cohesion. However, Orthodoxy's special status sometimes does not fall in line with state efforts to construct multifaceted Russian identity. The discourse on a separate Muslim identity has been developed within the concept of unity in diversity. This concept provides the state additional motivation to promote kind of Muslim education that would facilitate inter-faith dialogue and create interlocutors committed to such dialogue.

The State has a vested interest in training imams under a programme that would meet the requirements of its national security and social stability. Though some experts criticise the large-scale state funding of Muslim education which promotes values of inter-faith dialogue and harmony, it is indeed a prudent and productive step towards secular regulation of Muslim integration with Russian society in the interest of national security and social stability. In Russia where civil society has not been adequately developed, state partnership with Muslim organisations, state intervention in the sphere of Muslim education and social protection is no doubt a productive step. Muslim civil society organisations and clergy find their reputation tarnished in the eyes of some sections of Muslims if their association with the state is too close. That is why, the state and Muslim civil society, as well as religious boards, seek to build a mutual relationship which is productive, mutually beneficial without risking the reputation. There is an understanding between state officials and Muslim leaders that the social stability and spiritual revival of the nation require consolidation of Muslim structures of administration, which can be effective only in close cooperation with the state structures. Growing security concerns as well as issues of social stability, created largely as a result 'liberal reforms' of 1990s, justifies state's greater role in handling Muslim affairs in Russia.

Notes

1. Silantiyev, R.A. (2010), *Muslim Diplomacy in Russia (*Мусульманская дипломатия в России), Moscow: Moscow State Language University.
2. Ibid., p. 18.
3. Silantiyev, R.A. (2010), *Muslim Diplomacy in Russia (*Мусульманская дипломатия в России), p. 20, Moscow: Moscow State Language University.
4. Silantiyev, R.A. (2010), *Muslim Diplomacy in Russia (*Мусульманская дипломатия в России), p. 21, Moscow: Moscow State Language University.
5. Silantiyev, R.A. (2010), *Muslim Diplomacy in Russia (*Мусульманская дипломатия в России), Moscow: Moscow State Language University.
6. Ibid.
7. Ovlenskii B.A moya zhijhni, Moi Sovremeniikii, Paris 1988.
8. Ishakhov S.M. (1982), Russian Muslims and revolution, p. 384, Tomsk.
9. Bondarev I. (1982), "First experience of inter-faith peace keeping cooperation" in *Journal of Moscow Patriarchy,* (12).
10. Lenin V.E ovrashinieko vcem trudyatsimsya musalmanam rossii vostoka.
11. Gramika, A.A. and Panamareva B.N. (eds), "Istoria vneshnei politiki", SSSR vol.1:130-14.2
12. Ganiev v velikii sviin tatarskovo naroda Usuf Akshura //tatarskienov asti 2004 no 7.
13. Chervonaya S. (2003), "Pantyurkizm i panIslamizm va russiiskoe istoriiatchestevnie zapiski".
14. Gilyazov.I, Turkism: Stanovlenie E Razvitie, p. 32.
15. Iskhakov SM, Russiiskie musalmane i revolutsya, p. 57,
16. Silantiyev, R.A. (2010), *Muslim Diplomacy in Russia (*Мусульманскаядипломатия в России), Moscow: Moscow State Language University.
17. Salikhov R, mufti is parokhovoi slovodi, Vremya i Dengi 19 February 2003.
18. Silantiyev, R.A. (2010), *Muslim Diplomacy in Russia (*Мусульманская дипломатия в России), Moscow: Moscow State Language University.
19. Romanenko V S, Satrudnichestvo Sovietskoi diplomati i a musolmanskovo dukhovenstva SSSR v 20-e godi XX veka, N Navgorad,2006 pp. 14-15.

20. Silantiyev, R.A. (2010), *Muslim Diplomacy in Russia (*Мусульманскаядипломатия в России), Moscow: Moscow State Language University.
21. Kuzmin va, stranitsi diplomaticheskoe deyachelnosti KaHakimova, Isvestiya Uralskave Gasudarstvenova Universitieta 1997 no 7.
22. Vstnikh MID SSSR, 1990 no 21, p. 43.
23. SSSR i aravaskic starnih 1917-1960 dokumentii i materiali M 1961S-61-62.
24. Muhedinov D satrudinchstvo sovietskoe Diplomatii S 14-15.
25. Sinenko S G ukaz soch S203.
26. Arapov Da U Kasach GG ukaz Soch S 34.
27. Collected works of sinenko S G ukaz soch S203, Moscow.
28. http://www.centrasia.ru/newsAphp?st=1195631400.
29. Arapov, D. and Kasach, G. Collected works, Moscow, p. 99.
30. URL:http//www.ivran.ru/library/view_edition.php?edition_id=151.
31. Silantiyev, R.A. (2010), *Muslim Diplomacy in Russia (*Мусульманская дипломатия в России), Moscow: Moscow State Language University.
32. Gilyazov I (2002), "Tyurkism; stanovenie irazviti", pp. 58-59, Kazan.
33. Silantiyev, R.A. (2010), *Muslim Diplomacy in Russia (*Мусульманская дипломатия в России), Moscow: Moscow State Language University.
34. Silantiyev, R.A. (2010), *Muslim Diplomacy in Russia (*Мусульманская дипломатия в России), Moscow: Moscow State Language University
35. Vasan-girei D, Sovietskisayuzi IslamVesthnik institute pöizucheniyuisorii ikulturiSSSR 1954 no (3).
36. Silantiyev, R.A. (2010), *Muslim Diplomacy in Russia (*Мусульманская дипломатия в России), Moscow: Moscow State Language University.
37. Ibid.
38. Ibid.
39. Ibid.
40 Ibid.
41. Za satrudinchestvo i mir mezhdu narodami: konf predstavitieli vshekh religii va SSR Moscow 1972 p. 113.
42. Silantiyev, R.A. (2010), *Muslim Diplomacy in Russia (*Мусульманская дипломатия в России), Moscow: Moscow State Language University.
43. Silantiyev, R.A. (2010), *Muslim Diplomacy in Russia (*Мусульманская дипломатия в России), Moscow: Moscow State Language University.
44. Silantiyev, R.A. (2010), *Muslim Diplomacy in Russia (*Мусульманская дипломатия в России), Moscow: Moscow State Language University.
45. Sheikh-ul-Islam of two Centuries (Sheikh-ul-Islam dvukh stolietii) (2008), Baku p. 109.
46. Silantiyev, R.A. (2010), *Muslim Diplomacy in Russia (*Мусульманская дипломатия в России), Moscow: Moscow State Language University.
47. Abdulatipov, R.G. (2002), Faith of Islam in Russia (Вера ислама в России, p. 212, Moscow: Mysl.
48. Hunter, T.S. (1984), *Islam in Russia*, p. 291, New York: ME Sharpe.
49. Report of the 24th Congress of CPSU Moscow, p. 13, 1981.
50. Malashenko, A. (2007), Islam for Russia (Ислам для России), Moscow: Rosspen.
51. Abdulatipov, R.G. (2002), Faith of Islam in Russia, Moscow: Mysl.
52. Popov, V. (2003), "Russia is keen to join Islamic Conference" in the journal *Otechestveni Zapiski*, No. 5: 219.

53. Nezavismaya Gazyeta Religia, 26th December 2001.
54. url:http://www.ntv.ru, 8th November 2001.
55. Islama nizavisimaya gazyeta 6th July 1991.
56. Nizavismaya Gazyeta, 8th May 1992.
57. Malashenko, A. (2007), Islam for Russia (Ислам для России), Moscow: Rosspen.
58. Ibid.
59. Ibid.
60. Ibid.
61. Ibid., p. 140.
62. Silantiyev, R.A. (2008), *Encyclopedia Islam in Contemporary Russia (*Энциклопедия ислама в современной России), Moscow: Algoritm.
63. Ibid.
64. Ibid.
65. Ibid.

7. Conclusion

Approximately 15-20 million Muslims constitute roughly 14% of Russia's total population, and that makes Islam multi-confessional Russia's second most professed religion. Russia's interaction with Islam began in the 7th century much before Orthodox Christianity was adopted as country's official religion by King Vladimir of Kievan Rus. The reign of the Tatar-Mongolian Golden Horde during 13th and 14th centuries provided a strong impetus to expansion of Islam in Rus. In the year 1313, Golden Horde ruler Sultan Muhhamed Uzbek declared Islam as his country's official religion. As a result of this,a multitude of Turkic tribes from Crimea to Siberia adopted Islam as their religion. His son Zanikek continuing his father's tradition established warm and harmonious relations with Moscow metropolitan, Aleksei, who had helped in healing his wife. In the 16th century, the conquest of Kazan, Astrakhan and Siberian khanates led to incorporation of this huge territory with its Muslim population into the Russian Moscovite state. Russian kings more or less had a tolerant attitude to their Muslim subjects and seldom took coercive measures to convert them into Orthodox Christians, rather encouraging conversion through economic measures. However, strict measures were taken against conversion of Christians into Islam. Beginning from the second half of the 15th century, Tatar settlements appeared in Russian towns like Kashir, Serpukhov, Kolomna, Zvenigorod, Podolsk etc. Islamic norms were reflected in the family as well as in public life of these settlements. It must be noted that Christians and Muslims had peaceful co-existence in those places, largely thanks to Golden Horde's wise policy in this regard. However, Russian Czar, Ivan the Terrible had issued an order to convert the people in the conquered territories to Christianity. Russian authorities had thought that Islam could be uprooted in the Volga region and Siberia. Steps were taken to motivate Muslims materially in order to convert them into Christianity. There were discriminatory practices against Muslims. Czarist authorities took away the land from Muslims and gave it to those who got converted into Christianity.

Russian rulers gradually changed their policies towards their Muslim subjects in the 18th century. While Peter the Great facilitated translation of the Quran from French to Russian in 1704, his successors Elizabeth Petrovna,

Catherine the Great issued decrees in order to regulate Muslim religious and public life and permitted the building of mosques for their Muslim subjects. These decrees ensured official legal status to Islam in Russia. As a result of prudent policies pursued by the Russian rulers, Muslims joining Russian empire did not regret it. Muslim spiritual leadership in return did not support the uprisings against the Czarist Government, rather they extended assistance in establishing order and stability on their territory. Catherine the Great allowed the peaceful propagation of Islam in some parts of her empire and permitted building mosques and religious schools in Bashkortstan and the Kazakh steppes. This enlightened policy brought rich dividends for Russia in terms of economic prosperity, social harmony and stability. The turn of 20th century witnessed growing political activities by Muslim representatives. The factors that promoted this were Russia's defeat in Russo-Japanese war of 1904-05, developments in Muslim countries and uprisings by workers and peasants. The first Russian Revolution of 1905-07 compelled Czar Nikolas -11 to initiate certain political reforms that created space for political movement of Muslims. In 1905 the Muslim movement succeeded in building a unified political platform that demanded religious self-determination, fair land reform etc. The building of common platform was followed by a major initiative to convene the first ever Congress of Muslims of Russia (CMR) that appreciated the step for creating the Russian Duma and called for inclusion of Muslims in the reform process. The second congress held in 1906 took the decision to create a political Party, Union of Muslims (UM), which was liberal and pro-reform. The third congress held in Nizhni Novgorod, adopted a programme that was close to that of Constitutional Democrats. While Russia's Muslim political leadership developed a Muslim agenda through All Russia Muslim Congress, the Ittifak party tried to establish itself in Russia's newly constituted State Duma. Muslims had 25 members in the first Duma and 39 members in the second Duma. The Second Duma, despite the rise in the number of Muslim members, witnessed decline of the Ittifak party's influence as a result of infighting and factionalism. The dissolution of the second Duma by the Czar in 1907 coincided with virtual break up of Ittifak as an effective party.

The fourth congress held in 1914 was almost a non-event with just 30 delegates and failed in its attempt to revive Ittifak as a viable political party. Although Ittifak and the All Russia Muslim Congress lost much of its influence, nevertheless it remained as an united platform championing Muslim cause.

The fall of the Czarist regime and victory of the October Revolution offered plenty of opportunities to Muslims to obtain greater autonomy in the sphere of culture, religion and politics. Some Muslims even aspired to gain full independence, and some even achieved it for a brief period.

After the fall of Czarist regime, Muslims emerged as a strong political force between the period of the February Revolution and the October Revolution. The All Russia Muslim Congress got a new lease of life to influence the political developments in the country and its congress held in May 1917 gathered more than 800 delegates from host of Muslim organisations across the country. The congress despite differences on host of issues, took decisions in favour of an unified Russian state and formation of separate Muslim regiments in the army to serve in Muslim dominated territories. Delegates of the next congress recommended that the Muslims of inner Russia and Siberia should resolve issues concerning their territorial autonomy, religion, culture, education and language etc. The Congress took a decision in favour of setting up a Council, consisting of 12 members, headquartered in Ufa, to take steps for creating Muslim national-cultural autonomy. There was a strong move to create the Volga-Ural Republic with adequate autonomy.

After the October Revolution the Bolsheviks offered an opportunity to Russian Muslims to organise themselves politically and promised to provide national self-determination, particularly in religious and cultural spheres. The Bolshevik government issued a "Decree on the Rights of Peoples of Russia "that stipulated equality and sovereignty of the peoples of Russia and the right of non-Russian peoples to self-determination, including the right of secession. The Bolshevik leadership in its famous "Appeal to All Toiling Muslims of Russia and the East "promised religious as well as host of other freedoms to Muslims. The Muslims supported the Bolsheviks because they met their aspirations contrary to the White Guards. During the civil war Muslims on the whole fought on the side of the Bolsheviks. Reformist Muslims were convinced that Muslim revival would be much easier under the Communists than under reactionary While Guards. The nascent communist government declared to permit Muslims certain degree of cultural, religious and national autonomy.

Historically, Muslims had aspired for greater political and cultural freedom and autonomy. The idea to form separate units with majority Muslim population under the federal political system was always strong. There were proposals to form three major political –territorial units with dominant Muslim population, namely, one in Volga region incorporating Tatars and Bashkirs, the second in Central Asia, and third in North Caucasus.

However, there was a radical shift in the policy of the Bolsheviks about religion as a whole from 1928, and Islam was no exception on the issue. While the 1918 constitution had permitted both religious and anti-religious propaganda, Stalin launched a full-fledged onslaught against religion from 1928 from an ideological point of view in order to achieve the objective to create a "Soviet Man", forgetting all religious and ethnic differences. The attack against Islam was not exception. As a result, the country saw massive closures of hundreds of churches and mosques. This attack on religion affected the clergies from both Orthodox Christianity and Islam. The Law on Religious Associations, promulgated in 1929, stipulated state authority to supervise and regulate religious life in the country. All regions including Islam suffered as a result of this law which placed severe restrictions on religious practices.

During World war II, there was a serious change in the attitude of the government towards religions as it needed to mobilise the entire population using all means, including religious feelings. That is why there was a relaxation of restrictions on religious practices during the war years, and Islam of course benefited from this. The more or less relaxed atmosphere in case of religion continued after Stalin's death, during Khruschev's period too. The Breznev period did not see excesses in the sphere of religion though the atheism remained the state religion. The situation in it started improving only during Gorbachev's perestroika years.

In the post-Soviet period, there was an interesting change in the Islamic discourse in the context of Russia. The conventional view that the USSR was engaged in a coercive exercise to destroy and annihilate nations and religions has now been challenged seriously by the argument that Soviet authorities engaged in a systematic attempt at ethno-national construction and were significantly successful in this exercise. With the disintegration of USSR the salience of these Soviet constructed ethno-national identities has only grown. One way in which ethnicity continues to assert primacy over religious identity can be seen in the conflation of religious and ethnic identity.

An analysis of Russia's almost 1500 years of interaction with Islam brings out a number of conclusions and is significantly different and distinct from Europe's interaction with Islam. Islam is one of the traditional religions of

Russia, and it is considered more as a native religion than an alien one. Islam has contributed immensely to the evolution and enrichment of Russian culture and civilisation. Though Russia is primarily a Christian country with 80% population belonging to Orthodox Christianity, its civilisation is closer to European civilisation, and at the same time it is different and distinct from it because of number of factors —one of them being Islam. Russian history, culture, psychology, art and civilisation as a whole have been strongly influenced by Islam.

The discourse on Russia's evolution as a nation and formation of its civilisation is usually dominated by Russia's interaction with Europe and Christianity. The role of Islam in the evolution of Russian civilisation, formation of its world view, mindset, culture has not received adequate attention and is often seems to be ignored by scholars, with the exception of Eurasian school and particularly, one of its tallest proponents, noted scholar Lev Gumilev.

The Tatar –Mongol period and its influence on Russia is largely viewed negatively and is held responsible for Russia's alienation from Europe resulting in its backwardness. Some scholars believe that Russia's authoritarian political culture is a product of Tatar-Mongol rule.

While Islam became the official religion of Tatar –Mongol empire, under which Orthodox Christian Russia had to survive for almost one and half century,Tatar –Mongols did not try to destroy Christianity, or push it to the corner in Russia. When the Russian Moscovite state emerged as a strong state, following the defeat of the Tatar-Mongols, initially there was some kind of harassment unleashed against Muslims in Russia. However, subsequent Russian rulers, first and foremost, Catherine the Great took a number of steps to organise Muslim public and religious life in the country in order to integrate them with Russian state and promote co-existence of country's two main religions.

Muslim self-consciousness and political activities witnessed significant rise in the period between the two Russian revolutions. Muslim representatives took active part in the activities of State Duma that existed between the two revolutions. Muslims by and large supported the October Revolution and the Bolsheviks as their slogans for self-determination and greater autonomy appealed to them. Till 1928 Muslims supported the Bolshevik government. Muslims were alienated and antagonised from 1928 when Stalin unleashed his anti-religion campaign by destroying hundreds of churches and mosques and killing religious leaders. It should be noted here that Stalin's campaign was launched against all religions, and Muslims were never singled out or a special target as some scholars try to stress.

The state attitude towards religion took a positive turn after Hitler invaded USSR. The Soviet state wanted to mobilise all means (and believed that religion can be a strong instrument to mobilise people) in its war effort against Nazi Germany. That is why there were relaxations in the restrictions over religions and Muslims did reap benefits from this policy.

The post-Soviet period saw the mushrooming of Muslim political parties and movements which took active part in the political and social life of the country. These parties and movements took part in the national as well as local elections. A number of Muslim leaders became State Duma members; Muslim organisations also became active in the civil society movement of the country. However, a number of significant Muslim Political Parties and Muslim leaders have declined over the years.

Muslim revival took shape in the sphere of education also as a result of expansion of Muslim education. The establishment of a viable educational system that could help revive indigenous Islam of Russia and provide adequate number of qualified leaders for Muslim communities and institutions has been proven more problematic than building any physical infrastructure. But this was absolutely necessary from the political point of view to preventing infiltration of extremist elements among poorly educated Muslims. The major hurdles in creating an adequate number of Islamic educational institutions have been lack of sufficient funds, inadequate human resources (particularly the lack of qualified teachers) and political factors. When local funds are inadequate, foreign fundings should be welcome. However, foreign funds for creating educational institutions have diluted the educational agenda and helped promote extremism and fundamentalism. This has created a serious problem for the country. As per political considerations, both federal as well as regional authorities have some scepticism about building of Islamic educational institutions. This scepticism has grown in the back drop of some Islamic educational institutions serving as breeding grounds for religious extremism, fundamentalism and terrorism.

The Muslim revival in post –Soviet Russia could be seen in the media sector. DUMES revived publication of its newspaper in 1990 which was closed after some time because of financial difficulties. Its publication started again in 1997 with the help of Mahmedgalli Khuzin, mufti of Perm district.

Iman, the Muslim literature publishing house was inaugurated in Kazan in 1991; it also published a newspaper by the same name. Journal "*Islam Nuri*" started getting published in Kazan from 1993. Islamic Newspapers "*Vera* 'and "*Yakin*" got published from 1994. After the split in DUMES, the break away group of muftis started publishing their own newspaper. The Muslim Spiritual board of Bashkortstan founded the Russian language paper "Islam and Society" in 1992, and DUMER started publishing monthly paper "*Islam minber*" from 1994. Dagestan Muslims too started publishing their own periodicals from the beginning of 1990s.

By the end of 1990s, the majority of centralised Muslim organisations had their own newspapers. The most regular among them was "*Islam Minber*" which became the mouthpiece of council of muftis of Russia. Different Muslim communities too tried to publish their own newspapers, which did not last long.

Islamic revival could be seen in Muslim book publishing and Halal industry which saw its boom in the post-Soviet period.

Russia's state approach to Muslim integration with the society is a product of its distinct historical, cultural and political developments over centuries. It has been strongly influenced by the dominant role of religion in the history of Russia and the need to protect the Muslim population's cultural originality while integrating it in the interest of national security. The integration process in Russia takes place under state control in conditions of multi-ethnicity, multi-confessionalism, multi-nationalism and cultural diversity. The Russian approach to State –Islam interaction is complex, distinct because of Muslim's prolonged historical association with the country. The Russian integration process involves integration of not only Muslim migrants but also own ethnic Muslims, living on its territory for centuries, even before the advent of the dominant religion, which is Orthodox Christianity.

Muslim communities of Russia with their distinct ethnic, political, religious characters, have strong regional differences, ranging from moderate Islam in the Volga region to radical movements in the North Caucasus. The most striking difference can be witnessed between Muslims of the Volga region and North Caucasus in the context of integration. While the integration process has been more successful in the Volga region, the rebellious mood against the Russian state is evident in North Caucasus. That is why the state has to pursue different policies towards different regions for resolving the integration issue. The sense of belonging to the state is stronger and efforts to centralise regional administration are more acceptable in the Volga and Ural regions than in North Caucasus. While the separatists movement is almost absent in the Volga – Ural region, North Caucasus has become a hotbed of terrorism, extremism, separatism and thus is a major source of state security. Aware of the separatist mood and rebellious character, state does not try to enforce central authority in North Caucasus as much as it does in the case of the Volga-Ural region. The State desists from the attempts to undermine traditional sources of local and religious authority. Rather it tries to establish its authority there with the help of the local religious authority and judicious use of traditions.

Muslim integration in Russia has been the product of top-down assimilation process, combined with preservation of cultural autonomy. Starting from Catherine's period to Putin's presidency, the State has been engaged in a process of assimilation as well as of liberal accommodation while dealing with Muslim issue, in order to defend national security and internal stability. The repressive Soviet methods of dealing with religion for the sake of promoting atheism led to weakening of Muslim institutions

Radical Islam

Though Islam played a consolidating role in the fight of radical Chechen separatists against Russia, the slogan to build an Islamic State did not find support amongst the majority of Muslims. The propaganda of radical Muslim fundamentalists could not have much impact on most Muslims. Nevertheless, various interpretation of Islam and fight for its realisation have triggered differences among the Muslims of Caucasus. Differences of this nature can be found among Muslims of other regions of Russia as well. However, these differences are not so sharp among Muslims of Tatarstan, Siberia or Moscow. The issue debated among Muslims of these regions are how to practice shariat in a secular country, where Muslims constitute the minority.

The rise of radical Islam in Tatarstan, Bashkortstan, Ural region is attributed to functioning imams and madrasa teachers, who have received their education in Saudi Arabia, Tunisia, Egypt, Morocco etc. There have been reports in Russian press that militant muzahidins were trained in mosques and madrassas, which were under the control of radical imams, for taking part in military actions against official Russian troops.

One of the sources of expansion of radical Islam in Russia are the activities of dubious international Muslim organisations functioning in Russia. They spread Muslim fundamentalism and teach a non-traditional form of Islam to Russian Muslims. Muslim missionaries from foreign countries try to spread 'clean Islam', which hugely differs from traditional Islam practiced by Russian Muslims.[1]

Tatarstan became the worst affected region by increasing presence of proponents of 'clean Islam'. The full-scale penetration of Wahhabism into the republic began in 1993 when the Saudi charity organisation 'Taiba' signed an agreement with the newly formed Naverezhno-Chelno madrassa 'Ioldyz' for implementing education programme, which led to transformation of the madrassa into a training centre for militants.[2]

In the autumn of 1999, Denis Saitakov, a product of this madrassa became one of those suspected in the terrorist act that took place in Moscow. Subsequently, the involvement of some other students of this madrassa in terrorist acts was also proved. It has been also established that Chechen terrorist leaders Basayev and Hattab were imparting military training in this madrassa. Subsequently, this madrassa was closed by the special commission of the council of muftis of Russia and was converted into a female madrassa. However, this did not resolve the issue of spread of Wahhabism in NaberezhniChelny.[3]

After Naberezhny Chelny, there were reports about active Wahhabism centres in other regions like Nizhnekamsk, Kukmor, and Almetyevsk etc. There were reports about the successful penetration of Wahhabis in the power structures of different regions— even into the leadership of Kazan muftyat.

The Muslim community's unity was disturbed in many regions by the penetration of Wahhabism. There were reports about clashes between traditionalists and Wahhabis in many places including Moscow, Ulyanovsk, Volgograd, Perm, Izhevsk, Petrozavodsk, Ekatirinburg, Tyumen, Omsk and many other cities.[4] While discussing the radical organisations functioning in Russia, special attention should be given to organisations with Turkic origin that propagates ideas of Saed Nursi. Their interests were represented by organisations like 'Tolerance' in the western part of the country, Toros foundation and Eflyak company in North Caucasus, Sehat company in Volga region, Ufuk foundation in Ural and Siberia. These organisations were actively engaged in recruiting people for the Nurdzhular sect banned in Turkey for their extremist activities.[5]

The emissaries of Nurdzhular set up tens of thousands of schools and colleges in different parts of the country. These schools, colleges and other educational institutions, run by this sect, drew the attention of law and order department in 2003 for their propaganda of pan-Turkism in these institutions. In spite of the fact that this sect is banned in Turkey, its representatives could take their students from Russian regions without any problem homeland, where values of Nursism were being openly taught. The Neo-Sufi organisation of Turkic- origin Suleman Zhidar and some other organisations like Grey Fox of Bashkiria were engaged in propagating values close to Nursism.[6]

Starting from 2004, most of the arrested Wahhabis were found to be members of Khizbut –Tahrir which was dominated in the beginning by Uzbek dissidents coming to Russia.[7]

By then the party had its branches in most of the major cities of Russia. However, their presence was particularly strong in Tatarstan, Bashkortstan and Tyumen district. The relative weakness of Hizbut Tahrir in North Caucasus led to the belief that there was some kind of division of sphere of influence between various Wahhabist groups.[8]

Russian authorities rose to combat radical Islam since 1999, particularly after President Putin came to power. The Russian Government banned representative offices of Al-Harmein foundation, Al Igasa foundation andTaiba foundation; closed educational institutions run by Turkic sect Suleimanzhar and 'Nurdzhular'; it prohibited activities of odious publishing houses and media. Members of Hizbut Tahrir were also arrested on a mass scale. Certain legal steps were taken to ban Wahhabism.

In February 2003, the Supreme Court of Russia in an open session looked into the case for declaring certain organisations as terrorist organisations and banned their activities on Russian territory. According to the verdict of the SupremeCourt the above-mentioned organisations were declared as terrorist outfits with all its consequences.

Contrary to Catholic Church which pays significant attention to issues related to status other religions, the Orthodox Church does not have holistic doctrinal approach towards Islam. Eminent Church leaders of Russia emphasize their respectful attitude towards Islam. The Famous Archbishop Vladimir described Islam as a friendly religion of Orthodox Christianity, whose main features are enlightenment, religious tolerance and openness. Official social doctrines of the Orthodox Church and Russian Islam herald a new stage in the dialogue between Christianity and Islam. They maintain similar views on state-religion relations and social issues. None of them claim status of state religion and both of them recognise secular character of the state. Both religions advocate social partnership with the state and plead for constructive interaction between the two faiths.

Orthodox Christianity historically gained some experience of co-existence with Islam. Historical experience shows that there is hardly any country with significant Christian and Muslim population that has escaped inter-faith contradiction and tension. Russia can not really be called an exception in this context though its inter-faith harmony, it has to be admitted, has been far more stronger than in any other country.

A process of co-existence between Orthodox Christianity and Islam has been going on in a country with predominantly Orthodox Christian population. This process was complicated and not always a smooth one. The Inter-faith situation in Russia largely depends on relations between Orthodox Christian Church and Muslim Spiritual Boards; Orthodox Christians and Muslims. Today, these relations are quite healthy, sound, forward-looking and positive.

Islam and Muslims are not looked down upon as alien to Russian civilisation and society. It is widely believed that Russian spirituality and civilisation can hardly be complete without Islam and Muslim culture. Russian Islam emphasises mutually respectful dialogue and cooperation in the social sphere with members of other traditional faiths of the country.

Russian Muslims' efforts to gain adequate recognition and at the same time become an integral part of the Russian society have been hampered by number of factors. Firstly, because the intra-Muslim conflict and contradictions have weakened their bargaining capacity with the secular state and consequently damaged their position in the society;secondly, strengthening of radical Islam, rise of terrorism and extremism in the Muslim-dominated regions have dealt a serious blow to the status and privilege of Islam as a whole across Russia.

There has always existed a philosophical and ideological basis for dialogue between Orthodox Christians and Muslims, and it does exist today, because it is believed that these two religions are close to each other in terms of content and major principles. In this context, Orthodox Christianity and Islam constitute basic elements of Russian spirituality and civilisation.

Historical experience shows that there is hardly any country with significant Christian and Muslim population that has escaped inter-faith contradiction and tension. Russia can not really be called an exception in this context though its inter-faith harmony, it has to be admitted, has been far more stronger than in any other country. Here what is significant is the idea of spiritual revival reflecting fusion of religious and secular values.

The idea of inter-faith dialogue and multi-ethnic and multi-cultural strength dominates the state approach to Muslim integration. State authorities miss no occasion to reiterate that Russia's success lies in the strength of its moral values and ideals based on tolerance, inter-faith and inter-ethnic cohesion. However, Orthodoxy's special status sometimes does not fall in line with state efforts to construct multifaceted Russian identity. The discourse on a separate Muslim identity has been developed within the concept of unity in diversity. This concept provides the state additional motivation to to promote kind of Muslim education that would facilitate inter-faith dialogue and create interlocutors committed to such dialogue.

The State has a vested interest in training imams under a programme that would meet the requirements of its national security and social stability. Though some experts criticize the large-scale state funding of Muslim education which promotes values of inter-faith dialogue and harmony, it is indeed a prudent and productive step towards secular regulation of Muslim integration with Russian society in the interest of national security and social stability. In Russia where civil society has not been adequately developed, state partnership with Muslim organisations, state intervention in the sphere of Muslim education and social protection is no doubt a productive step. Muslim civil society organisations and clergy find their reputation tarnished in the eyes of some sections of Muslims if their association with the state is too close. That is why, the state and Muslim civil society, as well as religious boards, seek to build a mutual relationship which is productive, mutually beneficial without risking the reputation. There is an understanding between state officials and Muslim leaders that the social stability and spiritual revival of the nation require consolidation of Muslim structures of administration, which can be effective only in close cooperation with the state structures. Growing security concerns as well as issues of social stability, created largely as a result 'liberal reforms' of 1990s, justifies state's greater role in handling Muslim affairs in Russia.

Notes

1. Ibid.
2. Ibid.
3. Ibid.
4. Ibid., p. 140.
5. Silantiyev, R.A. (2008), *Encyclopedia Islam in Contemporary Russia* (Энциклопедия ислама в современной России), Moscow: Algoritm.
6. Ibid.
7. Ibid.
8. Ibid.